FARO...

The Cricketing Cavalier

THE AUTHORISED BIOGRAPHY

COLIN EVANS

To Jim
Cheers x
Happy 92nd Birthday
No Quick singles to reach 100 !!!

Max Books

First published in the UK in 2017 by Max Books

A CIP catalogue record for this title is available from the British Library

ISBN: 978-0-9934872-3-1

Typeset and Design by Andrew Searle
Edited and indexed by Ken Grime
Cover painting by Christina Pierce
www.christinapierce.com

Printed and bound in India

MAX BOOKS
Epworth House
34 Wellington Road
Nantwich Cheshire CW5 7BX
Tel: 01270 625278
Email: maxcricket@btinternet.com
www.max-books.co.uk

AUTHOR'S ACKNOWLEDGEMENTS

Farokh Engineer and I tossed up at the start of this book with an unusual coin, India's flag on one side, Lancashire's Red Rose emblem on the other. I hope a reasonable balance has been achieved.

For the Indian aspect I relied heavily on the classic *A History of Indian Cricket* by Mihir Bose (Andre Deutsch Ltd., 1990). Other sources included the website www.cricketcountry.com and Sujit Muhkerjee's book *Playing for India* (Orient Longman Ltd., 1972) while I am indebted to the author and historian Ramachandra Guha who allowed me to commandeer his humorous and perceptive essay *The Art of Wicketkeeping*.

Incidentally I hope my Indian friends forgive me on one issue. Towards the end of the 20th century the names of some major cities were changed - Bombay to Mumbai, Madras to Chennai, Calcutta to Kolkatta - but for convenience and, in a historical sense, for accuracy I have stuck with the old titles.

For the Lancashire perspective I delved into my own archive having watched Engineer from the Press Box for most of his time at Old Trafford and having reported on Lancashire for most of my career. It is an archive of personal experience along with interviews and conversations, old and new, with several former Lancashire players particularly Jack Bond, David Green, Warren Hegg, Clive Lloyd, David Lloyd, Harry Pilling, Jack Simmons and Barry Wood. The Lancashire club's historian Malcolm Lorimer provided a treasure trove of records and Brian Bearshaw's official history of Lancashire, *From The Stretford End* (Partridge Press, 1990) and David Lloyd's autobiography *Anything But Murder* (CollinsWillow, 2000) were also valuable.

There was also a cascade of information covering both India and Lancashire from ESPN Cricinfo (particularly several articles by Martin Williamson), the *Wisden Cricketers' Almanack*, and John Cantrell's well researched and engaging biography of Engineer, *From The Far Pavilion* (The History Press Ltd., 2005). I bow reverently to Michael Henderson who granted me full use of his superb article on Engineer, published in the Wisden quarterly *The Nightwatchman*.

I also thank Andrew Searle and Ken Grime for their contributions, and Lancashire CCC, particularly their library, which has provided information and images. Many others, particularly my wife Fi, have offered their encouragement and I am grateful to them all. If, unwittingly, I have omitted anyone or any source from this list I apologise and beg forgiveness.

Most of all of course, there is the man himself. Thank you Farokh for so much entertainment on and off the pitch.

COVER PAINTING

Acclaimed cricket artist, Christina Pierce, graduated from Central School of Art, London, Christina has exhibited extensively in the UK and abroad.Her paintings hang on the walls of both county and International players, as well as businesses and private collectors. Her exhibitions include the Royal Academy of Art, Lord's, The Kia Oval, RAC, Albemarle Gallery, Kent House, London, Hackwood Art Festival, Tao Gallery, Mumbai, Touring exhibition, Australia and many Benefit year events for England and County players.

www.christinapierce.com

DEDICATION

In ever loving memory of my parents MINNIE and MANECKSHA together with my brother DARIUS to all of whom I owe everything; with deepest affection and gratitude. To my immediate family, wife JULIE and my four lovely daughters MINNIE, TINA, ROXANNE, SCARLETT. Thank you all for bearing up with Dad. To my prophet Lord Zarathustra for his unstinting guidance and blessings.

Farokh

FOREWORDS

FAROKH IS not an engineer. He's a maestro and a wizard with the bat. And like all 'captains' of India he's a minor deity in the history of cricket. He's also a wit and a raconteur so this book can be recommended to everyone who loves the game of cricket.

Jeffrey Archer

CRICKET IS rich in characters-more so, I think, than in any other sport-and Farokh Engineer can take his proper place in the pantheon of them. Farokh is one of the great entertainers of cricket. Whether behind the stumps or with a bat in his hand, he commands both the attention and the enjoyment of his audience. He is the same off the field-buoyant and a bundle of fun, anxious to enjoy life to the full. As a wicketkeeper, Farokh was among the best I have seen: unconventional sometimes, but with astonishing reflexes as the impossible catch or stumping is made to seem commonplace.

Sir John Major

THE 1960s has to be the most glamorous era in Indian cricket. There were so many good looking guys playing for India that if people think women are flocking to the game now after the T20 revolution they are wrong. For in 1960s women of all shapes and sizes crowded the stadiums just to ooh and aah about the Indian players. Of course it was a different era in many ways but as a youngster growing up to see the reaction of the women to Tiger Pataudi, M. L. Jaisimha, Abbas Ali Baig, Hanumant Singh, Budhi Kunderan, Chandu Borde, Nari Contractor, Salim Durani to name just a few, was just jaw-dropping. Then there was Farokh Engineer, the original playboy of Indian cricket. He was among the first to model for a product and so successful was that advert that for years anytime the name Farokh Engineer was mentioned the first reaction was not 'oh the dashing wicketkeeper batsman' but 'oh yes the Brylcreem model'. These guys were dating film stars and leggy models as the cricketing grapevine would let us young upcoming cricketers know. If today most, if not all, the kids who want to play cricket want to do so for the IPL razzmatazz, glitz and riches, for us kids back then it was maybe, just maybe we might also get to do what the seniors were doing. Of course the major incentive was always the India cap and representing the country but if there was an added attraction, then why not?

Farokh has not changed a bit. No, that is not entirely true. He has changed ever so slightly. He wears a different size shirt and a different size trousers now. Having been a wicket keeper he does follow the ball wherever he goes but doesn't try and grab it in front of first slip, as he did so splendidly during his playing years. Speaking of first slip. Farokh is the reason I became a slip fielder for India. The skipper Ajit Wadekar was an absolutely brilliant catcher in the slips but after the first few overs he preferred to stand at short cover or short midwicket. As he explained later he just couldn't concentrate on field placements and bowling changes with the joke-a-minute Farokh Engineer standing by his side. So he moved away and asked me to stand next to Farokh. As Parsees call everybody 'dikra' which means 'son', Farokh, a Parsee to the core, would call me that and tell me stories and jokes that had me in splits throughout some long hours on the field but how quickly those hours would go by. Since then we call each other dikra, though of course he is way older than me!

It's been a fun time playing with Farokh and that was conveyed to the spectators as well.

I am sure this book will bring out all the fun and 'masti' that Farokh brought to cricket and continues to bring to life.

Sunil Gavaskar

I always enjoyed Farokh's entertaining batsmanship and the way he enjoyed the game of cricket. He is one of the game's great ambassadors on and off the field, always a delight to talk to, and without doubt he was one of the world's great wicketkeeper-batsmen.

Sir Donald Bradman

PREFACE

June 2017: I am writing this exactly 50 years after an Engelbert Humperdink look-alike strode to the middle of a little seaside cricket ground and proceeded to batter my sporting hero Brian Statham to all parts of the boundary.

'Engelbert' became better known to Lancashire fans as Farokh Engineer.

He was playing for India against Lancashire at Southport, a warm-up for the first Test of the 1967 series, and really gave Statham some stick in a brief but hugely entertaining display of pulls and drives.

I hated those rare occasions when Statham suffered undue punishment. Like most players those days he showed little emotion, either in success or defeat, but the pain could clearly be seen on his face as the Indian star treated even his best deliveries with apparent disregard. But there were two happy consequences of this performance. One - Engineer and Statham became firm friends. Two and more significantly - it hardened Lancashire's resolve to sign Engineer in the face of stiff competition from several counties.

Engineer forged an unforgettable Red Rose career and it was my pleasure to watch most of it from the Press Box. Sometimes, as Lancashire battled towards another one-day triumph, Old Trafford crackled with excitement. Coupled with his dashing style of cricket his name made life easy for the newspaper headline writers - Electric Engineer was one favourite.

But, in hindsight, I would swap all those golden memories with Lancashire for just one day of Engineer inspired drama on an Indian Test ground, say Eden Gardens in Calcutta or the Chepauk Stadium in Madras.

The only time I saw him in Test cricket was in England, usually in cool, damp conditions in front of relatively small crowds. What a difference in India! The sun blazing down, the tumult of 50,000 passionate fans, the sight of Engineer stunning the world's most lethal fast bowlers with the sheer audacity of his attack. Yes, I would have loved that.

Still, I was lucky enough to witness his unique brand of cricket. Perhaps even luckier for him to regard me as a friend. In conspiring on this book I feel we have got to know each other better in the last 12 months than in the previous half-century. Lots of laughs, some very meaningful debates about cricket, friendship and morality, and one or two sparky moments stemming from my pedantry and his scepticism of stats and 'official' reports.

His many admirers, some of whom have contributed to this book, all say: "He's a great guy." Or maybe: "Woh bahut achha aadmi hai."

Sir Don Bradman, for example, said: "I always enjoyed Farokh's entertaining batsmanship and the way he enjoyed the game of cricket. He is one of the game's great ambassadors on and off the field, always a delight to talk to, and without doubt he was one of the world's great wicketkeeper-batsmen."

But amid all the sumptuous tributes and compliments paid to him I have always liked best the under-stated Northern tone of little Harry Pilling who told me early in Engineer's days at Old Trafford: "He's alreet is Rooky."

Colin Evans

CHAPTER 1

"SO THE Queen walks up to me, offers her hand and says: 'Engineer, I've got some special news for you. It's a girl.'" Even now, almost 50 years after that jaw-dropping moment Farokh Engineer's face wears a look of astonishment. He shrugs and stretches, his right arm pointing in the direction of first slip as though preparing for one of the famous diving catches which made that particular fielding position redundant during his Lancashire and India career.

"Imagine that," he chuckles. "The Queen. At Lord's. Announcing that I'm a father. And that it's the daughter I wanted. Such wonderful news and I knew that my dear mum Minnie had kept her promise. She had told me just before she died that she would come back as my first child who would of course be named Minnie."

It was 1967. The India team had lined up to be introduced to Her Majesty before the start of the Test and Engineer, waiting to hear whether his wife had given birth back in their home town of Bombay, had spotted an official handing a telegram to the MCC secretary Billy Griffith who promptly whispered into the Queen's ear. Seconds later she was congratulating him.

You couldn't script it. Yet it is only one of a hundred or more wonderful tales which The Cricketing Cavalier reels off from the storybook of his life. Admittedly many have been sympathetically 'restored' but in the unique environment of Great Cricketing Tales a little spit and polish has never done any harm. Honest.

On and off the pitch, was there ever a more reliable entertainer than Farokh Manecksha Engineer? Reliable in that you knew there would always be something to cheer, to laugh about, to marvel at. Sometimes a rash attacking shot which made you groan in exasperation only for you to acknowledge in the same breath: "He can't play any other way." His exhilarating first-class cricket career ended in 1976 but the audience continues to applaud on his globe-trotting exploits as a cricket ambassador and raconteur.

An outstanding mould-breaking wicketkeeper and a brave, adventurous if sometimes reckless batsman he was a key figure of Lancashire's dominance of one-day cricket under the captaincy of Jack Bond. And he claims that he helped to transform Indian cricket not least by strengthening its backbone.

"I learned to stand up for myself and I persuaded others to do the same," he says. "I took on Dennis Lillee and Jeff Thomson in a game in Queensland. They were mightily quick and hostile. I was hooking them, Lillee came up to me, ball in hand and brushed my nose with it while giving me some terrible abuse. One or two words beginning with 'B' I think. I made a joke of it. In the end we all ended up having a laugh, Dennis included. He was only trying to wind me up.

"But I had realised long before that incident that it was absolutely essential not to buckle down to any kind of intimidation. I talked to my team-mates about it and kept talking to them. In the past India had been too soft. I'm not sure why. There were others who stood up of course but in general we were fragile and too easily folded under pressure. Maybe because we still considered the white nations as our masters, that they could say and do anything to us that they wanted. But gradually we began to give some of it back. We discovered new confidence. I like to think I played a big part in that."

He nearly took on the Queen as well. "She called me 'Engineer'. I was tempted to say that my name was Farokh or Mr Engineer. I didn't like it really but that is royal protocol and so obviously I let it go."

Not always a laughing Cavalier then....of course not. Engineer was a proud, deadly serious, highly combative cricketer although ideally he preferred to sledge with his bat rather than his mouth. He was determined to succeed and desperate for India to win respect as well as to win Test matches. But rarely did he lose his natural mischievousness, his warmth, his generosity, and his ability to make people smile. While now if he dived for a catch the floor would shudder under his weight and he might have difficulty getting up he can still stand tall and hold centre stage with his reminisces and views of cricket.

When he gave the M.A.K.Pataudi lecture at the Board of Control for India annual awards in February 2017 the Times of India report highlighted his gaffe in naming spinner Ravichandran Ashwin's home state as Karnataka instead of Tamil Nadu. But the Indian Express preferred to focus on the fact that he left the audience 'in splits' with his jokes. He divided opinion at that ceremony just as he did as a player, frustrating some perfectionists but delighting the masses.

Of course there are flaws in this extravagant larger than life character. Those who make it to the top of their particular tree need many qualities, notably deeply rooted self-belief. It manifests itself in different ways. Brian Statham, briefly Engineer's team-mate at Old Trafford and forever his much valued friend, was the quietest and most modest of top calibre sportsmen but he scoffed at false modesty. "I was good, I knew I would take wickets," he once confided. Statham, though, played down personal success. He cared more for his glossy family photograph albums than his rather worn and meagre cricketing scrapbooks. Details of his career had to be extracted from him slowly, carefully, like drawing a tooth.

In contrast the extrovert Engineer brimmed with confidence and personality. If sometimes now it overflows into self-congratulatory mode then at least he is able to recognise it and usually attempts to douse the blaze with a self effacing joke.

There is an argument that he was Indian cricket's most recognisable international star until the arrival of Sunil Gavaskar. "That's for others to say, not me," he insists. "But while I don't want to sound big-headed neither do I want to under value myself. I played for India for many years and I was the first Indian player to have success in one-day cricket. What happened with Lancashire cannot be under-estimated. We launched the one-day game and changed cricket. We played 60 overs, 40 overs and 55 overs matches. It was all so very new and it could have flopped. But Lancashire more than anyone made it a success. And look what it has led to. This was the start of big time one-day cricket. ODIs, the World Cup, Twenty20. England was the only country playing full-time professional cricket and for me, an Indian, to be involved was fantastic."

Engineer's move to England in 1968 did not go down well with certain factions in India and, in assessing his career, his triumphs with Lancashire are unlikely to resound throughout the sub-continent at this stage, almost 50 years further on. However it cannot be denied that he was a trail-blazer in two major cricketing nations.

Engineer was a Test ace in India well before he joined Lancashire after which, in nine seasons 1968-76, he became one of English cricket's biggest names, winning six trophies in the Gillette Cup and fledgling John Player (Sunday) League. It was a period which transformed cricket forever and the name of Engineer, initially a lone Indian among a galaxy of overseas stars, is inscribed on it just as it is on India's Vijay Balla (Victory Bat) monument which commemorates India's historic series win in England in 1971.

India has led cricket's progress in recent times. Jagmohan Dalmiya boasted shortly after being elected President of the International Cricket Council in 1997 that he intended to make the one-day international game more popular than Test cricket. He did. And then came the Indian Premier League, re-shaping a rather eccentric English idea into a bold, brash Bollywood showpiece. If the DNA for the glitzy success of T20 and ODI cricket lies way back in the days when Lancashire bestrode the one-day game, then, while in reviewing Engineer's career it might remain necessary to keep a grip on a jug of cold dousing water, it is also only fair to give full weight to his achievements as a pioneer. The first Indian to succeed in one-day cricket. The fact that it was for a county rather than at international level should not devalue the currency one bit. English cricket then was a massive stage, a Mecca, for the world's top players. It took Engineer's countrymen some years to catch up. Thankfully they did and then overtook everyone.

His popularity endures. Invitations flood in from all parts and in his native Bombay, decades after his retirement, he can still pull a trick or two. I was in that city's airport one day, tired after a long flight from the UK, frustrated with British Airways (bless 'em) who had failed to put my bag on the plane, and being informed that I had been 'bumped' off my connecting flight to Calcutta and would have to join the waiting list hoping for late cancellations. As that list consisted of two dozen shouting, demanding Indian citizens who were laying siege to the check-in counter I was about to cut my losses, find some lodgings and try again next day when I heard a familiar voice behind me. "Colin, what are you doing here?" It was 'Rooky' as we knew him then. (Now he prefers Farokh). Sheer coincidence. He was also on his way to Calcutta. I explained my predicament, "Leave it with me," he said. He disappeared behind the desk. Minutes later I had a berth on the plane. It is a story which does me little credit but it does highlight the influence that a cricket star has in India. Twenty years had passed since Engineer's farewell appearance and he was long settled in his adopted homeland of Manchester but he could still conjure an airline seat for a rather bedraggled, unknown Brit.

Engineer cemented his position in India's Hall of Fame as a wicketkeeper with flair and agility, leaping high and wide to grab 'impossible' legside catches and clicking off the bails in, as one writer put it, 'a flurry of gloves'. Alert, quick and hugely confident he was able to stand up to seam bowling and to cope efficiently with the multi faceted spin of India's renowned quartet of Bhawat Chandrasekhar, Bishan Bedi, Erapalli Prasanna and Srinivas Venkataraghavan.

As a batsman he had plenty of shots and bravado, hooking lethal fast bowling off the front foot in a time when batsmen had little protection either from gear or umpires. Although generally acclaimed for this crowd pulling approach he occasionally demonstrated a more careful technique when the occasion demanded it ….occasionally. His career batting figures for Test matches are interesting. An average of 31.08 does not tell it all by any means.

He was India's Cricketer of the Year in 1965, was the only Indian to play for the Rest of the World on their tour of England in 1970 and featured again for the ROW in Pakistan and Australia along with countrymen Gavaskar and Bedi in Australia 1971-72. In 1973 the Indian government awarded him the Padma Shri, similar to the UK's MBE, for services to sport. Off the pitch he adopted the role of ambassador for his team and the sport. It was not a conscious decision, simply a manifestation of his nature. Generous, always up for a good time, eager to help, never refusing an autograph, a cricketer who understood not just that spectators wanted value for money but that they were part of the game not an adjunct. Saluted in India and in England he was also warmly greeted everywhere else whether by Sir Don Bradman in Australia or by Wes Hall's mum in Barbados.

In debating world-wide celebrity status the impact of imagery and commercialism has also to be taken into account. What you are off the pitch can be almost as significant as what you do on it. Here Engineer had a useful start. Well educated, he had business acumen, and he could make friends easily. Whether in the sphere of cricket, business or high society he was a naturally skilled networker, eager to put himself about. Most of all he was a good looking bloke. He likes to point out that his skin is comparatively pale, a feature which counts heavily in certain sections of Indian society and when a het-up Lillee sledged him with the phrase 'black bastard' Engineer merely turned to the slip cordon saying: "Is he colour blind?" In all then a bit of a pin-up boy, ripe for marketing of himself, cricket in general and other products. As such he followed in the footprints of Keith Miller and Denis Compton when Brylcreem plastered his image all over the sub-continent. "I was the first Indian player to feature in a commercial advertising campaign. There was a huge placard of me hanging from a bridge on one of Bombay's main roads."

I hope that Indian critics - and Engineer has them - do not under-sell his time in English cricket. Only a handful of Indians played county cricket before Engineer and he was the first to leave a permanent mark on an era in which the one-day format blossomed and where overseas players made a much deeper, more colourful impression - at least with a more youthful cricketing public - than those players less sharply defined against the blurred black and white backcloth of Test matches. By the time of the first World Cup in 1975 Engineer was one of the most easily recognisable faces of the whole show.

Before Gavaskar there were plenty of other Indians who earned huge respect in other countries as well as being worshipped in their own. A lengthy list of superb batsmen and captains including Vijay Hazare, Vijay Merchant, Lala Amarnath, Vinoo Mankad, Vijay Manjrekar, Gundappa Viswanath, Ajit Wadekar, and Engineer's mentor Polly Umrigar - along with the spin quartet of Chandra, Prasanna, Bedi and Venkat who between them played 231 Tests and claimed 853 wickets. (This is not a comprehensive list and for those murmuring impatiently 'What about Tiger?' I will come to him shortly).

And even if you focused purely on entertainment value rather than sheer ability, Engineer was not the only one who could light up a packed stadium or turn heads in the street.

Like M.L. Jaisimha a stylish cricketer who, gushed one commentator 'had a slim figure which he maintained until his last day, the boyish good looks, the inimitable gait, the trademark silk shirt and scarf, the sleeves buttoned at the wrist or the collar turned up - all these attracted immediate attention.' Or Salim Durani, the first Afghan to play for India. He loved hitting sixes and when dropped for one Test fans mounted a massive protest chanting: 'No Durani, no Test.' Durani was handsome, too. In 1973 he appeared in a Bollywood film.

However in debating the first Indian to earn widespread star appeal at home and abroad I rely on only two candidates and neither is Gavaskar who arrived a little later although what he was to achieve eclipsed all. One of the duo in my frame wears a cap, the peak pulled over his right eye. There is the hint of a smile, perhaps slightly condescending as though the photographer has pleaded with him. The other subject stands relaxed, a wide grin, enjoying the attention....

India gained independence in 1947 but by the late 1950s their cricketers and many of their officials were still hampered by the psychological shackles of colonial domination. Too often they displayed a lack of spirit and ambition. Farokh Engineer was to provide both after his debut but thanks to the exasperating politics of selection in Indian cricket he played only 11 of his 46 Tests during the first half of the 1960s and in that period the Indian uprising was led by the suave and heroic figure of the Nawab of Pataudi, who was handed the captaincy at the age of 21 and became revered as Tiger Pataudi.

Educated at Winchester and Oxford, Pataudi played for Sussex at the age of 16 and won the heart of every cricket fan by appearing for India only six months after a car accident which had seriously damaged his right eye. Despite this permanent disability he played in 46 Tests, captained India in 40 of them, and was one of *Wisden*'s Five Cricketers of the Year in 1968. Rahul Dravid has described him as a 'romantic figure'. Neville Cardus, never one for under statement wrote: 'there was suppleness and lithe grace which concealed power, as silkiness of skin conceals the voracity of strength in a beautiful animal of the jungle.'

Engineer recalls how Pataudi once teased a couple of new boys on the Indian team by indicating the famous Victoria Memorial, a huge white marbled building in Calcutta, and inviting them for tea: "Come and see me at my home this evening." His respect for him is undiluted. "He was a very fine cricketer and a top-class captain. We all had great respect for him. Some thought he could be a little standoffish at times but he had a good sense of humour and I for one got on very well with him. We had an instinctive understanding out on the pitch. We didn't have to talk a great deal, just a look would confirm that we were thinking along the same lines, maybe about a change in the bowling or a fielding position."

He always elicits a laugh with his story of how Pataudi would grab any bat before walking out of the dressing-room. "Invariably it was mine but at least it meant someone was putting it to good use."

Pataudi was a charismatic figure, a character straight out of the 'Boys Own' magazine who shrugged off a desperate physical disability to lead his country with aplomb. Under him, India scored some of their greatest and defining victories and suffered one or two gallant defeats. Witty and wealthy, his already immense popularity soared in India when in 1969 he married the actress Sharmila Tagore. In England he was held in high regard. A brilliant batsman, he came from the 'right' background, public school, Oxford, a member of the elite. He looked good, tall and slim and immaculately attired. Maybe his wealth, education and elegance earned him fewer brownie points in the less conservative ranks of a British society which underwent radical change in the 1960s but what did count with them were his dignity and courage.

However he took no part in the revolution which changed the world of cricket. Pataudi played only five one-day games in England and a couple in India. In stark contrast, between the introduction of Sunday league cricket in 1969 and his retirement in 1976 Engineer was one of the most watched, most seen and most heard players of any nationality.

One match each Sunday was screened live by BBC 2. Millions of viewers switched on and eventually Lancashire proved the biggest draw both for the armchair fans and those who queued to get into packed grounds all around the country. When Lancashire won the first Sunday title it is estimated that they pulled in over 150,000 fans for their eight home fixtures. When in 1970 they retained it and launched their run of three successive Gillette Cup wins attendances mushroomed, then exploded. Once or twice the Old Trafford gates were locked with people still outside but usually they managed to squeeze them all in and over 30,000 packed the ground to the rafters for the decisive 1970 clash with arch rivals Yorkshire. I can only liken the atmosphere of that day to that of the 2005 Ashes Test at Old Trafford when thousands were locked out on the Monday as 'cricket fever' gripped England. However there are major differences. One: seat prices for the Ashes clash were slashed for the Monday, the last day. Two: while many more wanted to get in, the ground capacity was restricted to around 20,000.

There was more noise, greater tension and more satisfaction watching that Sunday Roses clash than the one at the 'other' Old Trafford 24 hours earlier where Manchester United met West Ham in front of 50,000 fans. I was at both matches. So were many others judging by the football crowd noise and drama which attended Lancashire's win over the old enemy. It was cricket but not as older fans had known it. Long after play had ended the ground, never pretty, looked as though it had been hit by a herd of rampaging buffalo and was still full of celebrating supporters, a press of autograph hunters waiting at the bottom of the dressing-room stairs. One or two players, not used to or not enjoying the attention, sidled past without speaking. I understand that now much more than then. They would have been tired and anxious to get some space for themselves. Then Engineer appeared. Although we barely knew each other at that stage he was more than happy to talk, breaking off here and there to sign an autograph or greet someone. He said: "Now I know what it feels like to be a soccer star."

Back to the present day and he is beaming at the memory. "It might be difficult now to appreciate what was going on at that time," said Engineer. "In cricket there was nothing like it anywhere else in the world and Lancashire were the stars of the show. We were mobbed when we won the league."

Players lacked experience in dealing with the pressures of this new phenomenon. One minute they were football's poor cousins, county cricketers meandering from one run-down venue to another, playing tedious championship cricket for the benefit of one man and his dog. Then suddenly they were stars, attracting massive gates, faces on nationwide TV, names in headlines. Some found it difficult. Some like Engineer took it in their stride. "One English tabloid offered me £1000 for a picture of me showing my bare torso with my daughter perched on my shoulder. I was happy to do that. "

Whether in India or in England Engineer was the beating heart of the team. Always involved, always determined to be at the centre of the party. He had motivational qualities which can never be reflected by mere facts and figures (he disdains bare statistics) and he developed valuable tactical relationships with three esteemed captains, Bond, Pataudi and Wadekar. No matter what the verdict on him as a player it is clear that he was a major figure in two remarkable phases, India's rise as a Test power and the volcanic surge of one-day cricket.

CHAPTER 2

WHEN A silly rumour that Farokh Engineer had died went viral on social media in October 2016 he responded in typical stand-up comedian fashion: "I'm more alive than ever - I'm 78 and don't need Viagra. It would only give me a stiff neck."

Engineer is a busy energetic bloke. In his company time passes quickly. Hours go filled with anecdotes. He often batted like a whirlwind, now he talks like one, effortlessly unleashing stories and opinions off the sweet spot. Entertaining is an understatement like describing the traffic in Bombay as occasionally busy. However Engineer is also a serious-minded commentator, who delights in debating cricket's problems and its future - of which he remains positive. So the laughs are punctuated with the occasional slight frown as he delves into the sport's issues.

While, for example, he excelled in the one-day game and would surely have been highly prized in the Indian Premier League auction he believes that the status of Test cricket should be jealously protected. At Test level he is saddened by the dramatic fall of attendances in some parts and the decline of the West Indies team, once the powerhouse of world cricket under the captaincy of his close pal Clive Lloyd.

"T20 and other One Day formats are deservedly popular with the masses and also with the majority of international cricketers as they offer so many benefits but Test cricket is Test cricket, the greatest challenge of all and should never be replaced by the shorter versions. There's room for all to flourish," he says.

Get him talking about match-fixing and he sits bolt upright lambasting the corruptors and the corrupted. In January 2017 he was mentioned as a possible candidate for India's new Committee of Administrators drafted in by the Supreme Court to clean up the national game. But sportsmen are best remembered for their deeds rather than their words. To those who have never experienced cricket in the sub-continent it is difficult to convey the impact made by a player like Engineer. Cricket is a 'religion' or a 'way of life' there - those are the usual ways of expressing how deeply the sport is embedded in the Indian soul but, to me, these phrases present a slightly faded watercolour picture when it should be daubed in vivid oils.

Thinking of cricket in India I go back to 1997 when Engineer, then acting as an ambassador for Lancashire, led a Red Rose squad to Calcutta for a one-day game against an India XI at Eden Gardens - part of a week-long commercial and leisure festival in the city. Known too easily for its slums and Mother Teresa's work with the sick and poverty stricken, Calcutta wanted to re-brand itself. The then British Prime Minister John Major was at the top of a long VIPs list and, knowing he was a cricket fan, the organisers had shrewdly made the match as a pseudo India v England centrepiece although the Lancashire lads had been told it was more of a fun friendly, part of the jamboree.

Engineer was in his element, setting up sight-seeing tours for the Lancashire committee and their wives, making sure the players had all they needed, even taking some of the committee to a tailor's to be fitted for suits. Fans surrounded him wherever he went. The players reckoned it was a pleasant way of spending a week in January before getting back to serious pre-season training back at Old Trafford. They lounged around the pool at the five star Oberoi Hotel, had a couple of practice sessions, attended one or two receptions. No pressure - after all the game promised to be a light-hearted affair, everyone to be introduced to Mr Major. Hopefully there would be a few thousand spectators just to provide a little atmosphere. At least that's what they thought.

It turned out somewhat differently. For the Lancashire squad the first worrying signs were the baying hundreds of fans outside the hotel and the excitement that the team bus caused during the journey to the ground, Outside Eden Gardens armed police escorted the bus and VIP limousines towards the entrance. Crowds were gathering at the turnstiles. Neil Fairbrother who had played in the World Cup in India and Pakistan only 12 months earlier looked pensive. Wicketkeeper Warren Hegg said: "I wasn't expecting this."

Fifty thousand fans turned up that day, easily the largest gate that Lancashire had ever played in front of. They shouted and screamed constantly. The chanting and heat turned it into a cauldron. With national pride suddenly at stake the 'friendly' turned into a real battle. Near the end as dusk began to fall the fans lit newspaper torches and, against this almost hellish backdrop of fire and deafening noise, Lancashire scrambled to a thrilling sweat-soaked victory which mirrored some of their most notable escapades in domestic one-day cricket. Afterwards, totally exhausted, Glen Chapple said: "I thought it was supposed to be a friendly!"

"It was," joked Engineer. "You should see what the really serious games are like."

An Indian cricket idol can count on an affluent, glamorous life akin to that of a Bollywood film star. He has the highest status in a country where status is perhaps the most prized possession of all and Engineer stamped his name on the Indian psyche in an era when Test cricket reigned supreme without rivalry from the one day international format, nor from other sports. Put simply - he was big.

In England he was quickly dubbed as a headline act. 'Engineer's daring 58 lightens the gloom'. 'Fantastic Farokh' roared the sports pages of the British Press, 'quality' and tabloid papers all paying homage to a special cricketer. The Old Trafford fans embraced him. Clive Lloyd's power packed hitting emptied the bars but as he loped from pavilion to wicket you did not feel forced to neck your drink and rush back to your seat. The West Indian star usually took his time to settle in before setting about the bowling. With Engineer taking guard you supped up double quick - the fireworks could start any second. Freddie Flintoff's entrance from the dressing-room provoked similar excitement although by then, 30 years later, there was one massive difference, the size of the crowd.

Engineer and his Kings of One Day cricket team-mates were sometimes roared on by 20,000 plus. Once or twice by over 30,000. Freddie could only count on that support when he appeared for England. It all ended on a slightly downbeat note at the end of the 1976 season after Lancashire had slipped to a disappointing defeat by Northants in the Gillette Cup final. Engineer, then 38, had already decided to retire and concentrate on a business career.

Eight years earlier his arrival at Old Trafford, along with Clive Lloyd's the following season and the emergence of Jack Bond as a shrewd, enterprising captain, had sparked off Lancashire's rise to dominance in one-day cricket. Engineer's exit with those of Ken Shuttleworth, Peter Lever and John Sullivan heralded the county's swift fall from grace. Apart from a Benson and Hedges Cup triumph in 1984, after a game so desultory that the man of the match award went to John Abrahams for his captaincy, Lancashire spent 13 years in the doldrums. Engineer left with a testimonial cheque of over £26,000, then a club record. It spoke volumes for the affection in which he was held.

Late in that final season of 1976 when England melted under a heatwave he gave me a lift in his Merc over the parched hills to Buxton where Lancashire were to appear at the Park ground for the last time. We chatted about nothing in particular but I remember saying: "Why pack up now? You've got at least another season in you." But the cricketing glint in his eyes had dimmed somewhat. "I've done everything I set out to achieve. There's nothing left to play for." I let it go for the time being. Mainly because his driving was the source of much dressing room banter and at that moment he was steering his Merc one-handed around a hairpin bend....

Now it is 2017, 40 years further on and Engineer, just back from a trip which took him to India on business and then to a Trinidad Test match, tells me: "I could have gone on for a couple of years. But you have to have ambitions and I had fulfilled all of mine. I didn't want simply to go through the motions, I had loved every minute of it. Yes, I had a ball."

When George Best arrived in Manchester as a skinny unknown 15 years-old in the summer of 1961 he got off the train at Victoria station and asked a taxi driver to take him to Old Trafford. He was duly driven to the cricket ground where Lancashire were involved in a championship match. "I don't think this is the right place," said George. "I want United's ground." The cabbie was puzzled. "Nothing going on there lad. Season's over. I thought you wanted to watch the cricket."

Thankfully Best eventually got to the correct stadium to launch a career which transformed United and invigorated a city which, after years of neglect, was to shine as a beacon of the Swinging Sixties. By the spring of 1968 United were preparing to face Benfica in the European Cup Final, slums were cleared and replaced by tower blocks, the nightlife buzzed and Coronation Street boasted 16 million viewers. The cricket club was a few years behind everything else but trying desperately to catch up. As Georgie Boy and the rest battled to victory over Real Madrid in the European semis, Lancashire embarked on a new era with Bond as captain and an astute ambitious businessman named Cedric Rhoades making his presence felt in the committee room. Moreover the club had signed Engineer and planned to bring in Lloyd the following season. Suddenly life looked a lot brighter at the 'real' Old Trafford. And about time....

Lancashire had endured a miserable period, rooted in the bottom half of the championship between 1961 and 1967. Particularly in the first half of the decade the finger of blame was pointed firmly at the committee leading to a successful members' rebellion, headed by Rhoades, in September 1964. Rhoades was elected to a new committee and Brian Statham took over as captain.

Younger players like David Lloyd, Harry Pilling and David Hughes were emerging but progress was slow and inconsistent so much so that even with Statham's inspirational bowling Lancashire could manage only placings of 13th, 12th and 11th under his charge. But Bond's promotion from struggling veteran batsman, rarely sure of his place, to captain proved one of the most valuable decisions ever made at Old Trafford. Some have described it as an out and out gamble - after all Bond was 36 with a career batting average in the mid 20s - but there is evidence to categorise it as a visionary move for Bond's leadership attributes had been noted when he had occasionally captained the second XI. Under Bond, Lancashire won five trophies in four years. Heady days. Incomparable days.

Some will say 'What about the 1990s?' when a magnificent team packed with internationals played in eight Lord's finals and also won the Sunday League twice. Powerful in every department, bound together by the little general Neil Fairbrother who, whether as captain or not, called for and sometimes demanded the same degree of team spirit which Bond had instilled 20 years earlier, they also earned the title of Kings of One Day Cricket. But, for me, it was not quite the same as the 1970s. Crowds had diminished and the game had become more professional resulting in a wider gap between players and spectators.

Success generates instant growth and, after so long in the doldrums, what happened in 1969 onwards was manna from heaven for supporters. Only a Roses match or a big Gillette Cup tie would get the turnstiles clicking over at Old Trafford until the birth of the Sunday League. Then, in the blink of an eye, Lancashire were transformed. They were winners. Engineer and Lloyd were heroes. But a hero is not always hugged as a family member. Engineer and Lloyd were not only welcomed at the door with open arms, they were pushed into comfy armchairs by the fire and handed slippers long before they decided to live forever in the North-West to be acknowledged as adopted Lancastrians.

Lloyd had a head start in the popularity stakes. He was a Test player who had done time in the hard-bitten Lancashire League where anyone lacking heart was quickly exposed. The 6 feet 5 inches tall bespectacled West Indian, not then the best in the world - that was Garry Sobers - was already well liked, an 'amiable beanpole', as he was described in one newspaper. Strangely, though reporters of that era were charged with establishing the facts, they sometimes got the facts wrong simply through a lack of source material. Engineer's forename was constantly spelled wrongly with such variations as 'Farouk', 'Farook' and 'Farookh'. As for Lloyd, describing him as a 'beanpole' would probably have seemed a reasonable compromise to a scribe unable to ascertain his exact height - better than reducing him to 'just over 6 feet tall' as per one article in the *Manchester Evening News*.

Lloyd was modest and polite yet you could have a laugh with him. Very soon into his full first Lancashire season (1969) he found himself batting with the 5 feet 3 inches Pilling, one of the smallest men ever to play county cricket, and quite often when they met in the middle of the pitch for a conflab it seemed that while, with head bent, he was listening attentively to 'Little Harry' he was also acting as his bodyguard. "I'd tell him to stick there while I got the runs," joked Pilling who usually started quicker than Lloyd. "He'd tell me not to bother ducking under the bouncers." This ungainly partnership earned Lloyd extra bonus points in the stands where Pilling, the local lad, was well established as 'one of us'. When Lloyd began to bang the ball out of the ground that front door, already wide open to him, was flung off its hinges.

It was a little different with Engineer, the lone Indian among the international brigade who were about to invade county cricket. Apart from a few clippings from newspapers, *The Cricketer*, and *Wisden* the first we came to know of him was on India's tour of England in 1967 but it was a short visit with three Tests spread over five weeks and none at Old Trafford. Apart from catching glimpses of him during BBC's Test coverage the only real chance for Lancashire fans to see him in action was a three day game at Southport and when the club announced his signing he was, for many of us, a vague figure with a weird name and no connection at all to the frozen north.

But the story intrigued me. I had seen Engineer playing against Lancashire at Southport, a day which I might wish to recount later but, while I had been impressed, I had no idea he would end up playing for the county. How would he cope with the weather? Would he be demand curry at lunch? It seemed a bit of a punt for both club and player. What I knew for certain was that it would liven up the old place. Old Trafford, seen through my rapidly maturing eyes rather than those of the skittish star struck schoolboy I once was, had eroded from a cricketing Taj Mahal into a cold, dismal arena only worth visiting to watch Statham or, at a push, Geoff Pullar. If anywhere needed a dash of spice it was Old Trafford.

In his first summer at Old Trafford, 1968, Engineer had a mixed time with the bat but kept wicket well and roped himself into Bond's team ethic forming long-lasting friendships in the dressing-room. The following season he was a driving force in the first Sunday League triumph and had quickly endeared himself to supporters with his spirited play and outgoing personality. I began looking for more Indian restaurants, arguing with dad who dismissed curry and its ilk as 'muck' although he smothered all his food in pepper. (Neither of us knew then that we had Indian blood).

Engineer first visited England in the summer of 1962. He tucked into it as though a banquet had been lovingly placed in front of him. Staying at the Edgware, London home of his brother Darius he watched cricket, played tennis, carved the Sunday roast. And he even enjoyed the climate. It is not surprising that he took to the British way of life. His family were Parsees, the high caste community descended from Persian immigrants who had settled in the Maharashtra and Gujurat regions of India. Most had finished up in the Bombay area. They were affluent, professional people who had prospered under colonial rule and regarded Britain as a paternalistic power rather than as unwanted invaders. In the late 18th century some took their occupations as surnames, eg Engineer, Contractor.

His father was Doctor Engineer. Dr Manecksha Engineer worked for the giant TATA company who were building a dam in the low lying hills on the periphery of Bombay's sprawling outer suburbs. Bhivpuri, the village where the family lived was only 150 feet or so above sea level but just high enough to catch a cooling breeze. They had a neat bungalow surrounded by a well tended garden. Nearby was a 60 feet waterfall, cascading streams and the jungle where danger lurked in the form of snakes and leopards. Engineer's memories of childhood are happy ones. Apart from a cobra which once danced in front of him on the lawn before sliding off into the undergrowth there was little or nothing to worry about. A personable boy he made friends easily, showed early signs of becoming a top-class sportsman, and was backed by a caring, supportive family.

Manecksha, tall, upright and bespectacled acted as the village's GP although his salaried job was looking after TATA employees. He read voraciously, played cricket and tennis. "He was an opening bowler," Farokh says. "Pretty useful with the new ball. He would bowl to me sometimes. I would give it a real whack and force him to run miles just recovering the ball. But he never complained. He didn't mind - all he wanted was for me to become a better player."

Dr Engineer was also a hot-shot with a rifle. When a leopard attacked some villagers they called on him to shoot it. "He took me with him. Some bait was laid and we climbed up a tree onto a platform and waited. He stayed very calm. The leopard came and he shot it."

His mum, Minnie sounds like the sort of gregarious multi-talented lady you would love to meet as long as you did as you were told. She came from a musical family which included the conductor Zubin Mehta, played the violin and could swing a tennis racquet with as much aplomb as Mehta's baton. She ensured her children stayed healthy by ramming home the nutritional benefits of pure honey and buffalo milk. And while she encouraged Engineer's dreams of cricket stardom she also made sure he did his homework first, even to the extent of locking him in the house by wedging a stopper in the top of the door.

Once when he did escape to play for his local club, Minnie stormed onto the pitch. "I was batting," he says with a wry smile. "'You - out!' she shouted, 'You're coming home, You haven't done your lessons'. I was annoyed and embarrassed. But eventually I passed my exams so I had her to thank for it." Minnie continued to drive her son, whether scolding him into more revision or, after a match, demanding to know why he had got out. "She wasn't happy if I had been dismissed cheaply." With parents like these it was little wonder that Engineer quickly made a name for himself in club cricket when the family moved from Bhivpuri to Bombay.

Britain had emerged victorious from World War 2 but had given up its empire with the 'jewel in the crown', India, gaining independence at the stroke of midnight on August 14, 1947. Jawarhal Nehru, the Prime Minister told his nation just before the clock struck twelve: "Long years ago we made a tryst with destiny and now the time comes when we shall redeem our pledge.......at the stroke of midnight hour when the world sleeps India will awake to life and freedom."

Yet that proclamation unleashed the horror of Partition with millions killed and forced to leave their homes. Engineer saw bloodshed in the streets. "It was terrible, Hindus and Muslims killing each other. But thankfully we got through it." The Westernised Parsee community escaped much of the religious strife which has constantly affected India. Engineer admits he is not particularly religious. "The Parsee religion Zoroastrianism was not rigid, nothing saying that you must do this or do that. It's said that the Hindus refuse to eat beef while the Muslims refuse pork. The Parsee however like their meat medium rare."

The Engineer family worshipped at one of the Parsee fire temples where the flame burns continuously. Dressed neatly in white shirts and shorts he ate food served on banana leaves at family birthdays and weddings.

It is, in his view, a simple culture based around the purifying concept of fire. Good thoughts, good words, good deeds - similar to most other religions, actually, but with a relaxed framework. "We lived in a Westernised way and came into contact with the British imitating many of their customs and traditions such as a good English breakfast. We celebrated Christmas, and the various New Years, Divali (Hindu), Eid (Muslim), and Nowroz (Persian). My only criticism of the religion is that it is extremely snobbish and too exclusive. Other religions try to spread their gospel and recruit new members but not the Parsees. It is dying as a result." Official figures show that at the start of 2017 the Parsee population in India had slumped to 61,000 not even a drop in the ocean compared to the national figure of 1.25 billion.

India in the 1950s took time to come to terms with its new independence. But Bombay, its commercial capital, had a quality and resonance of its own, highlighted by the iconic Gateway of India, the 85 feet high basalt arch on the harbourside which was completed in 1924 to welcome royalty and High Commissioners but became a symbol of Indian pride. And in Bombay a promising Parsee cricketer had a real chance to make his name.

CHAPTER 3

BOMBAY. THE home of Bollywood. What a place! Teeming with life, it stretches higgledy piggledy for many miles over what were three islands with the Arabian Sea shimmering at its side. Fabulous wealth, abject poverty, billionaire towers with heliports, slums with open sewers - all there, hope, pride and helplessness dripping off its face like beads of perspiration.

Western tourists were told: "You'll either love it or hate it." Most voted for the latter and shot out of town as quickly as possible heading for the beaches of Goa or north towards Rajasthan. But there is, and always was, much to admire about this seething metropolis of 12 million. Some wonderful colonial and modern architecture, a vibrant cultural scene - even apart from that of Bollywood - and a real fighting spirit. It has risen courageously above many crises including horrific terrorist outrages. For much of its history it feasted on textiles and commerce.

The author Salman Rushdie whose family moved from Delhi to Bombay in 1946 to 'feel safer' after Partition found himself in "a city going through a golden age - like an enchanted zone. It was a wonderful, exciting city to grow up in." They lived not too far from the Engineer home which was in the Dadar Colony, built around 1900 specially to accommodate 10,000 Parsees. Strict conditions were laid down by the authorities before construction started - no building to be more than three storeys high with plenty of space between each one and communal gardens to be laid out providing a breath of tranquility from the hubbub of the streets. It became a desirable area. The Engineers' flat was what estate agents term 'compact' but he was more than happy to sleep on the balcony, imbibing the sounds and scents of one of the world's most vibrant cities. Bombay allowed him to spread his wings. He was a self confessed showman, always ready to push the envelope. A place like Bombay was tailor-made for him.

"'Tailor made?' Don't mention tailors to me," he grins. "There was a guy called Eric the Tailor who made my clothes. I wanted short shorts, above the knee but he was an old-fashioned Parsee who was out just to please my parents so when I put them on they were well below the knee. Same with the shirts. I liked mine loose, Eric made them so big I could invite a few friends in. It wasn't funny being made to dress up like a Japanese general."

As for cricket, well he was a Parsee. And they had invented the game, hadn't they? It was a tongue in cheek claim based on the fact that Persians had played a game called chowgan although the only known similarity with cricket was the use of a round ball. However the Indian Parsees had taken to cricket like mutton to curry and in *A Chronicle of Cricket Amongst Parsees* written in 1897 Shapoorjee Sorabjee explained: "Parsee boys began with a mock and farcical imitation of European soldiers and officers playing at Fort George Bombay, their chimney pot hats serving as wickets and their umbrellas as bats in hitting elliptical balls stuffed with old rags and sewn by veritably unskilful cobblers. Some enthusiastic boys at first only gleefully watched from a distance … and then hunted after and returned the balls to the players. For such gratis services rendered heartily and joyfully the officers sometimes called them to handle the bat which was done with extreme pleasure and delight. Thus were learnt the initiatory lessons in cricket by the Parsees."

Early Parsee enthusiasm for cricket stemmed partly from their desire for a close alliance with the British. They had lived in western regions of India for many centuries after fleeing Persia but had never considered themselves a totally Indian community, nor perhaps had been considered as such by others. They sponged up British culture. Cricket was the game to play and in Bombay, during the Victorian age, its popularity and social value soared. Not that the colonials were always keen to encourage the locals. After all 'old boy' there were still certain social divisions to be maintained!

In the 1880s a controversy broke out over where the Parsees could play. They wanted more room for pitches on the Esplanade, then a wide expanse between Fort George and the sea, but that was where the Brits also played polo. An enraged N.F. Symons, the Polo Club's secretary wrote to the *Times of India*: "Do not allow the preposterous notion to take root that a few young Parsee cricketers are going to be allowed to oppose the whole European community and jostle the Europeans off the Esplanade, whether at polo, sports or anything else - the sooner these young Parsees come to their senses and become a little more modest the better." Quite!

But Parsee cricket developed quickly. In 1877 they played and lost against an English XI at the Gymkhana Stadium and they toured England in 1886, raising eyebrows, attracting some scorn but generally being treated regally. One game was in Windsor Great Park against a side captained by Prince Victor, the Queen's grandson. Two years later they returned, dubbed the Bengal Tigers because of their black and yellow striped blazers and won respect with their refusal to give up lost causes. 'Parsee pluck' was acknowledged by W.G. Grace among other cricketing luminaries.

This was a springboard for Indian cricket. As Hindus and Muslims took up the initiative, cricket blossomed into the national game and although the Parsee influence waned Bombay remained the vortex. (The Dadar area alone has produced several Test players, Engineer, Tamhane, Gupte, Desai. Gavaskar and Tendulkar). A talented, ambitious young cricketer could not have been better positioned.

Neither could he have had a more attentive, encouraging family. Dr Engineer calmly and quietly marshalled his son's skills, practising with him, gently steering him in the right direction. "He had a dry sense of humour," Engineer says fondly. "He was softly spoken, mild mannered. I'm a little different!" Mum Minnie pushed and goaded him all the way. It is obvious that Engineer loved both parents but his feelings for Minnie were on a different plane. He was playing at Jamnagar in Gujurat, about 500 miles from Bombay when he received a message that his mother was seriously ill and to return home asap. The local Maharajah lent him his left-hand drive Cadillac and a driver who took things far too carefully on the dirt track roads. Impatiently, Engineer took over the wheel and tore through the countryside to get to Ahmedabad airport where an Indian Airlines plane was kept waiting. Passengers had been told of the reason and one volunteered his seat to allow Engineer to get home. At the hospital he stayed with Minnie through the night, tears streaming down his face. Her last words to him were: "Don't cry son. I promise I will come back to you as your first daughter. When we had our first child I knew it would be a girl. Her name had already been decided. Minnie."

Engineer was also indebted to his elder brother Darius, a fine cricketer himself who may have made it the top only to fall foul of the political machinations which bedevilled the Indian game. It was Darius who 'discovered' Engineer as a wicketkeeper. "He was a terrific off-spinner who could turn the ball square. But club wicketkeepers had no idea of gathering the ball down the leg-side. Every time it was byes. One match the regular 'keeper was absent so I offered to take over the gloves. I knew the way Darius bowled and got a couple of legside stumpings which was virtually unheard of. Darius told me: 'You should take it up full-time. You would be brilliant.' I'd enjoyed it and it was a way of keeping a place in the side. So that was the start."

Engineer was gifted. Confident, he enjoyed making batsmen nervous. Most of all he had ultra quick and positive eye-hand co-ordination. In the pre sports science era we called it split second reflexes, a physical process which does not require brain power. You do not have to think about it - it just happens. The batsman edges a delivery and deep in the 'keeper's central nervous system a 'receptor' springs into action, signals are relayed via the motor neurone to an 'effector' and this produces the relevant response - the 'keeper is flying through the air in front of first slip, hands outstretched and a hundredth of a second later his gloved fist tightens around the ball. Though nowadays they tend to weep a little, Engineer had good eyes. And the neurone signals must have bounced around his central nervous system quicker than particles through the CERN Hadron Collider because his reaction time was so fast. So rapid in fact that it once saved his benchmate and future Bollywood star Shashi Kapoor from a serious facial injury.

"We were schoolmates and best friends sitting next to each other on a bench when a master hurled a wooden blackboard duster towards us. Maybe we had been causing a disturbance. Anyway it flew through the air straight at Shashi and would have smacked him straight in the eyes but I threw up a hand and caught it right in front of his face. He became a Bollywood megastar, along with his two older brothers Raj Kapoor and Shami Kapoor but if I hadn't acted he might have ended up in Hammer horror productions because that duster would have wrecked his good looks."

That particular school, Don Bosco High, was run by Jesuit priests whose main sporting interests lay in football, hockey, badminton and squash. His cricketing education came on the spare ground, backstreets and beaches of Bombay with trees and cans as stumps. He practised catching with an old raggedy ball which gave an erratic rebound off a garage wall. Often his father would bounce the ball to him in the living room risking glasses and crockery as his son dived for it. At other times Engineer had his head stuck into cricket literature memorising names and averages from Test cricket or maybe he would spend time re-arranging his collection of miniature signed portraits of top players that you could get from the city's petrol stations. In other words, he was just like so many other cricket-daft kids. Except when his portrait appeared in Bombay some years later it was on a huge advertising poster overhanging one of the main roads.

Engineer's competitive cricket began with the Dadar Parsee Colony Sporting Club. He quickly established himself as a batsman with a rapid 50 off an old borrowed club bat. That persuaded his father to buy him a new one which he used to good effect over the next couple of years. There was little genuine pace bowling to deal with but plenty of top-class spin and some awkward seamers, especially in games played on matting pitches. Few batsmen were prepared to launch all-out attack but Engineer went for it full blast just as he did with life in general. Allied to his unique brand of wicketkeeping it got him noticed and soon he was invited to the Brabourne Stadium as one of the small annual intake of trainees under a Cricket Club of India development scheme.

His first setback was to be dropped by Dadar in favour of a more experienced 'keeper. Bitterly disappointed he joined a rival outfit Sassanian for a season and avenged himself by getting a big score when they clashed with Dadar in a cup final. Not surprisingly Dadar soon took him back and from them on little got in his way, not even grizzly old Nergish - the auntie whom Engineer detested. She stuck her oar in throughout his childhood, trying to persuade his parents that he should give up cricket to concentrate on his studies. Maybe Engineer did need the occasional kick up the rear when it came to school and college work but not from Auntie Nergish. She was his father's elder sister, a headmistress. Also, according to Engineer, a 'bit of a tyrant'.

"We had to visit her on birthdays for our present and for me it was always some pyjamas. She knew I hated them. I always slept in shorts. But every year it was pyjamas. But the worst thing was having to kiss her, she clamped her whiskers onto your face and drew six ounces of blood from each cheek. You could feel your life draining away."

Auntie Nergish apart, life could not have been sweeter. There were friends including Shashi Kapoor and lots of girls (but no sex apart from an occasional 'kiss and cuddle'). Sex was taboo. Engineer was viewed as a suitable husband for a number of young women whose parents made representations on the subject to Manecksha and Minnie. But Minnie dismissed them. "My Farokh is only young and he's got a life to lead" she told them. Engineer agreed wholeheartedly. His ambition to be 'someone' burned as fiercely and as constantly as the flames in the fire temple. Sure, he lived for the moment whether relaxing on the balcony listening to his Latin American dance music, which he still loves, lazing on the beach, chilling out with his pals - a typical (of his class) Bombay teenager. But, though undoubtedly talented and cocky, there was a tender spot in his make-up which needed massaging and still does. He was highly sensitive. Criticism was hard to take, especially if he felt it undeserved. One way to combat this was to make it to the top, sweeping away any doubters.

Engineer's path to stardom was traced out on a cricket pitch. By the mid 1950s he was well known in Bombay as a player for the future and it was mainly due to his cricketing ability rather than his academic achievements that he was given a place at Podar College of Commerce and Economics where the Vice Principal Professor Chandgadkar was to play a vital role in his development. Determined to make Podar a team to be reckoned with, the cricket-mad prof promised Engineer a free scholarship. "It wasn't the most popular college at the time - for example Sydenham College was regarded as the high class college and all the pretty girls then went there. Which would have suited me just fine! But Professor Chandgadkar persevered and suggested rather heavily that I would have no problems getting into the college no matter what my exam results." He quickly installed Engineer as captain and soon he was picked for the Bombay University side, a big stepping stone for any aspiring Indian cricketer. As for the professor he also made his way to the top as an administrator with the Bombay Cricket Association and India's Board of Control. "He was very enthusiastic and knowledgeable and made a tremendous impact on my career."

His debut in first-class cricket was one to savour at the time and certainly one to remember, India's Combined Universities taking on the West Indies tourists in December 1958. Talk about a baptism of fire. "We were a bunch of callow youths," he remembers with a wry smile. "They had Garry Sobers who had recently scored 365 not out against Pakistan to beat Len Hutton's world record. Their batting was strong. Rohan Kanhai was to hit 256 in six and a half hours the following month at Calcutta. But it was their attack which spelled big trouble. Wes Hall, Charlie Griffith, Roy Gilchrist. All of them fast, all ferocious. All trying to knock your head off. They wanted to maim you first and then get you out. There was no limit for bouncers or beamers and they took full advantage of that.

"It wouldn't perhaps have been so bad because the original plan was for the Windies to field a below strength side but then on the eve of the match the mayor made a speech. He over egged it and claimed that the tourists would be facing a team stronger than the Indian Test side! A few of us looked over our shoulders and wondered who he was talking about. Then we realised it was us. The Universities. Ha ha! The Windies weren't having any of that. They played Hall who had demolished the Test team in the second Test only a few days earlier along with Griffith and they brought back the lunatic Gilchrist who hadn't played in that game and was itching to get at us. Itching to get at anyone. He was that sort of guy."

Hall was tall, powerful and rapid. The first Test had been drawn but in the second at Green Park, Kanpur he had blasted India's batting apart with 6-50 and 5-76. Yet it was the stocky 5 feet 9 inches high Gilchrist who threatened mayhem. "He was the fastest bowler I played against, a real terror," admitted India's Chandu Borde. "We had never played that kind of bowling before. His motto was to hit the batsman so that he would be scared and get out … a lot of batsmen were out before going onto the field."

Already on that tour Gilchrist had been suspended for one match, the second Test, - by his own captain Gerry Alexander for bowling beamers and refusing to apologise after a row with team-mate Basil Butcher. But now he was on the rampage again, against a bunch of students. Engineer was one of his victims, bowled for a duck, in his tally of 6-16 as the Universities tumbled to 49 all out in their first innings.

"It was scary. Three of our side were hurt. We were having to push batsmen out into the middle. I was batting at number nine and by the time I got out there I wasn't apprehensive at all. I suppose it didn't really matter too much because we were on the point of being bowled out anyway but the fact is I was never afraid of fast bowling, not even from him. I just had a go and was bowled. He got another with the next ball. The hat-trick was on. Our number 11 was backing away towards square leg leaving all three stumps totally unprotected but for some reason Gilchrist sent down a bouncer which was so wild it was called a wide. I did wonder then what was going through his mind."

The students did better second time around. Hall and Gilchrist claimed only one wicket between them in 13 overs. "There was a big horse race on that day and they wanted to be there but we spoiled it for them. They must have thought 'We'll soon sort these kids out' but we were stubborn." After seeing off the new ball Engineer and one or two others enjoyed themselves against the spin of Sonny Ramadhin and Willie Rodrigues although not enough to prevent an innings and 152 runs defeat. Engineer now appreciated what world-class pace was all about. The experience might have planted seeds of doubt in the minds of less forceful batsmen, persuading them perhaps that survival in the face of such hostility was the key but his mind was already set.

"I refused to be dominated. Right from the moment I first picked up a bat I wanted to hit that ball as hard as possible. I used to make my dad chase all over the place when he bowled to me in practice. Not even bowlers of the calibre of Hall, Griffith and Gilchrist would make me change. In fact they made me more determined than ever. They could bounce me all day. I was going to hook them all day. Let battle commence."

Even with modern protection - helmet, huge gloves, padding etc - this declaration of intent might be seen as a mite foolhardy both in terms of keeping his wicket intact and of staying out of hospital. However Engineer's armour consisted only of a pair of thin cotton gloves with rubber spikes and the traditional 'box'. His sleeves were rolled up to expose elbows. He did not even have a cap to knock off. The only orthodox way to escape being bruised and battered by someone like Gilchrist was to duck, weave and dive. Engineer, though, eschewed orthodoxy. He vowed that one day he would exact revenge on Hall and co.

Roy Gilchrist had a violent streak. He broke bones and spilled blood, not just with the cricket ball although he was dangerous enough with that. Once, playing in England's Lancashire League he fought with one batsman on the pitch, taking a bang on the head from his rival's bat and giving one back with a stump. Another confrontation with an opponent caused a club match to be abandoned only 20 minutes after it had started. And in 1967 he appeared in court after assaulting his wife with a steam iron. Farokh Engineer however earned his respect.

"There was an incident," explains Engineer, "when we got together after an explosive day's cricket. He seemed to want to apologise to me for some of the things that had gone on during the game." It happened almost four years after the Combined Universities clash. India had been whitewashed 5-0 on their 1961-62 tour of the West Indies and it was blatantly obvious they needed more experience against fast bowling. Their solution was to import four West Indians to play in domestic cricket for a season. 'Gilly' was one and Engineer came face to face with him for the second time in his career during a match between South Zone and West Zone.

"He was bouncing away quite merrily until I hit him for two consecutive sixes. The crowd went wild. So did Gilly but in a different way. Next delivery he just kept running without letting the ball go, got right into my face and gave me a mouthful. He was raging. He said what he would do to me if I went for another big shot. Other players came rushing up. But he had picked on the wrong bloke to threaten. I could take it and I could give it back if necessary. I knew by then that you had to match aggression with aggression but never to lose control like him. So I spoke quite politely and diplomatically when I told him where one of the stumps might end up unless he backed off.

"Thankfully we got through the game without further trouble. But I wondered what might happen later because both teams were staying in the same hotel and there was a cocktail party that night. All evening Gilchrist kept glaring at me. I thought he was pig ignorant. Shortly after I went to my room there was a knock on the door and I asked who it was although I had a sneaking suspicion. 'It's me man,' he said. 'I want a drink with you.' I thought oh oh trouble but I let him in. He put a bottle of rum and two glasses on the table and we had a few drinks. It seemed to be his way of making up. At one point he showed me photos of his family - he was obviously missing home and was almost in tears. But, apart from that, he hardly said a word. He seemed content just to sit and drink. I finished up feeling a little sorry for him. There was a human element about him after all and after that I regarded him somewhat differently. But it was a strange evening."

Later that season they found themselves in the same invitation side at Hyderabad on a pitch so pedestrian that not even Gilchrist could push the ball through to the 'keeper. Engineer sorted it by standing up to the stumps and then pulled off a clever legside stumping. Gilchrist was not amused. "He was one of the fastest in the world, if not the fastest and he felt I had demeaned him. I tried to explain it was the slowness of the pitch but he wasn't having it."

Not many knew how to deal with Gilchrist. During my days as a general news reporter I bumped into him after a court case in Manchester and asked him for a comment. Gilly glowered, his shoulders hunched and he suddenly got taller. I realised he was on tip-toes. "Get out of my way man," he said. I jumped to one side. Anyone who stood up to Gilchrist has my undying respect.

CHAPTER 4

INDIA FOUND it difficult to breed fast bowlers. Their best during the 1960s was Ramakhant Desai, all of 5 feet 6 inches high earning him the nickname Tiny. Despite his diminutive physique he could still unleash a useful bouncer but he had little support in the seam department and had to toil long and hard on unresponsive tracks. The stamina draining workload and lack of help forced him into early retirement at the age of 29. India much preferred guile to pace. Spinners plied their tradecraft throughout every echelon of the game and when one of them Subhash Gupte produced an astonishing performance during the catastrophic home Test series against West Indies in 1958 it led to a new wave of young slow bowlers. Gupte bewitched the likes of Garry Sobers and Rohan Kanhai in the first innings of the Kanpur Test claiming 9-102. One of those listening to the radio commentary was a certain Bishan Bedi who said later: "I was so inspired that I took up spin bowling. It spurred me on."

Desai was about to break into first-class cricket but he was a rare representative of a type of bowling which was anathema to many in Indian cricket. While a few decent seamers earned a living, all out pace was virtually redundant. Which made life tricky for batsmen when they faced up to the pace of foreign attacks - and difficult also for wicketkeepers who had to deal with an assortment of clever spinners every match. Despite the skills needed behind the stumps, a 'keeper also had to score runs to catch the eyes of the selectors both at regional and at national levels. Too often the focus fell on his batting. Engineer's style altered a few perceptions.

"I broke the mould as far as wicketkeeping was concerned. Traditionally Indian keepers were pretty static but I had been a good goalkeeper and diving for the ball was second nature. The fans hadn't seen anything like it and they loved it. It wasn't playing to the gallery. If I went for a catch I went full tilt no matter how impossible it might seem to get it and if I pulled it off, well it gave everyone a massive lift." Engineer's reputation as a batsman who could quickly change the course of an innings was well-known but there were others who could don the gloves and usefully wield a bat as well. Eventually he pushed his way into the Test reckoning because he was the best keeper in town.

"I was born to be a wicketkeeper." It sounds trite - is anybody born to be anything? After all, his early forays on the club and college pitches of Bombay were as a big-hitting batsman and occasional leg spinner. But some strands of his DNA helped to make him a huge success behind the stumps.

Obviously it was not all down to Mother Nature. Anyone can improve their reflexes simply by practice and throughout his childhood Engineer worked on catching technique with a mis-shapen ball, having to adjust to its irregular bounce. Blend in his confidence and constant desire to be in the thick of the action and you have the perfect mix for wicketkeeping. The *Daily Telegraph*'s M.H. (Mike) Stevenson, writing at the time that England's Alan Knott reigned supreme reckoned that... "Farokh Engineer, arguably one of the two best wicketkeepers in the world, is everything that one means by the world 'natural'.

Stevenson continued: "Basically there are two kinds of keeper, the unobtrusive and the flamboyant......Engineer belongs to the latter category. I wonder how he would have turned out if he had been coached. Something in his psychological make-up precludes his being able to achieve a position where he is waiting calmly for the arrival of the ball like a (Don) Tallon, an (Keith) Andrew or a (Wally) Grout." Stevenson marvelled at the 'flurry of pads and gloves' and the 'predatory shriek' that signalled another batsman's exit at Engineer's hands.

Sujit Mukherjee, the respected Indian critic, was slightly less enthusiastic. At around the same time as Stevenson's eulogy, Mukherjee stated in *'Playing For India'* that India had never produced a world-class wicketkeeper 'in spite of the raptures of Sir Neville Cardus over Farokh Engineer.' Perhaps Mukherjee disliked Engineer's style for in laying down the criteria of a world-class gloveman he said: "Wicketkeeping ought to be an occupation which matches the Indian temperament. It is a slow and patient business, a waiting and watching game which stretches time out of shape and demands attention to the trivial and respect to the ordinary."

Engineer, thankfully, ripped up Mukherjee's job description. His style definitely did not 'match the Indian temperament'. Indeed as Australian star Neil Hawke said: "He's the most Australian Indian I've ever met. He was one of us."

In contrast to Mukherjee's conservative yearnings, Crawford White of the *Daily Express* reckoned Engineer's ability to orchestrate the crowd with his outrageous showmanship was a significant factor in India's performances. White was covering England's 1973 tour. India had just levelled the series with victory in Calcutta and the sides were ready to clash at the Chepauk Stadium in Madras. White's preview of the game paid this tribute: "Clearly if this is the turning wicket the locals say it will be India's task should be easier. Especially as England have a phobia about Bedi and Chandra to beat, as well as the pressure hurled at them by the packed 45,000 strong crowd who will be right down to the boundary edge. In one of my dispatches to England I described this pressure as Farokh Engineer's 45,000 Choral Society. In Calcutta it was 70,000!

"In any other country in the world," White wrote humorously, "a batsman can pad the ball away and nothing is said. But if an England batsman does it here, Engineer's hands go to heaven, the crowd go up with him and then the rest of the Indian team join to claim for lbw. Engineer is really the conductor of the greatest partisan chorus I have ever heard and, if he keeps it up, he will merit an Oscar for all action ballet."

Here Engineer suffered from the commentator's curse - with Bedi, Chandra and Prasanna bowling he had a rare off day when the match began although he ended Lancashire team-mate Barry Wood's 73 minutes stay with a neat catch. Throughout that series however Engineer outshone Knott who for once let his standards slip. "Knott had a less of a tour than is usual with him and he made a number of errors," said *Wisden*. ...."it was not a matter of concern for he was clearly suffering from surfeit of cricket. Knott's need was simply for a break from the never-ending strain of the game."

Warren Hegg, Lancashire's wicketkeeper from 1986-2005, backs up Engineer's belief that he was born to the role. "When I was a kid I loved batting but I wanted to be more involved in the game. Then when I joined my local club Stand, the professional Jim Kenyon saw something in me and said: 'Get behind the stumps. I felt straight away that that's what I wanted to be. I never looked back and I think it's absolutely true that keepers are born to it. I know that I never had any problem catching a ball and it seems that is down to seeing things quickly and responding. There's no time to think. Your body and hands move and suddenly the ball is lying there in your gloves. Or not! Looking back at my career I think I dropped only six clear chances in 20 years. I remember them all. Each one hurt.

"Technique behind the stumps, the way you crouch, your position, the way you rise to take the ball - that is something a keeper has to work on. You can have the fastest hands in the West but it doesn't matter if you have taken the ball too far away to bring it down smoothly and execute a stumping. Tell you the truth, the specialist technique of wicketkeeping has suffered in recent times with the spread of Twenty20. I know Farokh had to deal with some wonderful Indian spinners.

"I was still a kid when Farokh packed in. I wished I had seen more of him in action but I have heard so many stories and it's obvious that he was a unique cricketer. After all this time, 40 years since his retirement, he is still well loved in Lancashire and he is a tremendous ambassador for the club and cricket in general."

Hegg referred to it and Engineer has always underlined that one of the most important aspects of wicketkeeping is the intense involvement in every game. "It can exhaust you," Engineer admits. "You need immense powers of concentration especially if the spinners are on all day as they often were in my time. The ball is coming at you so much and the flight and pace is so different with each bowler. And if there is turn in the wicket that makes it even more tricky. In India the pitches were unpredictable. They could be two-paced, the bounce up and down. The heat was also a factor if you are in the field all day. Many a time the temperature was 100 degrees.

Batsmen don't have to face every delivery and it's rare that they are at the crease all day. Bowlers get chances to rest. Not so if you are a keeper. It's not only the ball coming towards you that you have to think about. You are watching the batsman's technique, looking for flaws to be exploited, and you should have a good working relationship with the captain. I was lucky. I played with a number of good captains and got on with them.

"Wicketkeeper is the most important position. If his head goes down, so does the whole team's. He can make or break it. He's the central figure and his enthusiasm, or lack of it, is easily seen by every other member of the side. A good keeper takes difficult catches and whips the bails off if the batsman strays just an inch but it's also about motivating team-mates, keeping them going through a long hard day. You can't just stand there moaning about bad luck or giving a bowler a dirty look when he's struggling to get the right line and length. Being extrovert helps, not allowing things to get you down. Most of the keepers I knew were extroverts, Alan Knott, Rodney Marsh, and later of course Adam Gilchrist. Maybe not Bob Taylor so much."

In his fine essay The Art of Wicketkeeping, Indian writer Ramachandra Guha said:

"*In the small town in northern India where I grew up, the preferred punishment for an errant child was known as the uttakh bhaitakh. Squat and stand, up and down, up and down, twenty times in succession, and preferably with hands on ears. Fine preparation, one might say, for that most complicated of cricketing tasks - keeping wickets.*

"*The demands, both mental and physical, of wicket-keeping greatly exceeds those of batting, bowling or fielding. There is the additional weight one carries, the pads and gloves that are not required by your team-mates. There is the low posture, made more uncomfortable by proximity to smelly and unwashed batsmen.*

"*A wicket-keeper must be vigilant and he must be fearless, alert to the need to go up or sideways, willing to be hit on his heart or on his head. He must focus, and focus relentlessly. Regardless of the state of the game and the shrieks of the crowd, he cannot ever give it less than one hundred per cent. And sometimes, even that might not be enough. While the bowler can rely on another spell, and the batsman can look forward to the second innings, the stumper's mistakes are remembered long after the event. 'He dropped X when he was five, and the blighter scored a double hundred'. A triple hundred, actually.*

"*Go back to Lord's, 1990, when poor Kiran More missed Graham Gooch before he had reached double figures. Gooch went on to score 333, and the Indian cricket fan, always so quick to judge and to condemn, prepared to forget More's many previous contributions to Indian cricket.*

"*A respect for wicket-keeping and wicket-keepers was drilled into me early, by my father. The first big match he witnessed was played between Rest of India and the then Ranji Trophy champions, Maharashtra, in 1941. The Rest of India were captained by Lala Amarnath, who at various times in the match batted, bowled, fielded and kept wickets. Ever since then, my father regarded the ability to keep wickets as the pinnacle of cricketing achievement. My own, modest experience as an active cricketer confirms this. There is nothing I found more taxing on the field of play than standing behind the stumps.*

"*How has one day cricket affected the duties of the wicket-keeper? It has made a hard job harder still. In conventional cricket, he could put his feet up after two hours, when lunch came or tea was called. But where innings are played without a break, he has to do three hundred uttakh bhaithaks in succession, while remaining focussed for a full three and a half hours. Moreover, the number of sit-ups required go up with every wide or no ball. Then again, he has to be prepared to run to the wicket for each delivery, whereas in Tests, he would at most be required to do so once or twice an over. He has to dash and dive to receive hundreds of throws, and make some himself. He must learn how to whip off a glove, and convey the ball with pin-point accuracy to the bowler's end.*

"In contemporary cricket, it is the wicket-keeper's job, and his alone, to keep spirits up, to cheer and exhort any and all of his team-mates. Among the basic requirements of the job is a knowledge of all the swear words that have been left out of the Oxford English Dictionary. From the moment a batsman comes to the crease till the moment he departs, the stumper has to lead the chorus calling into question the batsman's skills, aptitudes, morals and lineage."

Guha, who in 2017 was handed a place on India's new Committee of Administrators, told me: "Farokh was a boyhood hero (he scored a fifty in the first Test I ever watched, in Delhi in 1972), and many years later, in 2013 I think, I took my adult son to see him at his home outside Manchester and he was very kind to the lad (and to me). I hope he remembers our visit - in any case, give him my warmest regards."

Guha's essential qualifications for a keeper are: 'The concentration of a heart surgeon, the reflexes of a fighter pilot, the guts of a boxer. Must be able to do four hundred uttakh bhaithaks in succession, in daylight or under floodlights. Should have demonstrated the ability to run the hundred metres in under eleven seconds, from a squatting start. Applicants with eyesight other than 20/20 will not be considered.'

Engineer would have satisfied most of those requirements. Possibly not the ability to sprint 100 metres in under 11 seconds. His Lancashire team-mate and Test opponent Barry Wood recalled: "He was always up for a laugh and during one rained off match we had races at Old Trafford against the Notts' players. Rooky entered every sprint and lost every one, even to 'Knocker' White who was slower than he looked!"

But to compensate for that he could offer extra qualifications - the stamina and courage to stand for a day in a half in sapping conditions, trying to stay bright and snappy as India's spinners wheeled away, then - innings over - to start all over again, this time as his team's opener facing demon fast bowling. Wood added affectionately: "A great bloke and a very talented and proud Parsee. He is among the top three wicketkeepers I played with and against, the others being Knott and Bob Taylor."

Knott was also a fine batsman. But he did not have the added responsibility of opening the innings. Engineer did for half his Test career and in many one-day games for Lancashire. "I didn't think anything about it. That was my job and I wouldn't have had it any other way. I was proud to play for my country so I was not bothered at all about the workload. Sometimes I batted at eight or nine so I was able to put my feet up for a while but I was restless watching. I wanted to be out there doing something. Opening the innings had a certain status about it and it gave me the chance to attack the new ball which I relished. Not that I adapted my style. It didn't really matter where they put me, there was only one way of batting for me."

And only one style of keeping. Showy maybe but highly effective. Knott and Engineer vied for the title of greatest but did the Englishman ever grab a 70,000 crowd by the collar and pull it to its feet?

Every sport has to entertain otherwise it will die. Indian cricket had its conservative observers who wanted Engineer to cut the histrionics. Maybe, they claimed, he would be an even better keeper and a more consistent run-maker if he toned things down a little but perhaps they misunderstood the man.

CHAPTER 5

INDIA HAD been blown away by the West Indies in 1958-59, devastated on and off the field to the extent that the Lok Sabha (Parliament) staged an emergency debate on the debacle. The following summer they were crushed 5-0 in England with Lancashire's Brian Statham, Tommy Greenhough and Geoff Pullar among those taking advantage of India's brittle batting and ineffectual attack. Pullar hit 75 at Headingley and 131 at Old Trafford, Statham took 17 wickets in three matches, and leg-spinner Greenhough did better than any of the Indian spinners with 14 dismissals in three appearances including 5-35 at Lord's. But as a new decade approached so did new hope, highlighted by a wonderful first ever win over Australia at Kanpur where the tourists, chasing 225 to win, collapsed from 49-1 to 105 all out.

By then Farokh Engineer was pushing hard for a Test place. But when the selectors brought in a new keeper to take over from the long-serving Naren Tamhane it was not Engineer but a player still to make his first-class debut. Budhi Kunderan, who had defied his father in embarking on a cricket career, was a precocious and versatile talent, quick and resourceful in the field and a gifted batsman. But he was still learning his trade as a keeper. To be suddenly elevated into the Bombay Test against Australia was a fairy tale. India obviously reckoned he had a bright future but Engineer refused to be shoved into the shadows.

"I was determined to succeed. Budhi was a great cricketer. We played for the same club for years. He should have played more Tests but not at my expense. He was a very stylish and attacking batsman and an outstanding fielder in any position. But I was the number one wicketkeeper. When we played together for the Cricket Club of India I was always the keeper and Budhi was a brilliant batsman and cover point fielder. Eventually I established myself and he was my understudy."

Kunderan's story was a rags to riches affair worthy of investigation if only because it highlights the old anomalies of Indian cricket. An outstanding athlete he was mainly a self taught cricketer. When he moved from the south of India to live in Bombay he was quickly snapped up by the Railways club, coached by the hugely influential Lala Amarnath who was also chairman of India's selectors. Within a short time he was acting as India's 12th man for the first two Tests against the Aussies before displacing Tamhane for the third.

The Kunderan family lived in a modest tenement in central Bombay where Budhi and six siblings usually slept in a corridor. Under the regulations he could not claim a hotel room on expenses as his home was in the same city as the venue but to ensure he got to the ground in time each morning he slept under the stars in a garden close to the Brabourne Stadium. For his Test debut at the age of 20 he borrowed a pair of gloves from Engineer. He used a club bat and pads. And his cap was donated by Behram Murzban, principal of the Bharda High School. The match was drawn, Kunderan's performance being of little note except to get out, hit wicket, as he stepped back to pull Ian Meckiff. But a week later at the Corporation Stadium in Madras Kunderan showed what he was capable of. Promoted from number nine to opener he blasted the fearsome Australian attack for a dazzling 71 out of India's 149. "......I played my normal club cricket," he explained. "I got 14 runs in the first over off Meckiff. Suddenly the whole crowd was screaming. I was slashing outside the off stump, over the slips for four, over the covers for four. I just played my shots."

Over 40,000 hailed him. Here was a player with the potential to help India regain the pride and confidence they had recently lost. Yet Kunderan was to play only 16 more Tests, three of them as a batsman while others kept wicket. And after marrying a Scottish woman he quit India for good, raging against the 'disgusting' politics. After settling down in the UK he finished up appearing for Scotland in the Benson and Hedges Cup, taking on Lancashire in a dismally slow group game at Old Trafford in May 1980.

Engineer remained in close touch until Kunderan's death from cancer. "He was made into a wicketkeeper by Lala Amarnath and confided in me time and again that he never really relished that role. Had he been allowed to play as a batsman, coupled with his brilliant fielding in any position, I'm sure he would have played many more Tests. Ideally for India we should have played together, me as wicketkeeper, perhaps with Budhi as my opening partner instead of me being selected for some Tests and Budhi for others. We opened together for the Cricket Club of India and really enjoyed it. We complemented each other, always ready to rotate the strike and having the ability to score quick runs.

"I especially drove up to Scotland when I heard he was critically ill and when I left him after spending and reminiscing for a couple of hours I just knew that we would never see each other again. I had tears in my eyes driving back home. He sadly passed away shortly afterwards. Budhi was a truly great guy and an outstanding cricketer who will always be remembered. May his soul rest in peace."

Although determined to fast track Kunderan into the Test spotlight, Amarnath was also one of Engineer's biggest fans. That Brabourne Stadium Test in January 1960 was pivotal for both of them. "The Sunday of the Test was a rest day for the teams but I did a spell in the nets. Amarnath watched me and was impressed," said Engineer. "Later he selected me for the Indian Starlets team to tour Pakistan. I knew it was my stepping stone to the top and I worked hard. I know I did well on that tour. At the official functions Amarnath introduced me to other people as 'Farokh Engineer, the next Indian wicketkeeper for years to come'. I was riding high. But a couple of months after that tour the politics kicked in again and he was dropped from the selection committee. A new face appeared. I had to start all over again. Thankfully he came back after a while."

With arguments persisting in the selection room not even Kunderan was sure of his place. He finished off the series against Australia but in the tedious five match slog with Pakistan India used him, Tamhane and Nana Joshi who was dropped like a hot potato after missing a simple chance to dismiss Hanif Mohammed for 12 in the Bombay Test. Hanif punished that error to hit 160. There was no consistency. Engineer, meanwhile, had to grit it out patiently. Not easy for a character like him.

India played few games in those days - only eight between Kunderan's debut in January 1960 to December 1961, a period of almost two years, when Engineer got the call he had dreamed of. And which he felt was fully deserved. Tamhane's style of safe, reliable keeping was out of favour. And Kunderan had recently failed with the bat although in their wisdom the selectors had dropped him so far down the order that he had little chance to make an impact. So when England launched the second part of their sub-continental tour having already visited Pakistan, Engineer got the nod. He was to play in the first Test in front of his home town fans at the Brabourne Stadium. And against a powerful England side led by Ted Dexter.

"I could not have wished for better. I had been made to wait but it was worthwhile." Engineer commuted by train from Dadar to Bombay's Churchgate station. From there it was a short walk to the ground. Bombay had, and still has, some of the busiest railway services in the world. Normally he would have been vying for space with thousands of other passengers, maybe even hanging on grimly at the open door, one fist clutching bat and pads, the other clinging onto one of the door frame for dear life. But, as the news swept the city that he had been picked for India, the ride got a little easier.

"When I got to the station I was surrounded by people all asking questions. Usually when the train came in they would all make a mad rush for it but this time they let me go first. One man even wiped a seat clean for me. A star cricketer in India is treated like a god and if you do well you will be praised to the skies. But if you have a bad day you can be buried. Luckily I had more good days than bad."

However despair lay just around the corner. On the eve of the match Engineer was enjoying a net when a delivery from one of the quicker bowlers Raj Singh Dungarpur smacked him in the eye. "The manager Colonel Adhikeri had a idea to sharpen our reflexes and so on the eve of the Test in fading light he asked Raj to bowl bouncers from halfway down the pitch. Can you believe that? It was asking for trouble but the Colonel was worried that England had two fast bowlers, David Smith and Alan Brown, who were expected to send down a few bouncers. Anyway Raj got one to fly from around 10 yards. It was getting late, the light wasn't good but I was a compulsive hooker and went for it. Unfortunately I slightly mistimed it, it flew off the top edge and straight into my right eye. It was a bad one. Dad was there and he put some stitches in and got some ice on it. But he told me straight that I had no chance of playing. As well as being hurt I was totally shocked. This was supposed to be the greatest day of my career. My debut. I insisted that I would be ok. He pointed out that keeping wicket with two eyes was difficult enough, with just one it would be impossible! And dangerous. Anyway hoping beyond hope I reported for duty next morning. The eye was the size of a balloon but I said I was ok, gathered my things up and walked out of the dressing room for a knock-up. But I was on a loser. As soon as everyone realised they told me I would have to sit it out. Budhi took my place. I have rarely felt so low."

As a tour manager and top ranking administrator Raj Singh became one of India's foremost figures but never represented his country as a player. Engineer cherished him as a friend. "He liked heated discussions about the game. We would be on the lawn at the Cricket Club of India in Bombay and he would conduct the debate. The waiters all had starched white cotton uniforms and turbans. He would snap his fingers and they would bring bhel puri and coconut water. Music played in the background. All very colonial. Raj Singh was a Rajasthani prince. He could organise things - if Ted Dexter went on a tiger hunt it was Raj Singh who fixed it."

Kunderan took full advantage of that lucky break with a superb wicketkeeping display, three catches and two stumpings one of which ended Geoff Pullar's hopes of a century although the Lancashire opener quickly made up for that in the following match. If Kunderan had added a decent score to that haul he might have kept Engineer out of the side for the rest of the series but he fell lbw to left arm spinner Tony Lock for five in the first innings and did not get a chance in the second when India batted out comfortably for a draw after following on.

Engineer's injury healed quickly enough for him to play in the second Test at Kanpur. England had dropped one of their two fast bowlers Brown who had struggled with the conditions in Bombay and were hoping to make inroads with one new ball specialist Smith, supported by the medium pace of Barry Knight and Ted Dexter with David Allen and Lock providing the spin. India won the toss and batted. And batted. And batted. It was that type of pitch - over 1200 runs for the loss of 23 wickets, including a couple of daft run outs in India's second innings. When Engineer walked a little nervously to the crease on the second day the scoreboard read 414-7 from almost 180 overs and his boyhood hero Polly Umrigar was at the other end with a painstaking unbeaten century. The fans, dazed by the lack of entertainment, freshened up as Engineer emerged, knowing his reputation for big hitting. But the wicket was a rice pudding. Smith, the only bowler with any genuine pace, was fielding on the boundary trying to recover from a stamina sapping performance of 44-11-111-0 and Lock had the ball, having just dismissed Dilip Sardesai (hit wicket).

Engineer and Lock had met the evening before the game at an official reception, the Governor's cocktail party. Lock had seemed friendly. "We had a glass of pop together. I thought he was an extremely nice chap." Passing him on his way to the crease and feeling nervous Engineer looked towards him hoping for a bit of encouragement. How naive. Unbeknown to the newcomer, Lock was one of the most fiercely competitive cricketers ever known. His former Surrey team-mate Mickey Stewart said: "He gave his heart, body and soul to his team."

Engineer pulls a face as he recalls the incident: "He scowled at me and bombarded me with abuse. Really nasty. Almost racist. I was puzzled because he had been so nice to me at the function but I was also angry. There were three balls left of the over and I was surrounded by close-in fielders. Maybe out of nerves or simply through immaturity I had a swipe at the first. Luckily I hit it and it went for four. I dealt with the next two in similar fashion and the crowd were going wild. I know if I hadn't made contact I would have been lbw. Lock knew it as well. He was getting mad, giving me some terrible abuse with every ball. All in all a fairly quiet start to Test cricket! Polly Umrigar came up to me at the end of the over and said: 'You need to calm down a bit.' I did but neither did I want Lock to get the better of it. I stayed there for quite a while and got a few more boundaries but eventually he talked me into giving it away. I was 33 and jumped out to try to hit him over the top, missed and got stumped by John Murray. But I felt I had done well for the team. I hadn't let anyone down. And anyway I knew we were about to declare."

That salutary experience served Engineer well for the rest of his career. Lock grabbed hold of him at a function after the match and said: "Well played you bugger." Engineer asked about the verbals. "I knew you were nervous," said Lock. "I just wanted to make you more nervous! And it nearly worked - I nearly got you with that first ball."

A lesson not to be forgotten. "I decided there and then that I would never lose my cool again," Engineer adds. Yet he sometimes got out to rash shots. "Only because I was that sort of player - never because I was irritated by a bit of sledging."

England were glad to get away from Kanpur. Forced to follow-on for the first time ever against India they dominated the rest of the game with Pullar, Ken Barrington and Dexter compiling patient centuries, but it was not a match to cherish with the crowd causing constant problems, flashing mirrors and biscuit tin lids into the batsmen's faces. Fires blazed in the stands, fights broke out and play was interrupted several times. Engineer though can only look back on it with pride.

"I was playing Test cricket with some great players. Look at that side, Jaisimha, Contractor, Manjrekar, Durani, Umrigar, Borde, Gupte - these were household names in India, revered by millions. I had made it. I knew there was a lot of hard work still to do. In fact I didn't realise just how hard it would be at times considering the politics which played such a huge part in things. But I was there."

Disgusted by some of the fans' antics England were also embarrassed by having to follow-on. India hoped for something even better in the third Test at Delhi where the Nawab of Pataudi made his debut but another draw was on the cards before rain turned the ground into a quagmire, wrecking the last two days. However as 1962 dawned so did a new era for Indian cricket.

One familiar face missing as India strode out for the fourth Test at Eden Gardens, Calcutta was that of Subhash Gupte, one of their greatest spinners and many years later rated by Garry Sobers as a better 'leggie' than Shane Warne. Gupte was the victim of an unpalatable episode in which a hotel receptionist in Delhi complained of being harassed by a phone call from one of the Indian team. It was traced to the room shared by Gupte and Kripal Singh. Although Singh was the real culprit, Gupte was also censured for failing to stop him and both were kicked out of the side. Gupte never played again, a sad and pointless end to a wonderful career.

Despite his absence India played well on a pitch which at last offered some help to the bowlers and won by 187 runs, only their second victory over England. Engineer helped Durani to a five wickets haul with a catch and a stumping. They followed that up with an equally impressive display to win the finale in Madras by 128 runs to complete a famous 2-0 series triumph, one which pointed to a much brighter future. It might have been so different but for the natural flair of a batsman playing only his fifth Test innings. Engineer will forever remember the occasion.

India, boosted by the win at Calcutta, went on all-out attack. Previously they had concentrated on all out defence. Almost 300 runs for the loss of seven wickets on the first day - sensational! Pataudi led the surge with two sixes in his maiden century and right at the start of the second day Engineer blasted the England attack, hitting four boundaries in the opening over from Barry Knight. In an encore of Kunderan's showstopper two years previously Engineer went on to make 65 with 11 fours adding a record 101 with 'Pat' for the eighth wicket and taking the game away from Dexter's side. England put up little resistance after that.

"There were 40-50,000 in the ground. All on their feet screaming. I was hitting it all over the place. England didn't have a clue what to do. Tony Lock took some punishment - he didn't like it. We had been 277-7 when I joined Pataudi and it could have gone either way at that point. If they had snapped up the last three wickets and restricted us to around 300 then they had the depth of batting to cause us problems. But this time I wasn't joining Polly Umrigar and there was no-one to tell me to slow down. So I went for it. Also I didn't like some of things Knight was saying to me. I got my own back on him. Pataudi himself was an attacking player but I left him behind. Eventually we got well over 400 and it seemed to knock some of the stuffing out of them. Only one of them got past 50 when they batted. In the end we won easily."

India celebrated their first series success over a major Test nation. The fact that it was against the old colonial masters made it even sweeter. England could claim that they were not at full strength - their fast bowling duo of Fred Trueman and Brian Statham had opted out of the tour and their squad included four newcomers - but there were no excuses. They had been outplayed. This, then, was a watershed. Not all went India's way over the next few years but they had stepped up a level. Engineer, still a beginner in Test terms, was right in the thick of it, already a player you would pay good money to watch and a motivational figure for team-mates.

CHAPTER 6

'THE SLOW dogs of cricket' - that's how India were labelled by English critics in the 1950s. As *Wisden* put it: 'defeat was the horrid ogre in their path, and to ward it off they retired into a cave, pulled a massive rock over the entrance and attempted to defy all efforts to dislodge them'. India always had plenty of batsmen with good technique. Some added a touch of flair. But too often safety first tactics were the order of the day and scoring slowed to the pace of an octogenarian snail. Such criticism seems a little unfair on reflection. India struggled in English conditions, finding themselves in one damage limitation exercise after another but at least they showed a determination not to simply throw it away.

Another accusation, sneeringly muttered rather than written, was that they lacked physical fortitude against hostile fast bowling - an insult generated by the events of the 1952 series in England where a rough and ready Yorkshireman, still doing his National Service with the RAF, burst onto the Test match stage. Fred Trueman, later to be called Fiery Fred, left India shellshocked, cruelly exposing their vulnerability. He had a powerful frame, a mane of coal black hair and, most of all, a classic side on action which enabled him to bowl at terrific speed but with precise control. A great career was on its way. India had seen nothing like it. They could not cope.

At Headingley he created such pandemonium in his opening spell of the second innings that the scoreboard read 0-4. At Lord's he claimed eight victims in the match and on the Saturday of the next game at Old Trafford he had this astonishing analysis, 8.4-2-31-8 as India slumped to 58 all out. Thoroughly demoralised they did little better following on, crumbling to 82. Usually this is recorded as the first Test side to be bowled out twice in a day. But the detail is more revealing - those 20 wickets tumbled in just 220 minutes.

There were mitigating factors. Trueman was on fire - 'bowling downhill at extreme speed and making the ball whip from the ground and often rear up nastily'. Help came from a greasy pitch and some breathtaking catches by a ring of close-in fielders. But the Press rounded on India for 'irresolute batting'. Other critics, including his own captain, singled out Polly Umrigar for the way he backed so far to square leg that Trueman had a clear view of all three stumps.

Looking back at the reports of that 'Black Saturday' I feel almost sorry for the Indians. Picture the scene - a gloomy Old Trafford and those who have known gloomy days at Old Trafford know just how off-putting it could be for anyone visiting Manchester for the first time (or even the second!); a spiteful pitch with the ball spitting and rearing up like a cobra; an intimidating and accurate fast bowler; no helmets, sparse or no padding and little idea of how to get out of the way of a red leather bound missile coming straight at your head at around 90mph. Avoidance is not all about reflexes. It is also about experience. When to duck. When to sway. Umrigar, a tall powerfully built man with thick biceps was thought physically best suited to stand up to Trueman's blitz, although he was a bigger target than most of his team-mates, and he was a top-class batsman - a lifelong hero of Engineer's - but something about the Yorkshireman had unnerved him and he accrued a miserable 43 runs from the series, seeing his stumps shattered three times after backing away.

India needed to develop their own fast bowlers to hit back at opponents and to give their own batsmen the necessary experience but, sadly, it did not happen. Wes Hall and Roy Gilchrist went on their rampage in 1958-59 with a barrage of bumpers and beamers, aided by surprisingly lenient umpires, and a terrible incident on the 1961-62 tour of the Caribbean again shattered their fragile confidence. This time Nari Contractor was hit on the head by a ball from a fierce and controversial newcomer Charlie Griffith and needed emergency surgery with a metal plate inserted into his skull. He never played Test cricket again.

Engineer rated Contractor as a top-tier opener who would duck rather than attempt to hook a bouncer. "He was very accomplished at leaving and this time he ducked as usual but the ball didn't get up as much as expected. It sort of skidded. There were no speed guns in those days but it was so fast that delivery it must have been 100mph. It hit him on the temple just below the ear. We all heard the thud of it. Nari went down on his knees and we knew something was seriously wrong. In fact we saw red. We rushed out onto the pitch but Nari got up and said he was alright. But there was blood.

We got him back into the dressing room and he was resting but suddenly he started to scream in agony. At the hospital they found he had an unusual blood group and asked for donors. Frank Worrell offered and stayed all night there. Griffith was there as well. He was in tears. It was terrible. Nari was a great player and a lovely very unassuming man who was respected by all."

India were whitewashed 5-0. But there was some hope. Younger, more aggressive players were emerging. Engineer had already made an impact, hooking fast bowling almost arrogantly at times. He hammered 50 and 43 at Sabina Park, Jamaica, batting at number nine. And there was Salim Durani who, like Engineer, had shone in the 2-0 series win over England and was hailed as a champion on his return from the West Indies following a gladiatorial century at Port of Spain Trinidad where he drove and hooked Hall to distraction.

Indian cricket enjoyed a surge of popularity at the start of the 1960s. Although the average daily wage stayed under four rupees the country's economy was growing so there was more middle-class cash around and fans queued all night for tickets. In Bombay particularly the game was kissed by a breath of romance. Bollywood film stars infiltrated the VIP stands and the once unimaginable happened when a young woman clambered over the boundary fence to kiss batsman Abbas Ali Baig on the cheek after he had scored a half century against the Aussies. In the city streets stall holders tuned into radio commentaries, pulling in crowds of workers who drank sugar drenched chai, scoffed deep fried snacks or chewed on betel nut which left blood red stains on their gums (and on the ragged pavements when they spat it out) and smoked their bidis. Players, especially the handsome cavalier type were adored. A perfect setting for the likes of Engineer and Durani.

Some things did not change however. Protectionism, favouritism, narrow-mindedness, inconsistency - these and other negative aspects continued to deflect India's progress. Durani 'moved at ease with kings and paupers' claimed one report, highlighting his social dexterity while admitting that his performances on the pitch were of similar ilk, rich one day, poor the next. He was much loved, starred in a Hindi film and was at ease whether on the back of a scooter or in the passenger seat of the Maharajah of Jamnagar's limo but, for a number of reasons, his Test career of 19 matches in 13 years turned into a roller-coaster.

As for Engineer he was not even selected for almost three years. The fact that he went on to play 46 Tests, the same number as Pataudi, underlines his contribution to India. One wonders how much more he could have given but for India's political/personality shenanigans although that could also apply to a number of players, including Durani.

Initially Engineer lost his place for the last two Tests of the West Indies series. No complaints. While he had stood up to Hall he had been cheaply dismissed three times by Lance Gibbs, twice being stumped. Kunderan returned and cemented his place in the next home series with a record-breaking 192 against England at Madras. Engineer resigned himself then for a lengthy wait on the sidelines. "Kunderan and I were buddies as well as rivals. When he got that 192 I thought that was it for me. For a while anyway. I knew I was a better 'keeper than Budhi. So did the selectors but that innings clinched it for him. I wished him well but privately I was itching to get another chance and I was forced to wait far too long."

Selection was a dodgy, sometimes incomprehensible affair. "At times it was hard to believe what was happening. It was disgraceful. Diabolical. Players were picked sometimes because of who they were rather than what they had done on the pitch. Favours were given out and returned. Cliques were formed. There was so much wheeling and dealing. A number of players suffered. I'd like to think that it's a lot different now but before my time and during my time there were very questionable selections."

One which stretched eyebrows was that of 'Prince' Indrajitsinhji a useful 'keeper and middle order batsman who enjoyed a successful career in domestic cricket but was not in Engineer's class, nor Kunderan's. For reasons never officially declared, Kunderan was snubbed for the first Test against Australia in February 1965. He had kept the gloves for seven Tests and in the recent home series with England had totted up 527 runs with two centuries at an average of 52.7. The case for him to continue as M.L. Jaisimha's opening partner was rock solid. Whether he should continue behind the stumps as well was debateable with Engineer hovering impatiently in the wings but to promote Indrajitsinhji above them both seemed bizarre.

Engineer still bristles at the insult. "I was furious. How could they possibly pick him ahead of me? I don't want to sound big-headed but a professional sportsman has a pride and a faith in his ability and this selection didn't make any sense at all. Australia were the toughest team we played against and we needed our best players. Indra had done ok in the domestic matches but everyone knew he was not up to it at Test level. Budhi had scored stacks of runs in the previous series against England. I had been playing well and it was accepted that I was the top 'keeper. So why were we were both left out? It was unbelievable and heart-breaking."

Indrajitsinjhi played in all three Tests against the Aussies, claimed four catches and three stumpings and made 32 in five knocks - hardly enough for the selectors to feel smug about. And yet smug they were for he emerged as something of a national idol when India, chasing a target of 254 on the last day of the second Test, slipped to 224-8. Indrajitsinjhi, relegated to number 10 after failing as an opener in the first game, joined Chandu Borde and stuck there under enormous pressure while Borde farmed the bowling and led them to a famous victory. The crowd went wild. The nation rejoiced. Here, surely, was the day when Indian cricket could stand with pride among the world's other great Test playing countries.

The aggrieved Engineer celebrated with everyone else but felt that the point still had to be made. "Indra did what he had to do but it was Borde's experience which really counted. He made sure that Indra faced as little of the bowling as possible. We might have won more easily if Budhi and I had been playing. There was a feeling that if our batsmen hit form we could take Australia and I'd be doing myself an injustice, Budhi too, if I said that the selectors were justified."

Australia might also point to the fact that they played with only 10 batsmen throughout the match having lost one of their chief run-makers Norman O'Neill through illness. Even so, after that extraordinary win, Indian fans celebrated in style and for a brief moment Indrajitsinjhi shared in the glory. But the fact remained he was not of the required calibre. It did not take long for even the most prejudiced selector to accept that. He appeared in only two more Tests, once when Engineer dropped out with injury, and finished with a total of 51 Test runs at an average of 8.5.

There is no doubt that it helped your prospects if you were a prince or a wealthy, influential landowner like the legendary 'Vizzy' who persuaded India to elect him as captain of the 1936 tour of England even though he was little better than good club standard. Actually he did not do badly on that tour and later he was knighted as Sir Gajapatairaj Vijaya Ananada the Maharajahkumar of Vizianagram, became president of India's Board of Control, a member of the India Legislative Assembly and a broadcaster whose most noted comment was a long, drawn out 'oooooooh'. Engineer remembers him as a 'great character' who would present tiger skins to visiting captains and managers. The joke was that cricketing squires like Vizzy had more Rolls Royces than runs.

If Engineer had failed to satisfy the selectors in the Caribbean he at least made some lifelong friends among the West Indians. Wes Hall, Frank Worrell, Garry Sobers and many more. When he returns to that region he is greeted warmly.

"Hall and I got on famously. In the Jamaica Test he was bouncing me and I was hooking him. Indian batsmen usually didn't hook him but I did. When we went to Barbados Wes said his mum had heard about me and would like to meet me. I thought that was a real honour. Wes Hall taking me home to see his mum! We drove down some bumpy lanes through Bridgetown. He was a tall bloke, we were in a small car and his head was banging against the roof. It was the same when we got to the house. He had to duck to get through the door. He was almost scraping the ceiling, the place was that tiny. His mum, too. She was frail. 'So you're the man who has been hitting my son all over the place. No-one does that,' she told me. I felt like I was being told off. But we got on so well. Ever since then Wes and I have been very close friends."

Worrell was another. Engineer was idling by the hotel pool a few days before the first Test when he was surprised to see Worrell approach. "I was on my own. All the others had been to the West Indies previously, had made friends and were out on the town. 'Hello Farokh,' he said. I was surprised to find that he even knew my name. 'Hello Mr Worrell,' I replied. 'Call me Frank,' he said. 'Come on, get changed. You're coming out with me.' We went out in his white Jag. What a night! He was a little the worse for wear when we got back to his home and I helped Velda his wife to get him to bed. It was the start of a long friendship with both of them. After Frank died whenever I went to Barbados I would call on Velda, give her a carton of cigarettes, and then go with her to put flowers on Frank's grave. He was a great man. She was a great lady."

Engineer returns often to the Caribbean usually via Florida where he stays with daughter Tina, her husband Gavin and grand-daughter Zia and spends as much time as possible on the golf courses. One day he was invited to play on the Ryder Cup course at Kiawah Island.

"The Ryder Cup had only finished the day before and so it was a real honour to be treading in the footsteps of some of the world's greatest players. To start with I was on my own but a younger guy, an American with his cap pulled down over his eyes, walked up and asked if he could come along for the ride. I introduced myself as Farokh and he said: 'Great to meet you Frank - I'm Kev.' We had a great morning even though we both played absolute rubbish. The fairways were narrow with marshes on either side and we kept losing balls. And all the way along he continued to call me Frank. I got fed up correcting him. Later on my wife and I invited him to have a drink with us and we were sitting around a table when she suddenly started kicking my leg. I couldn't understand what the problem was. Then she said to him: 'Excuse me but are you by any chance Kevin Costner?' I was astonished. He laughed and said: 'At last - someone has recognised me!' We have stayed friendly ever since. He still calls me Frank just to wind me up."

Engineer's exile from Test cricket spanned March 1961-March 1964 a period in which India played only 10 matches, most of them in two home series against England and the Aussies. He bitterly resented being on the sidelines. "They were the two most powerful sides. From a personal view I wanted the chance to prove myself against them but there was something else. These were the colonials who had looked down on us for too long. I thought they still had the master-servant attitude towards us, that India wasn't quite on the same level. It was a superiority thing, rather than outright racism. England rarely sent over a full-strength team. They thought that we should roll over for them and too often in the past we had. I didn't want that. I loved the English way of life, that's the way I was brought up but I considered myself an equal not something inferior. Standing up to them and beating them on a cricket pitch was the best way to do it. In the mid 1960s I didn't get the chance. I have few regrets or complaints about my career but that is one."

England's patronising of India is highlighted by *Wisden's* account of their 1964 tour, a test of endurance for the tourists who suffered badly from illness and injury. All five matches were drawn with India's left-arm spinner Bapu Nadkarni sending down a record 21 consecutive maidens to Brian Bolus and Ken Barrington in the opener in Madras. *Wisden* recorded: "An eight-week tour of India containing five Test matches was an interesting MCC experiment in January and February 1964. It is the general wish today to shorten overseas tours. A five-Test series could, obviously, be crammed into a shorter period but whether such congestion of important fixtures is desirable is very much open to question.

…An additional hazard in India is the risk of stomach trouble, which, in fact, struck severely at this MCC team. Having learned from experience, MCC arranged for their team - and the attending writers - to take tinned food from England for use in the more remote cricketing centres, where European cooking is not understood. There was some slight criticism from touchy folk in India, but that should not prevent MCC acting similarly on future tours. The tinned food in some places was very necessary."

The report goes on to mention 'drugged' pitches, interminably slow batting from both sides - although England (of course) were the only team showing intent - the admirable leadership of the tourists under M.J.K. Smith and the gutsy performances of several players particularly off-spinner Fred Titmus who sent down 400 overs 'and every single one of them tidy' and opener Bolus. The only hint of reproof for the tourists was reserved for none other than Colin Cowdrey who flew out to replace the injured Barrington and scored successive centuries in his first two matches since being injured by a Wes Hall delivery the previous summer. Cowdrey, it appeared, was far too slow with 107 in 380 minutes at Eden Gardens. And when acceleration was needed at Delhi his 151 spanned 375 minutes, though 98 runs came from boundaries.

I find *Wisden*'s tone towards India a tad sniffy. Yes they had gifted batsmen and spinners. But…."The cricket was disappointing and on occasions tediously boring, particularly the final days at Delhi and Kanpur. It was not surprising that, when all interest had gone from those games, Smith used bowling that enabled India's batsmen to treat the spectators to a lighthearted exhibition of hitting. Unfortunately those spectators, and even some officials, continued to take the proceedings seriously and imagined that the batsmen were proving their superiority to England's best."

Pataudi came through a lean spell to hit 203 not out, the highest score by an Indian against England but 'the second hundred was made very easy for him.' In scoffing at the fans' reaction perhaps *Wisden* displayed a lack of appreciation for the role of cricket within Indian society. A Test match in an Indian city was a cause for celebration, an occasion to lift the spirits, five days where supporters who could afford the ticket prices could leave the daily grind behind. No other sporting event matched it. Crowds often reached the 50,000 mark. It was estimated that the aggregate attendance for that particular tour was one million, a massive money-spinner. Many of that one million watched from stands so shorn of facilities they had to urinate into empty coconut shells. The seats were often hard wooden planks. The heat was stifling, the cricket mind-bogglingly tedious. Come a bit of entertainment, a few expansive shots and they went bananas. Who could blame them? It did not matter one jot that boundaries were being flayed off exhibition bowling.

Engineer comments: "It has all changed of course. For many years England cricketers and fans have loved India because of the hospitality and the experience of big passionate crowds. It is a place to prove yourself as a cricketer. England would not have enjoyed being beaten the way they were in 2016 but I'm sure they learned a lot from it."

Rameshchandra Gangaram Nadkarni, the bowler who pinned down Bolus and Barrington, took his nickname Bapu from Mahatma Gandhi who had been called Bapu (Father) by his millions of followers. Nadkarni, a left arm spinner and decent batsman, had rather less admirers but wore the same kind of traditional underwear as Gandhi, a long triangular shaped cloth which he carefully draped around his body before pulling on his flannels. "We could not help staring whenever he got changed," grins Engineer, his team-mate in Bombay's Ranji Trophy side.

Nadkarni employed unerring accuracy rather than turn, pitching the ball on a coin in the nets. Vijay Manjrekar joked: "The only time he turned it, it was declared a national holiday." Against England in 1964 his length was immaculate and with a severely weakened England hell-bent on stonewalling there was little chance of a runs feast. Even so his analysis for the first innings takes some believing, 32-27-5-0. One of those five runs came early in his spell. He then delivered 21 overs and five balls before Barrington stole another single. The *Times* writer noted: "He was immediately taken off as though being altogether too expensive."

South Africa's Hugh Tayfield had sent down 137 consecutive dot balls against England eight years previously but they were in eight ball overs and unbeknown to him Nadkarni's tally had created some kind of world record, beating the 17 successive six ball maidens by Somerset's Horace Hazell against Gloucestershire in 1949. No-one really bothered about it though. "I only came to know about it later," Nadkarni explained. "In the evening the official scorer came up to me and told me that I had set a new world record with the most economical spell." Congratulations were few and muted. "A few of my team-mates took a dig at me. At that time there was no media coverage and things like these went un-noticed."

Nadkarni pinned England down for the rest of the series with spells of 6-4-6-2, 4-2-8-0, 14-11-3-0, 42-24-38-2 and 57-30-97-3 - an economy rate of one an over. Imagine sitting on a hard bench, watching that and then finding that your coconut shell was overflowing.

Engineer was used to playing with Nadkarni and when they linked up for India in February 1965 they produced a show-stopper which re-launched Engineer's reputation as an extraordinary batsman. He went in at number nine against a value for money New Zealand attack and hammered 90 in 115 glorious minutes. Nadkarni, with no option but to play second fiddle, helped him to pile on 143 for the eighth wicket, an Indian record beating the one they made against Ted Dexter's England in 1961 but the packed Madras crowd rose to acclaim Engineer. One Indian newspaper described it as a 'display of thunder and lightning..... hooking viciously and driving majestically. Engineer's cavalier innings ended 10 minutes after the interval. With his sights trained on his century he mistimed a drive off Yuile and Pollard at extra cover held a brilliant tumbling catch.'

Unfortunately the series, like so many others, ended limply and Engineer briefly lost his place again to Kunderan. But his fireworks at the Corporation Stadium remained the highlight of the season. "It was fantastic to be back in Test cricket after almost three years. I don't know what the attendance was, 40,000, maybe 50,000, but the atmosphere was terrific. I knew I had to do something special. They had picked Indrajitsinjhi and Kunderan. It seemed they had come to their senses about Indrajitsinjhi but Budhi was still a rival in terms of batting. I was in good form, had been playing particularly well for Bombay as had Babu. So I felt confident when I went to the crease. Maybe the crowd remembered what I did against England on the same ground a few years earlier because they gave me a huge welcome. That helped. And having Nadkarni at the other end was re-assuring. New Zealand had a tough side, very competitive with players like Dick Collinge, Dick Motz, Bert Sutcliffe and John Reid but it had to be my day. I started with a four and went on in the same way, clattering the boundary. The cricket had been pretty dull until then so the crowd loved it. I suppose a century was there for the taking but I didn't know what the nervous nineties meant. I didn't have that problem. I hit the ball cleanly but Pollard took a great catch. I was not that disappointed. I had played brilliantly and I thought to myself: 'Now drop me if you dare.'"

Which they did! After New Zealand's tour India had to wait almost two years before playing again and when West Indies visited in 1966-67 the tangential process of selection provided Kunderan with another chance to establish himself as the 'keeper/batsman. Again Engineer was left wondering what he had to do to cement his place. Kunderan did not let anyone down, 128 runs in four innings against the fearsome Hall-Griffith combo only to fall victim to another mystifying switch which in turn led to one of Test cricket's most awesome batting exhibitions.

CHAPTER 7

CRICKET IS a game which lends itself to humour. Many of the best after dinner speeches are dotted with well embroidered yarns, embellishments hanging off them like tinkling bells. I see no great harm in that. It is just a good laugh - as long as the basic truth, the root of reality, is preserved. An old cynic like me will chuckle at such stories without ever accepting they are the truth, the whole truth and nothing but....

Yet whenever Farokh Engineer regales me with an outlandish tale I smile and want to believe or at least sit back and enjoy it. Because he is an endearing man, because I have known him for almost 40 years and because there is usually a gleam in one eye, a tear in the other as he leans back and conjures up another magical moment. Ok, the watering eye is due to an over-active tear duct rather than pure emotion but the overall image is of a passionate character revealing an old flame of his.

However his recollection of one of Test cricket's most remarkable innings is spell-binding and does not need any embroidery.

January 13, 1967: Madras is steaming. It is holiday time, the Festival of Pongal (Harvest), and families are digging into bowls of the regional delicacy, a rich, ultra sweet blend of jaggery and rice which tradition states has to be left to boil over the rim of the pot before it is removed from the stove. On Marina beach a few stall holders are setting up early - evening is usually the best time for business but this is holiday time - and a few groups of kids are playing cricket with rudimentary bats and balls, state elections are in full swing, movie idol turned politician M.G. Ramachandra and a rival are having surgery after a shooting incident and their fans are rioting. At Chepauk Stadium, a stone's throw from the beach and the home of MCC, the Madras Cricket Club, India are preparing to take on the mighty West Indies in the third Test of the series. The temperature is rising towards 90. The whole city is on fire.

For some of the players this few minutes of waiting for play to start is always a nervy time. Today particularly as the captain has won the toss and decided to bat, an obvious decision for the Nawab of Pataudi to make but the relaid pitch is likely to be fast and bouncy, so different from most others in India, and the Windies' attack is the fearsome Wes Hall and Charlie Griffith. It could go disastrously wrong….

Here is Engineer's vivid account of that day: "I had been out of the team for the first two Tests. They had preferred Budhi Kunderan and he had scored a few runs, 79 at Bombay in a big ninth wicket stand with Venkat but Wes Hall had got him in both innings at Calcutta and you could never tell with the selectors, what impressed them and what didn't. Anyway they brought me back for Madras and asked me to open the innings. I had never opened before. I had played once at number three and once at five but most of the time I had been down the order. So why was I suddenly put at the head of the innings? It seemed strange. I had not played for a while but I was constantly fighting for a place, putting people under pressure, and I got the feeling that some of those in authority wanted me out of the way completely and this was the best way to do it - put me in the firing line against Hall and Griffith with the new ball on a pacy pitch. If I failed they would have every justification to kick me out again. Probably forever. I was suspicious of the selectors' motives. At the same time a guy like me could not have wished for better motivation. I would show 'em. They were not going to get rid of Farokh Engineer so easily.

"The Windies' bowlers were looking at that pitch hardly believing that it was so green. They had hammered us in the first two matches, now they were thinking that they would roll us over again and have time to go fishing or something. The ground was absolutely packed. My dad was there. The atmosphere was amazing. This was make or break for me."

What happened next was nothing short of sensational. Engineer demolished the most feared attack in the world. Hall's first spell was 0-35 from six overs. Griffith had 6-0-46-0. After an hour India were 72-0 with Engineer on 57. Clive Lloyd, soon to be his Lancashire team-mate, was in the Windies' side and said: " He was very unlucky not to join the select band of batsmen who scored a century in the first session of a Test match. And it was against some of the greatest bowlers. There was Hall and Griffith supported by Sobers and Lance Gibbs with his vicious off-spinners."

Engineer takes up the story again: "I faced up to Hall with most of the fielders behind me, four or five slips, a gully, third man and he came running in. I thought: 'This is it'. It was short and it bounced. I hooked it. Hall muttered something. But that set the pattern for the rest of the morning. I gave him and Griffith so much stick.

"It was one of those days when I could not go wrong. Hall and Griffith were always intimidating and the pitch was the liveliest they had bowled on in India. But that suited me. The ball was coming onto the bat and I refused to let them get on top. They bounced me but I hooked and pulled them. I was using the pace of the ball but I also drove them back down the ground. The adrenaline was rushing through me. The overs rate was quite slow at first, there were a lot of no-balls and I didn't have much of the strike. Sardesai at the other end was just blocking it. I was getting impatient and I made the most of every ball I received. I got to 50 and he wasn't in double figures. The fans in Madras still remembered the 90 I hit against New Zealand two years earlier and they were seeing me take the bowling by the scruff of the neck again. They were going crazy.

"I kept looking at my bat to make sure it wasn't broken. It was a light bat, about two pounds eight ounces with a small sweet spot. You had to get it exactly right but if you did the ball flew. I didn't even know who had made it. It had my autograph on it but in those days all our bats were made in the Sielkot region, near the border with Pakistan. There were a number of bat manufacturers up there - the wood came from Kashmir - and we would be just presented with them. There was no choice as such. That bat must have been well made - it took a lot of punishment that day but it stood up well.

"The funny thing was that when I hit Hall to the ropes I heard Griffith laughing. Then I gave Griffith the same treatment and Hall laughed. They were taking the piss out of each other. But perhaps they were just covering up. I had hurt them. I can't believe they had suffered this sort of treatment before."

Approaching lunch Engineer was on the verge of history. Only three batsmen at this point, all Australians playing against England, had scored a century before lunch on the first day of a Test - Victor Trumper (Old Trafford 1902), Charlie McCartney (Headingley 1926) and Don Bradman (Headingley 1930). Only two have achieved it since, Majid Khan (Pakistan v New Zealand, Karachi 1976-77); and David Warner (Australia v Pakistan, Sydney 2017).

For Engineer, in his first appearance as an opener and against West Indies, this was the chance of cricket immortality.

"I got to 92 with plenty of time left to make 100 before lunch. I never suffered from the nervous 90s. I never got bogged down. If I got that close I just went for it. But this time I ran out of luck. There was time for two overs. I tried to hit a four but Rohan Kanhai made a brilliant stop at square-leg and kept it to a single. Sardesai played out the rest of the over. Last over before lunch and the same thing happened. I drove and there was another superb piece of fielding at extra cover, I think it was Clive Lloyd, and again only a single. Sardesai played it out again and I went in with 94.

"Some of the lads were unhappy with Sardesai but he was playing for the team, not just for me. I understood it. He did a great job. Anyway I was happy enough with 94 not out. I felt I had proved something. I had destroyed the Windies' attack. There was no going back for me now. No way they could ignore me. This was the last match before the tour of England. That is what I wanted and now it was guaranteed."

"I hadn't got that century before lunch but I was determined to get it as soon as possible afterwards. The first ball I faced was from Gibbs. I thought to myself 'This is it. It's him or me.' I went down the pitch and smashed it straight down the ground for a six. The noise in the stadium was incredible. Clive and some of the other West Indians congratulated me."

Strangely, there is Indian government film footage which indicates that Engineer completed his century with a single but Lloyd said in the Indian magazine SportsWeek: "Who will ever forget his 94 not out before lunch? He cut, drove, hooked and pulled with such venom and so narrowly missed joining a very select band. Anyway he did get his hundred first ball after lunch as he thumped Gibbs for a mighty six."

Cricket writer K.N. Prabhu who covered the match wrote: "His bat spluttered runs like a Catherine Wheel. In an era where the helmet had not made its presence on the cricket field, Engineer played pedigree hooks, cuts and drives that left the fielders standing….the entire West Indies team joined the crowd in giving him a fitting ovation."

Lloyd was one of the first to shake his hand. They were to share in many celebrations in years to follow.

What Engineer has forgotten is that he battled on for some time after an attack of cramp. He was limping at one stage which makes his feat even more worthy. Not only did he get his century but he stayed for another half hour or so, almost hobbling at one stage as he turned for a second run.

Sardesai went, Ajit Wadekar got a duck, and India had 143 on the board at close to a run a minute when Engineer succumbed to Sobers.

"It was only afterwards in the dressing-room that it all hit me. First I felt so proud to have scored a century like that. Then I felt disappointed again that I hadn't done it before lunch. But now I know it was all for the best. Would I deserve to have my name alongside the great Don Bradman's? I don't think so. But the satisfaction was immense. If there had been a plan to get rid of me it had backfired to some tune and looking back 50 years later I see how that innings changed my entire life. Incredible."

'One of the great epics of Test match batting," observed one Indian commentator. Sadly there were no TV cameras present. Nothing to fully record the event, the government film being savagely edited to produce just a few highlights of the whole match. What it does show is Engineer going out to bat with Sardesai at the start of the day. As they walk onto the outfield, Sardesai looks straight ahead, grimly determined. Engineer turns and smiles at the camera. He looks relaxed enough to be playing a game on nearby Marina beach. How could he do that? The pressure on him was intense. This was the last chance saloon. Fail and he faced Test oblivion for there were influential people who did not want him around. And waiting for him were Hall and Griffith, a new cherry and a strip of lightning. Plenty for most batsmen to worry about. Yet he could still play to the gallery.

If India had won that game surely now there would be a statue to Engineer standing tall and proud outside the ground but after being tied in knots in the second innings by Bedi and Prasanna West Indies were saved by an unbroken eighth wicket stand of 77 between Sobers and Griffith. Sobers was dropped twice before reaching 10, the usually ultra reliable Rusi Suti missing the easiest one but India were also frustrated by the controversial tactics of Griffith sinking to his knees and blocking the ball with his body, provoking widespread criticism.

Engineer gives a different viewpoint. "To be honest it was so blatant everyone was laughing. It was like a footballer nowadays taking an obvious dive. Prasanna was flighting the ball and one delivery brushed Griffith's pads, barely touched them, but he went down as though he was hurt. It was a Bollywood performance. Some of our players were falling about laughing. Sobers too. We thought we had them but had to settle for a draw. That would have been one of the greatest wins."

Madras has stayed in Engineer's affections. "It was a lucky place for me and the team. There were two grounds. We usually played at the Corporation Stadium but the Chepauk had more history. We only lost once in Madras when I played." That was to the Australians early in 1970. Engineer played in three Madras victories and two draws scoring a total of 421 at an average of 42.1.

Within a few months of his Chepauk feat Engineer was talking terms with Lancashire and just over a year later he arrived in Manchester to take up residence and to learn how to make a coal fire.

Madras to Manchester. What a difference. My great great grandmother Amelia and her family made a similar journey 100 years earlier. Born in Madras, an orphan at the age of 18 months, she was brought up in the city's Female Asylum (orphanage) and married an English soldier. They and their children came to England in the 1860s and settled in Bury, Lancashire. Which gives me a historic link to both India and Lancashire of which, just like Engineer, I am extremely proud.

To complete the chain of coincidence, Amelia's brother Edmund was a pioneer of the Indian Electric Telegraph Department. But before joining that part of the civil service he was an assistant apothecary, a doctor, studying at the Madras Medical College near Chepauk. I have no solid evidence but there is a possibility that he played cricket along with other officers of the East India Co. Just in the way Engineer reminisces of his towering six off Lance Gibbs I lean back sometimes and imagine Edmund playing a game in Madras and cracking the ball to the boundary. An even longer flight of fancy has me wondering whether Farokh Engineer looks down on my ancestor's last resting place....

Edmund and his wife were killed by rebels in the First War of Independence (called by the British the Indian Mutiny) of 1857. By then he was in charge of the telegraph department in Indore, between Bombay and Delhi. Within literally a few yards of where I believe they died, close to the former British Residency and the Nehru cricket stadium, is a massive shining white sculpture, the Vijay Balla, the Victory Bat, commemorating India's 1971 triumph in England. Inscribed on it are the names of India's victorious squad of that year, including Engineer's.

Daydreaming over, I find myself back in Engineer's kitchen. He is dawdling over the kettle.

"My wife (Julie) has told me off for always giving you cheap instant coffee. She says I've got to make you proper coffee from the cafetiere. But I'm not sure how to use it." After a while he comes up with a tasty brew. Lukewarm but tasty. While I am sipping it we enter into a potentially thorny debate about the book. I am anxious to go into more detail over his performances. He is not so sure. "Why? Readers don't want to read figures."

We have touched on this before. I am not a statistics fan but how can you write a cricket book without them? Engineer is dubious. Maybe, I think, he realises that on paper those batting statistics do not always serve him well. Too many low scores, too many run outs, too many stumpings. I appreciate his doubts. If used against him by a prejudiced judge they could present a picture of disorder, eccentricity and a distinct lack of self discipline. Though he might not like it, Engineer's Indian service demands detailed analysis and when the figures are fleshed out I think he will emerge the better for it. I will try to do it in later in this book. For now, I gently push the mug of coffee aside and say: "Okay, let's go back over that Madras innings. What were you saying...."

"It changed my life."

CHAPTER 8

MANCHESTER. WHAT a city! The Bombay of England?...not quite, but still an exciting place to be in the 1960s. It's reputation for dirty weather persisted and much of its Victorian architecture was covered in inches of muck. But, thanks to massive regional hand-outs from Harold Wilson's 'Backing Britain' Labour government, the city and its environs had entered a new development phase which went hand in hand with the cultural revolution sweeping across Britain. Tower blocks reached for the clouds while diesel and electric trains buzzed into ultra modern railway stations. Asian cuisine restaurants increased in number and quality, department stores grew bigger and bigger, long-haired youths in strange clothes hung around coffee shops where posters advertised the weekend's entertainment at any number of all-night discos. A garish red neon sign hung over the Granada TV studios where a 'soap' called Coronation Street was beamed into 8.5 million homes. And, of course, there were two great football clubs, United and City, and one of the most famous cricket grounds in the world, the home of the Lancashire county club. This city, known in Victorian times as King Cotton, still had a long way to go to retrieve former glories - indeed trading in cotton at the Exchange came to an end in 1968 - but it still had plenty to feel proud about.

Engineer says: "It has even more to be proud about now. I love the place and like everyone else I was devastated by the terror attack in June 2017. Mumbai also has suffered from terrorism and worked hard to recover from it. Manchester has done the same. It's a spirit of unification that links both cities."

Unfortunately, Lancashire County Cricket Club had had to be dragged into the new era kicking and screaming all the way. "The Lancashire of the 1960s was just a cottage industry compared to later, run on a Victorian shoestring," explained David (Bumble) Lloyd who was just starting to make his way in the game. "There was no shop, indeed no club merchandise to speak of and certainly no computers. The odd, old-fashioned typewriter was the solitary concession to technology in an office where almost everything was written by hand. Scorecards and other club mailings were printed on an ancient Caxton press."

For the first half of the Swinging Sixties Lancashire stayed stuck in the past with no money to invest in the ground and a team rooted in the bottom half of the championship with an old-fashioned, amateurish and sometimes heavy-handed committee in charge. Sick and tired of the way the club was being run and with its lack of success (their last County Championship triumph had been in 1934) its members rebelled to kick out the committee and install a more businesslike one. However things continued to go wrong. Then - an astonishing turnaround, propelled by the surprising success of one-day cricket, changes in the captaincy and chairmanship and the arrival of two players, Farokh Engineer and Clive Lloyd.

It is difficult to judge which was the most significant area of progress. Jack Bond emerged as the club's most influential and successful post-war skipper, Cedric Rhoades proved a dynamic, enterprising and - it could be argued - a visionary chairman, and one-day cricket came along at just the right time for a youthful, energetic Lancashire side well versed to playing the limited-overs game for their league clubs. But with their overseas stars, well…. as Bumble put it 'We won the pools.'

Despite a strange report in the *Manchester Evening News* that he would sail from Bombay Engineer and family flew into Manchester on a cold, damp March afternoon in 1968. Their new home was a semi-detached in the suburb of Timperley, rented by the club and where neighbours had laid out a 'Welcome to Lancashire sign'. Engineer has never forgotten that heart-warming start to life in the north west of England. "It was bitterly cold but they all came out to greet us. It was the best possible welcome. I felt right at home straight away and I've never lost that feeling. In fact over the years my love for the county has grown. I had one problem however. The house had a coal fire and I had no idea how to light it. We don't have many of them in Bombay. One of the neighbours showed me how to lay the paper, sticks and coal. We had a good chuckle about it.

"I had heard about the people in Lancashire, that they were so friendly so I wasn't too surprised at the way they treated us. Even so it made me feel humble. They had read about me in the papers but they didn't know me at all really and yet here they were going out of their way to help. Of course it was totally different from Bombay and India, but my family had always lived in a Westernised way. Bacon and eggs for breakfast, things like that. My brother Darius had moved to London some years previously and had settled down so we did not anticipate any problems. The weather? No. It was freezing when we arrived but it did not worry us and when it rained, well you haven't seen rain until you have experienced an Indian monsoon! The truth is that I was excited to be in England. I was to play cricket for what I considered was the biggest county and at a famous, historic ground. Life could not have been better."

A few weeks after Engineer's arrival the right-wing Conservative MP Enoch Powell stirred the race pot with his Rivers of Blood speech in which he warned against increasing immigration. During 1968, Britain took in 84,000 immigrants, most from the Commonwealth, and the National Front party were actively campaigning not only to limit numbers but to reduce them by deportation. However Engineer did not suffer from personal racism.

"Possibly this was because my skin is lighter than many Indians. I suppose I might have been mistaken for an Italian or Greek or other Continental. It was only when I opened my mouth and wiggled my head that they realised I was Indian. I never encountered any problems in England because of my colour. I was accepted from the beginning. Some players rubbed me up but in a good natured way. Clive Lloyd had to accept this too. But I've always liked pulling people's legs and if you give it out you have to be prepared to take it. People from the Asian communities often asked if I suffered any problems. When I said no, they thought it might be because I was someone in the public eye. Perhaps they were right."

There was one incident which might have turned nasty, recalled by an un-named Lancashire fan: "At some point in the 1960s my great uncle Tommy turned up at his social club in Rawtenstall to find a scrum at the door - an Asian man wanted a drink but no-one would sign him in. Tommy said: 'I'll sign you in' and when they entered together they were mobbed. Turns out it was Farokh Engineer."

Engineer's reference to the 'colour' of his skin might raise a few eyebrows but he is being merely factual about it. In some areas of India, geographic and social, a paler skin is considered desirable and even emphasised in the Bollywood and TV world of Mumbai. On my first visit to the sub-continent

I was surprised by the number of 'whitening' agents on open sale but percentage wise I guess there are more tanned all over Brits than pale-faced Indians.

He was lucky in avoiding outright racism. The Asian influence on Manchester had grown rapidly in the 1960s. More and more Chinese and Indian restaurants were appearing laying the foundations for the city's Chinatown and Curry Mile but race was definitely an issue. The Race Relations Act had to be tightened up, leading to Powell's speech, the voice of the National Front, formed in 1967, became more strident and the D'Oliveira Affair was just around the corner.

Lancashire cricket had not been immune to racism. In the late 1930s the county club considered the signing of the West Indian all-rounder Learie Constantine who was then playing in league cricket. The idea was quickly binned after a dressing room protest. "The thought of a black man taking the place of a white man in our side was anathema," admitted one player. "We Lancastrians were clannish in those less enlightened days." Yet when Mahatma Gandhi made a whistle-stop tour of the county's cotton towns in 1931 he was treated like a movie star. One image from that trip shows him dressed in his dhoti surrounded by admiring women textile workers. What a pity he did not visit Old Trafford.

By 1968 things had improved. Although much work remained to be done Manchester was at the forefront of a new racial tolerance. Manchester's club scene was the best in the country and youngsters danced the nights away to the rhythm of America's black musicians, blues and Tamla Motown. The American record company Stax, the first of its kind to employ black and white executives in the same office, accredited Manchester with indirectly aiding the civil rights campaign. And at a time when black players were rarely seen on professional sports fields in Britain Lancashire were one of the clubs who campaigned for overseas stars to be allowed into county cricket paving the way for, among others, Engineer, Clive Lloyd and Garry Sobers who joined Nottinghamshire after the Old Trafford committee had refused to match his financial demands. Several years earlier John Kay the *Manchester Evening News* cricket writer had helped Basil D'Oliviera, classified by South Africa's apartheid regime as a 'Cape Coloured' to find a more integrated home in England.

As well as revising out-dated registration rules, the Test and County Cricket Board also re-vamped the county game by introducing the Sunday

League, a 40 overs competition, sponsored by the cigarette company John Player, building on the popularity of Rothman's International Cavaliers' Sunday matches and to start in 1969. All this promised a whirlpool of excitement compared to the pedestrian progress of English cricket over several decades and Engineer could not wait to get into action.

Many Red Rose fans had already seen him smashing the ball to the boundary during the previous season of 1967 when India toured England. It was an ill-fated tour, marred by poor weather, injuries to key players and by 'Boring Boycs' - England opener Geoff Boycott. This obdurate Yorkshireman scored 246 not out in the first Test on his home ground Headingley. Engineer accumulated 196 runs from the whole three match series. Yet Engineer returned to India with accolades ringing in his ears while Boycott was vilified and even dropped for one Test, a decision which stained his career. How could this be? The distinction between self preservation and an almost suicidal desire to entertain could not have been more graphic.

Boycott spent nine and a half hours - 572 minutes - at the crease during the first two days of the Leeds Test. Completely out of touch but never threatened by a severely weakened Indian attack he refused to take any risks, patting juicy half volleys back to the bowler although he speeded up, comparatively, in the second half of his marathon. By the end England had amassed 550-4 but no-one really cared. England were struggling to attract the fans. This was death watch cricket.

When India replied the contrast was startling. They, too, were well short of top form having had little batting during their rain-hit warm-up games but Engineer slammed 42 off 62 balls in 79 minutes against a high-class pace attack of John Snow and Ken Higgs. Following-on 386 behind, Engineer ignited a remarkable Indian fightback. *Wisden* reported: 'When India followed on shortly after lunch on Saturday, Surti, with the twelfth man Venkataraghavan as his runner, went in first with Engineer but soon edged Snow to the wicket-keeper. Then the England bowlers sampled the brilliant form Indian batsmen often display on their own sun drenched grounds. In a scintillating record second-wicket stand of 168 for India against England in two and a half hours, Engineer and (Ajit) Wadekar struck boundary after boundary. Engineer hit fourteen 4's.'

Snow and Higgs were again punished as Engineer's 87 led India to 173-1 before he offered Brian Close a return catch. Pataudi's century lifted India to 510 their highest total against England forcing them not only to bat again but to work hard for a six wickets win. All that effort and further injuries consumed India who folded to a 3-0 series defeat, only once more going beyond the 200 mark but Engineer continued to earn praise. *Wisden*: 'While Pataudi stood out by himself among the batsmen, the number one wicket-keeper, Engineer, often gave the side a fine start with his enterprising stroke play.'

Despite falling cheaply in both innings of the second Test, Engineer ended the series as the sixth highest run-maker from both teams and his strike rate of 61 was the best, with England's Colin Milburn second. The 18 stones Milburn was the most extravagant English batsman of the times. Like Engineer he was an opener who put his body and soul into an attacking shot and, also like Engineer, he had stood up bravely to the West Indies pace attack. Unfortunately Milburn featured in only the last Test at Edgbaston, combining in an unlikely opening partnership with Boycott.

For all his rapidly widening reputation as a batsman worth watching what intrigued me about Engineer's performance at Headingley was -'What was it like standing behind Boycott for the best part of 10 hours?'

"Bloody boring. I kept suggesting he played a few shots and all he said was: 'It's nowt to do wi' thee'. It was difficult to get on with him off the pitch. We were complete opposites and we would never be on top of each other's Christmas card list. And he could bore you to death on it. But you had to admire Boycott as a batsman. His technique was so good, so straight and so fully behind the ball that I couldn't see it. I had to move sideways."

Lancashire officials and perhaps more significantly the captain Brian Statham had seen Engineer in close-up a few days before the opening Test when India played a three day game against the county at Southport - an interesting rather than exciting match but Engineer did enough with the bat, hammering Statham for boundaries in the second knock, to make people sit up and take notice. Worcestershire, Hampshire and Somerset were among the clubs vying for Engineer. Don Kenyon, the Worcester captain, wined and dined him. Kenyon had led his side to successive championship triumphs in the mid 1960s and, as an opener who relished the challenge of fast bowling, he saw in Engineer a kindred spirit. The commentator John Arlott invited him to his Hampshire home, plied him with Beaujolais from his impressively stocked wine cellar and said: "Farokh, you should be playing county cricket, you would be very popular." Umpire Syd Buller said something similar to him during the Headingley Test. Somerset made him a big offer, then Lancashire entered the auction.

"It was good to be courted by so many. A massive compliment. But while I had often thought about playing in English cricket it was something I had to consider carefully. In India I had a regular job with TATA-Mercedes Benz and usually played cricket at the weekend unless it was a Test series. Basically I had played cricket for fun, having to turn out six or seven days a week sounded more like a job."

Engineer had to weigh up the options. He was firmly established in India, a star cricketer, whose face appeared in all sorts of marketing campaigns and he had lucrative employment outside the game working for the TATA conglomerate who controlled Mercedes Benz operations on the sub-continent. English cricket however fascinated him. "It would be a great opportunity. England was the only country where you could play full-time professional cricket and I reckoned that no player could be considered complete until he had played the county game. It was all about playing in different conditions on uncovered pitches and against some of the best bowlers in the world, like Brian Statham and Fred Trueman. I told Lancashire that when I got back home I would talk to TATA about releasing me from work for the summer."

Statham and Trueman had opted out of England's tour of India in 1961-62 when Engineer made his entrance into the Test arena and all three were missing when Ted Dexter headed the 1963-64 touring party so Southport, a genteel west coast resort better known for its annual flower show than for cricket, hosted a memorable first meeting of two players of vividly contrasting styles and characters, one already a Red Rose hero, the other to become one.

"I knew of Statham obviously. One of the great, great bowlers. He opened the Lancashire attack, I took strike and I hooked him and pulled him. I could hardly believe I was whacking this wonderful bowler over mid-wicket. I don't think he could believe it either. I gave him a return catch in the first innings but I had another go at him in the second and dished out even more stick. Hit him out of the attack. I can still picture him, a bit perplexed about my strange technique. He never showed a great deal of emotion but afterwards we had a drink and I thought: 'What a lovely fellow.' He was the Lancashire captain, coming to the end of his career really, and he made it obvious that he wanted me at Old Trafford.

"As it happened we only had one season together before he retired. He took well over 2,000 wickets for Lancashire and England and he often told me: 'I would have had a lot more if you had been playing with me.'" Statham was not the sort to butter up someone. Neither would he have wanted to slur other keepers who he had played with but when it came to taking difficult catches, particularly down the legside, Engineer was in a class of his own.

Engineer did not take long to decide Lancashire was the club for him, settling on a three years contract 'without knowing exactly how much money I would be getting. It wasn't that I was naïve about money. I had business experience after all. But I have always taken people on trust. If they make a promise I believe they will keep it and the chairman Tommy Higson told me I would be well looked after and that they would get me a job with Hawker-Siddeley and a semi-detached house. That was good enough for me. Why Lancashire? I suppose even as a kid in Bombay I had supported them. I knew about Cyril Washbrook and Statham. And there was the off-spinner Roy Tattersall who toured with England in the early 1950s. I saw him play in the Bombay Test where he took a few wickets and there was another match where he sent back the first five. Geoff Pullar was another Lancashire player I knew. In fact he made a century in my Test debut. It seemed to me that Lancashire produced a lot of good cricketers. Keeping wicket to bowlers of the calibre of Statham and Ken Higgs certainly intrigued me."

CHAPTER 9

LANCASHIRE ALREADY had a good wicketkeeper when they pulled in Farokh Engineer. Keith Goodwin was adept - in 1967 when Engineer was touring with India he caught well and pulled off neat stumpings in the county championship - and he was also extremely popular. A former Lancashire bowler told me: "I liked Keith. You could count on him and he was a team player, always ready to help." The problem was that Goodwin was a batting bunny. In 1967 he boasted an average of 7.5 from 29 first class matches - and that was his best campaign. He finished with a career average of 5.77 and yet continued to go in at number nine above Brian Statham and John Savage.

Tail-enders were not expected to occupy the crease. Championship matches lasted only three days and often less because of waterlogged pitches. Truncated games were kept alive by contrived declarations or by forfeiting an innings and while batting was often difficult on rain affected wickets the priority was to keep the game moving. Statham, for example, was enjoying a little knock late one day when the captain Cyril Washbrook sent out a terse message: 'Tell the silly bugger to get out now - he's got to bowl for the last half hour!' Statham had just hammered 62 in 31 minutes with two sixes and 12 fours! Often Goodwin did not have to bat, or if he did he remained not out - 42 of his 149 first-class innings for Lancashire ended that way.

Sometimes he became desperate. Going for an impossible second run during a game against Hampshire at Southampton even the square leg umpire, Dickie Bird, urged him to retreat and save himself. "I was so involved with the game that I forgot I was umpiring," said the embarrassed Bird. "I shouted to him 'No Goody, get back, get back.' He took no notice, carried on running and I had to give him out. The Hampshire fielders just fell about laughing."

Engineer also grins at the time when he was injured and Goodwin replaced him for a game not knowing that Engineer and David Lloyd had developed a little catching routine called the shimmy. "It was very simple. Normally the keeper takes the ball and tosses it to first slip and it's returned to the bowler. But Bumble would whip it back to me instead. Unfortunately he forgot to inform Goodwin about the shimmy and Keith got it full in the face."

Goodwin's 100th match for Lancashire, the finale to the 1967 summer against Somerset at Taunton, said it all. Not required to bat at any stage he still made his mark with five dismissals in an innings for the second time that season. Lancashire's committee recorded his success with the gloves in matter of fact language but noted their 'disappointment' with his batting. By then Engineer had been recruited and Goodwin's future looked dicey. He stayed at Old Trafford until 1974 playing 22 more games.

Goodwin's predecessor was a different kettle of fish altogether. Geoff Clayton, sturdy, abrasive and nicknamed 'Chimp' for the manner in which he crouched behind the stumps, was a good 'keeper, rated as one of the best three in the country. In 1961 he held onto 86 catches. And he could bat. Unfortunately Clayton was trouble. His belligerence came to the fore in a Gillette Cup tie against Warwickshire in 1964 when in protest against their ultra defensive fielding tactics he blocked and blocked, eking out 19 runs in 20 overs and leaving Lancashire well short of their target. The Old Trafford crowd went wild and it turned into a near riot with fans gathering outside the pavilion to howl for Clayton's head. Washbrook, a strict disciplinarian and by then the team's manager, orchestrated an autumn purge which resulted in the sacking of Clayton, who joined Somerset, and three other senior players.

Engineer's engaging personality contrasted sharply with Clayton's. Goodwin had always struggled to reach double figures - Engineer was a world-class opener. Here, at last, was a wicketkeeper-batsman who would stamp his class on county cricket and help to build a trophy winning side.

Lancashire and county cricket in general faced huge challenges. Some of the most radical measures in the game's history were announced in late 1967, an embrace of overseas players, the expansion of one-day cricket, a new point scoring format for the championship. One target was to raise technical levels, another to bring in more fans after years of dwindling support. One newspaper columnist said pointedly: "May the spirit normally

Coming back from hunting leopard; Mum Minnie and Dad Manecksha;
"Dreaming of Test Cricket?"

Mum with her two sons Darius and Farokh.

Teenage portrait of Farokh.

The Parsees, 1886.

PLAYED AT SHEFFIELD PARK, MAY 24, 25.

Parsee Cricket team in the 19th Century.

First overseas tour with India to East Africa (Farokh back row fourth from right).

| Wednesday 18th January 1967 | MATCH DRAWN | Hours of Play
10-30 a.m. to 12-30 p.m.
1-15 p.m. to 3-15 p.m. & 3-35 p.m. to 5-05 p.m. | Umpires:
Samar Roy
S. K. Raghunatha Rao | The numbers put on Scoring Boards correspond with the names of players on this card |

INDIA

			1st Innings	2nd Innings
1	D. N. Sardesai	c Hendricks b Gibbs	- 28	lbw b Hall - 0
2	F. M. Engineer	c Kanhai b Sobers	- 109	c Butcher b Hall - 24
3	A. L. Wadekar	c Hendricks b Gibbs	- 0	c Sobers b Gibbs - 67
4	C. G. Borde	c Kanhai b Hunte	- 125	c Lloyd b Gibbs - 49
5	Nawab of Pataudi (Capt.)	b Hall	- 40	c Sobers b Gibbs - 5
6	Hanumant Singh	c Kanhai b Griffith	- 7	b Griffith - 50
7	V. Subramanyam	c Sobers b Hall	- 17	c Lloyd b Griffith - 61
8	R. F. Surti	not out	- 50	c Hendricks b Griffith - 8
9	E. A. S. Prasanna	b Bynoe	- 1	c Sobers b Gibbs - 24
10	B. S. Bedi	c Griffith b Gibbs	- 11	c Nurse b Griffith - 8
11	B. S. Chandrasekhar	c Hendricks b Sobers	- 1	not out - 10
	R. Saxena		-	-
	(12th Man)			
		Extras	- 15	Extras - 17
		Total	404	Total 323

Runs at foll { 1-129 2-131 3-145 4-239 5-257 6-292 7-379 8-382 9-403 10-404
of wickets { 1-0 2-45 3-107 4-123 5-192 6-245 7-266 8-281 9-297 10-323

	O	M	R	W	O	M	R	W
Hall	19	1	68	2	12	2	67	2
Griffith	23	4	96	1	14	2	61	4
Sobers	27.2	7	69	2	27	11	58	—
Gibbs	46	10	87	3	40.4	13	96	4
Lloyd	13	2	39	—	12	3	24	—
Hunte	10	2	25	1				
Bynoe	5	4	5	1				

WEST INDIES

			1st Innings	2nd Innings
1	C. C. Hunte	c Subramaniam b Chandrasekhar	- 49	c Surti b Prasanna - 26
2	R. Bynoe	lbw b Chandrasekhar	- 48	c Surti b Bedi - 36
3	R. B. Kanhai	c Borde b Surti	- 77	c Pataudi b Bedi - 36
4	B. F. Butcher	b Prasanna	- 0	c Surti b Prasanna - 24
5	C. L. Lloyd	b Surti	- 38	b Bedi - 24
6	S. M. Nurse	b Chandrasekhar	- 26	lbw b Bedi - 0
7	G. S. Sobers (Capt.)	c Engineer b Chandrasekar	- 95	not out - 74
8	J. L. Hendricks	c Engineer b Surti	- 0	lbw b Prasanna - 9
9	C. C. Griffith	c Surti b Bedi	- 27	not out - 40
10	W. W. Hall	b Prasanna	- 31	-
11	L. R. Gibbs	not out	- 1	-
	B. Davis		-	-
	(12th Man)			
		Extras	- 14	Extras - 1
		Total	406	Total 270 for 7

Runs at foll { 1-99 2-114 3-115 4-194 5-246 6-246 7-251 8-324 9-404 10-406
of wickets { 1-63 2-71 3-118 4-130 5-131 6-166 7-193 8- 9- 10-

	O	M	R	W	O	M	R	W
Surti	19	2	68	3	9	1	27	—
Subramaniam	7	1	21	—	7	3	14	—
Chandrasekhar	46	15	130	4	12	2	41	—
Bedi	19	3	55	1	28	7	81	4
Prasanna	41	11	118	2	37	9	106	3

India v West Indies scorecard when Farokh scores 94 before lunch.

India in Australia 1967-68 (Farokh seated far right).

A young Farokh at Tower Bridge in London.

Farokh second right with,
left to right, Nadkarni,
Buggie, Desai and Borde at
the Taj Mahal.

Farokh in characteristic style. Another one bites the dust.

Above: Edwards ct Farokh b Sullivan, The Oval 1970.

Below: Stumped by Farokh - "Raise your foot at your peril".

Rest of the World XI 1970
Standing: B Hassan (Kenya - 12th man), I Alam (Pak), MJ Procter (SA), RG Pollock (SA)
CH Lloyd (WI), GD McKenzie (A), BA Richards (SA), FM Engineer (India).
Seated: RB Kanhai (WI), EJ Barlow (SA), GStA Sobers (WI), LR Gibbs (WI).

Farokh being presented to the Queen at Lord's in 1971.

Farokh Engineer ... among the best

Majestic Lancashire get a taste of that old glory

CRICKET

Lancashire go to the top

Lancashire rally under Engineer's guidance

Engineer steadies wilting Indians

Engineer sweeps Lancashire home by nine wickets

ENGINEER TO THE RESCUE

Fearless Farokh hors de combat

Saturday Review

Engineer is best wicketkeeper

MASON

were bowled out for 202 by Ken
Kanhai was the only batsman

Headline Grabber!

Above: Farokh in action in the 1970 Gillette Cup final.

Below: Lancashire in 1971.

LANCASHIRE **Standing:** B. Wood, J. Simmons, D. Lloyd, D. P. Hughes, J. Sullivan, F. C. Hayes, K. Shuttleworth.
Seated: P. Lever, H. Pilling, J. D. Bond (Captain), F. M. Engineer, C. H. Lloyd.

Above: With his Lancashire teammates at the Old Trafford nets,

Below: Farokh in full flow for Lancashire at Old Trafford.

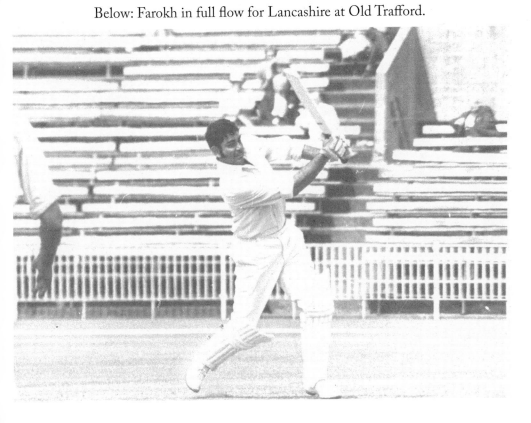

The Pied Piper of cricket.

PRIME MINISTER

MESSAGE

Farokh Engineer is one of our best-known
sportsmen. As batsman and wicket-keeper he
represented India with distinction in international
cricket and endeared himself to millions.

My good wishes for the benefit match in
which reputed players from many cricketing countries
are taking part.

(Indira Gandhi)

New Delhi,
February 17, 1984

Opposite below: Mrs Indira Gandhi wishes Farokh good luck before a Test
and, above, a letter from Mrs Gandhi in 1984.

Judging a Miss United Kingdom beauty contest with Sid James,
Mike Winters and Freddie Starr.

Watching cricket and having a laugh with Peter Reid and Gary Lineker.

With friend
Garry Sobers.
"The Greatest
All-rounder.
Thank God he
didn't decide to
keep wicket as
well."

Farokh Engineer

associated with the cricket of such Commonwealth countries as Australia and the West Indies permeate our less adventurous natives likewise."

Doubts remained. And there was alarm in the powerful Lancashire League who warned counties against poaching their overseas stars, including Clive Lloyd who was contracted to Haslingden, Asif Iqbal of Pakistan who was on Burnley's books, and Australian Neil Hawke who had an agreement with Nelson. Generally, though, the overhaul was regarded as essential for the future of cricket. Meanwhile Lancashire had launched their own rebuilding programme. Statham, nearing the end of an illustrious career, relinquished the captaincy, opener David Green who was once considered his natural successor had been given the elbow and had signed for Gloucestershire and while the committee suffered plenty of justified stick for that decision at least they came up with an intriguing alternative in Jack Bond whose leadership qualities had been noted during a stint in charge of the second XI. With Engineer itching to get started, Clive Lloyd booked in for the following year and a number of promising youngsters in the pipeline, things were on the up. Some aspects of cricket and Lancashire specifically were not to change for many years.

David Lloyd compared life at Old Trafford to the Victorian age. David Green went back even further - 'medieval' - and when Engineer was given his first in depth tour of this world renowned stadium his heart might have sunk if he had been a different character. Work to build a new office block was still in progress, the terraces needed a lick of paint, office equipment was out-dated. The Press Box had new wooden benches but it still resembled an outsized garden shed perched precariously on top of the Ladies' Stand. On wet days it leaked, reporters had to change seats to keep their notebooks dry.

Derek Hodgson of the *Daily Telegraph* gave it a place in cricketing history when he wrote of the gale which wrecked a championship game against Notts in 1983: 'Not that the Manchester Press corps were entirely alive to the cricket as the monstrous wind threatened to blow in the back of their wooden hut and carry it, and them, off the top of the ladies' stand and into the Ship Canal. While the loss of a few cricket writers might cause little comment the destruction of the Press box, a temporary structure erected in 1946, would certainly alarm the National Trust.'

The ground was virtually empty when Engineer was first shown around. Typewriters clattered, phones rang but you needed a vivid imagination to picture a mid-summer's day with a 20,000 plus crowd. Yet his first impressions were positive. "I loved it immediately. Better than Lord's. Everyone was so welcoming. I knew I was going to enjoy it." He was, of course, special. And special people get special treatment. Lancashire gave him a well paid three years deal. The staff were primed to look after him. But there was more to it than a few friendly hellos.

"I knew beforehand that Old Trafford was steeped in tradition. But the sense of history I got when walking around the pavilion for the first time was extraordinary. All the photographs and paintings of old teams, players and officials. Some of cricket's greatest had walked down the stairs, though the pavilion stand and onto the pitch. You could hear people chatting about the Tyldesleys, Washbrook and Paynter. And, from a player's viewpoint, the facilities were good and compared favourably to what I'd got used to at the Brabourne Stadium in Bombay. The dressing-room had a balcony, there was a dining room - and the food was good though maybe not enough curry - and there was an indoor school with nets and squash courts. As for the pitch, it was a sporting wicket. It rewarded effort. All in all I felt privileged to be playing there."

Those who have loved Old Trafford, and I count myself as one, have always had to ignore its many ugly components. 'Loved but unlovely.' Its spectator facilities, or rather lack of them, were criticised even then and continued to be until its recent and long overdue modernisation. In 1968 loud heckling noises from south of Watford threatened its future as a Test venue, pushing Lancashire into frenzied activity. The same thing happened in 2006. Building work quickened, pots of paint were piled up ready to refresh the terraces in time for the Ashes Test in June and the office staff worked hard to market and sell tickets. Cash, they knew, was short. Lancashire had to pull in belts and yet invest for the future - it was a tricky time.

None of this played a part in the manner in which Engineer was received. What hit him immediately was the genuine attitude of the people who worked there. Nothing fancy, nothing artificial, nothing over-cooked. A cuppa in the office, a chat here and there, lots of smiles. Lifelong friendships were formed in those early days. Later Clive Lloyd and Wasim Akram experienced similar superglue emotions and, like Engineer, stayed stuck to Old Trafford and the north-west forever although, unwittingly, the club made a terrible blunder with Lloyd's first accommodation - Flat 1, Unit Two Sauna. For a few nights he slept on a 'massage' bed.

However all went well with Engineer's arrangements. "They couldn't do enough for me. But I never got the feeling that they were just playing up to me because I was the star of the show." Another ticked box was that Lancashire's Bert Flack was the country's top groundsman. A few years earlier the Old Trafford pitch was one of several named and shamed as poor but the redoubtable, heavily whiskered Flack had laboured to put it to rights.

As part of his deal, Lancashire provided Engineer with a car, a red Escort from the Ford dealer Quick's but, first, he had to take his test. "I wasn't worried about it. After all I had drove around Bombay for years and if you can drive there you can drive anywhere in the world. It's crazy traffic, you have to be quick and confident just to survive. So I was full of confidence on the day of my test. It was warm and I had the window down and the radio on. Most of the time I had just one hand on the steering wheel. After all that's how you drive in Bombay. I thought it was all a formality. I didn't even think about speed limits and things. At the end the examiner said he knew I could drive but then asked me if I'd ever read the Highway Code. I said: 'What's that?'. He gave me a little book and told me to read it, then said I'd have to take the test again."

Engineer's exploits behind the wheel became woven into Old Trafford folk-lore. "The first morning I drove to the ground I saw a young lady walking along the road. I have to admit that for a few seconds I took my eyes off the road. She was blonde and curvaceous. I took a good look at her as any self-respecting man would do but then to my horror realised that the car in front of me had braked suddenly, apparently because a dog had run in front of him. I skidded straight into his boot. Luckily no-one was hurt and Norman Quick the boss of the car company couldn't stop laughing about it. I got another car. I don't know what happened to the young lady. I promised myself it was the last time a blonde got me into trouble but I was wrong."

David Lloyd still jokes about Engineer's driving. "It was the road system that mystified him. He lived on the south side of Manchester and the only journey he was confident about was the one to Old Trafford. He conquered the M6 so he pointed his car in the right direction when we were playing down south but crossing the Pennines to Leeds for a Roses game completely defeated him. It took him four hours."

Having a house and car laid on by the club re-assured Engineer that Lancashire would stick to their promise of looking after him. Indian cricketers were not used to such luxuries.

Budhi Kunderan complained after a tour of England: "We felt a sense of inferiority even before we got on the field...when the English came to India they were so well treated, everything was provided for them. The day we arrived in England we had to go a sports shop to get some equipment. I had to save from the £1 a day allowance to buy a bat. We had gaberdine flannels that would stick to our knees so that we could not bend down. Our allowance was so meagre that from the moment we checked into a hotel we would have to go looking for a cheap meal."

Engineer had done better than most back on the Indian domestic circuit, thanks to his job with Mercedes which he took seriously and his Brylcreem advertising. "Normally if a cricketer is given a job the company does not really expect him to do any serious work. I could have drunk coffee all day and chatted to the bosses about cricket because they were all big fans, then maybe had a very lengthy lunch or a net session with the firm's team or maybe the state side. All very relaxed. But I had business ambitions. I asked for work and I went into sales and marketing. It was good experience for a future outside the game." Posing as the Brylcreem Boy did not bring in riches but it did give him extra exposure as the debonair pin-up of Indian cricket. Other advertising jobs came in, affording him a more comfortable lifestyle but not enough to own a car. A scooter was still the best option for short trips.

Cricketers' contracts in England usually covered the summer only. Winter jobs were necessary to pay the household bills. David Lloyd worked in the Old Trafford office, Harry Pilling made coffins for an undertaker, Statham worked as a part-time brewery representative. The 1968 championship season was not scheduled to start until May 4. Players began to drift back to Old Trafford in late March when John Kay the *Manchester Evening News* correspondent wrote: "Although I understand Peter Lever and Keith Goodwin have had talks with club officials about their prospects for the future all Lancashire's players have signed contracts for the new season. Goodwin, obviously feeling the special registration of Indian Test player Farokh Engineer would mean he might lose his first team place has been considering a possible move. But Lancashire's attitude is that if Goodwin is in good form behind the stumps Engineer might win a place for his batting alone. So Goodwin has decided to stay at Old Trafford." Of course Goodwin did not stand an earthly.

Ronnie Davies, the club's treasurer, told the members in his annual report that Lancashire had lost £9,510, the second largest deficit in their history due to bad weather, a poor fixture list and the lack of a Test in 1967. But, he added: "We are far more optimistic about the prospects for 1968. Engineer will be available for all matches and although Clive Lloyd is still Haslingden's professional and cannot play regularly until 1969 he will play in non Championship games." And so on May 15 Engineer and Big Clive shook hands in the Old Trafford dressing room to renew a friendship already formed on the world's Test stage. The opposition were the touring Australians, a non championship fixture allowing Lloyd to make his Red Rose debut and to mark this momentous occasion the Manchester weather appeared in full battle dress. It hosed down.

Ian Wooldridge of the *Daily Mail* was one of a possee of Press men keen to see the Aussies in action and hoping for some Indian-Caribbean fireworks to feast on. Instead he and his colleagues decamped from the chilly, leaking Press Box to mingle with the players in the pavilion bar. This is how he started his report:

"The lunchtime score at Old Trafford, Manchester, yesterday was 19 Guinnesses, 13 halves of draught Worthington, nine rum and cokes, seven cold lagers, and a pink gin for the only Old Etonian present. After an eternal silence an Australian said: 'That bloody Bradman must have been good. He got 1,000 in May and I haven't held a bloody bat yet.' Nobody laughed. Outside the streets shone like a guardsman's toecaps and you would have sunk to your shoelaces had you set foot on the outfield. It was raining again on Bill Lawry's Australians. So far they have played 11 hours cricket in 21 days."

They managed to squeeze in 230 minutes on the third and last day, just time enough for Lloyd to get out for a single playing early at a ball from Freeman and offering a simple catch to cover and for Engineer to enjoy 17 overs behind the stumps watched by a small huddle of patient fans in the pavilion stand. It is the essence of the man that he gained only positives from this first rain drenched game at Old Trafford. "We were stuck inside most of the time playing cards mostly. But it gave us time to bond. And that is so important. Clive and I were the new boys. Sure, we were big names but we had to fit in, to show the rest of the lads that we were team players, not just individuals looking to make a few quick bucks. For county players this was a new thing, working with overseas players. And it wasn't all about what you did on the pitch. It's about the sort of person you are. Whether you get on with other people, whether they get on with you, gelling together as a team. I thought I fitted in. It felt right to me. It was pouring down and we hardly played but I had a big smile on my face."

The smile stayed. But Engineer had problems in his first season. He played in every game, his wicketkeeping was adjudged outstanding, he got on like a house on fire with team-mates and quickly built a vital understanding with captain Bond but harsh critics pointed at his batting record - 672 championship runs at an average of 16.87 did not meet all expectations. Those apparently modest figures should be taken in context. Runs were at a premium during that waterlogged summer with only Harry Pilling reaching 1,000 in the championship and Bond topping the averages with just 26.6. Also Engineer was never sure where he would appear in the line-up - Lancashire juggled it around, using him as an opener, at 4, 5, 6, and 7, hardly helping him to find consistency. There again, his natural inclination to attack, hooking and flat-batting pace and charging at spin often proved his undoing on England's bowler friendly pitches. His top score was 65 during 85 minutes of 'dare-devilry' (*Daily Telegraph*) at Worcester. Even so this swashbuckling 'Parsee pirate' as one Indian writer described him was a permanent fixture, now on the verge of Lancashire's most successful post-war period.

Lancashire never viewed Engineer as a regular championship opener despite his success at Test level, preferring David Lloyd and Barry Wood both of whom could get their heads down when necessary and pick the 'right' balls to hit, giving Lancashire a solid start whatever the conditions. Their names remained glued to the team-sheet for a decade although Engineer was to get his chance in one-day cricket. "I didn't mind where I batted. I always gave my best. All that mattered was that I was playing for the biggest club in the country. The start of the season was a bit gloomy simply because of the weather. It poured down. Three of the first four championship matches hardly got off the ground and I thought that things weren't going to be as rosy as I imagined. I was run out twice - and not through language difficulties. The reason was that I kept slipping. I still had short studs on my boots after playing on the hard surfaces in Australia the previous winter and I couldn't get a grip."

(Engineer had had problems with his footwear the previous winter on a Rest of the World tour to Australia where none other than Sir Don Bradman chastised him for playing in rubber soled shoes. More comfortable than orthodox cricket boots, thought Engineer, until Bradman appeared in the dressing-room and gave him 'the greatest roasting' he had ever suffered. "He absolutely chewed me up. Then he asked me whether I was free that evening! He picked me up from the airport, drove me home and gave me carrot juice and a vegetarian meal, I assumed because he thought that that's what all Indians had. Very nice of him but I had been playing all day and what I needed was a couple of good cold beers. And a big steak. Then he pulled out a rusty projector to show a slideshow of his batting. He gave a commentary explaining this shot and that. Told me I was too flamboyant. It was getting late. I was tired, thirsty and starving! It was a memorable evening but when got back to the hotel the first thing I did was to order a beer. After that we always got a Christmas card from Sir Don and Lady Bradman.")

One match which did beat the weather gave Engineer his first taste of Roses rivalry - and of Fred Trueman.

"We were at Headingley getting changed when Fred walked into our dressing-room. I was surprised to put it mildly - he was stark bollock naked apart from the tobacco pipe he was chewing. Here was one of the most famous fast bowlers of all time, someone I had always wanted to meet, someone with a fearsome reputation standing right in front of me without a stitch on. Brian Statham introduced us and I was very polite and said: I'm very pleased to meet you sir.' Fred looked at me hard and said: 'Don't you f... ing creep to me sonny!' He promised that my stay in the middle would be a very short one. Of course when I went out to bat I cracked the first ball to the rope but he got me before I could really get going. Afterwards he asked me what I wanted to drink. I had a beer. The rest of the Yorkshire lads were shellshocked - they had never known him buy a drink for an opponent. Fred and I were to have some good times together. Even now I can hear that gruff Yorkshire voice of his."

As Engineer got to grips with English cricket the newspaper headlines were all about football. Manchester City won the league title and United topped that by beating Benfica at Wembley to lift the European Cup. The city buzzed. Top cabaret acts appeared at clubs like The Golden Garter and youngsters danced the night away at Oasis, Takis, The Twisted Wheel and other discos. In London theatre-goers flocked to see the nudity in the musical Hair following the relaxation of censorship laws. The Church of England had lifted the ban on women priests. But despite this whirlpool of change, in and outside the sport, cricket and the Old Trafford club in particular found it difficult to completely ditch a more conservative way of life. The younger players grew their hair longer - Barry Wood once received a letter from an ex Test star informing him that he would do a lot better if he paid the barber a visit - but there were few other concessions to the 'Swinging Sixties'. Females were barred from the pavilion, even those wearing dog collars, and were for another 30 years until the rule was tested and found wanting when a male member in drag attended the AGM. The second XI had a separate dressing room, called the dogs' home, from the first XI; a strict dress code was still in place with players instructed to wear blazers at lunch; and in the stands polite applause was the order of the day. Despite the surge of overseas stars, few black faces were seen on the terraces. But 'La la la Lancashire', the chant of the one-day brigade, would soon echo around the ground and for Engineer that first season was one to archive for the rest of his life.

"One of the great thrills of my career was keeping wicket to Statham. It was his last season and so I didn't catch him at his absolute peak but it was still magical. I remember the first ball I ever took from him. It pitched on middle and leg and suddenly I saw it flying away down the legside. That surprised me. I hadn't expected the ball to move that much off the pitch. I gradually got to know his bowling and I got a number of legside catches off him, through anticipation. I felt a touch of nostalgia keeping to him and it was a privilege to play in his last match against Yorkshire at Old Trafford.

"In that one season with Brian we travelled together to most of the away fixtures, stopping off at any number of out of the way pubs. He liked a beer and a cig but he never put on an ounce of fat and he could bowl all day. I don't think he truly realised how good he was and he was so unassuming. Years after we had finished playing we were both in Barbados and I saw him in a crowd looking completely lost. I thought 'They don't even know who he is'. Me, I love people to recognise me. But Statham wasn't bothered. I wish I'd had had his qualities."

As I have mentioned earlier, Statham once told me that he did know how good he was. He was certainly modest, but not falsely modest. I once asked him of his early impressions of Engineer. "Extrovert, a bit of a showman I suppose. It was just that we English players rarely showed any great emotion. A handclap, a pat on the back if we got a wicket, little else. We didn't go in for showing too much emotion out on the pitch. Rooky was different, a bit louder if nothing else! But it worked because he was good for team spirit. We groaned a few times when he got out to a daft shot but every time he went to bat and every time he dived for an impossible catch he gave you hope. I played with a number of good keepers but I did wish I had played with him more often."

CHAPTER 10

INDIA'S PERFORMANCE in the January 1967 Madras Test suggested they were on the up and West Indies heading down. "There were big cracks in their team. We had opened them up," claims Farokh Engineer. But India lost their next seven matches.

"We went to England in the first half of that summer '67. It was wet and cold. Miserable weather. The pitches were ideal for English seam bowlers, a nightmare for our spinners. We didn't have much of a chance really. Me? I loved every minute. Offers rolled in."

England comprehensively won all three Tests. By six wickets, an innings and 124 runs, and an innings and 132 runs. But it was a series to forget for both teams. Attendances were hit by the weather, the inevitability of the result and by Geoff Boycott's go-slow in the first game at Headingley. Dire warnings were issued about the future of cricket.

There was criticism of India's officials for arranging a tour in the early season when they needed pitches to be as dry as possible for their spinners. Bedi and Prasanna had linked up beautifully to push West Indies to the brink of defeat in Madras, Chandrasekhar was a handful for anyone and Venkat was keen to impress in England after destroying New Zealand with 8-72 on his debut in 1965. They all bowled superbly but England were strong in batting and the conditions were unfavourable. India were also so badly hit by injuries that just before the final Test at Edgbaston, the captain Pataudi asked Budhi Kunderan - Engineer's deputy who had played in the previous game at Lord's as a batsman: "What sort of bowler are you?" Kunderan said he wasn't sure. He ended up opening the attack, sent down four overs at a respectable cost of 13 and never bowled again.

"It was chaos," admits Engineer. "You could not blame Pataudi. We had so many injuries. A couple had to bat with runners at Edgbaston. The whole thing was a mess really."

Kunderan was biting about it all: "The day we arrived in England we had to go to a sports shop to get some equipment. The Indian Board did not provide any. Even the clothes we had were not suitable for cricket in England. We had gaberdine flannels that would stick to your knees. We had a sleeveless sweater and a full sleeve sweater but they were not woollen and did not keep out the cold. Some of the boys suffered terribly with the food. Venkat and Chandra being vegetarian could not eat ham or any of the cold meat salads which were served a lot during cricket matches. For much of the tour they were living on bread and butter. They were almost starving by the end. The manager Keki Tarapore did not help. He did not organise any practice facilities and went around telling the English: 'We have come to learn, we have come to learn.' He was always crawling to the English."

If Kunderan was over the top with some of his criticism, Engineer would agree with the general intent of his message - that India still had to shake off its reputation as whipping boys and that the people in charge of Indian cricket had to get their act together. Engineer remembers the riots in Calcutta during the series with West Indies when fans vented their anger over the black market in tickets.

"There were some disgraceful things which led to that incident. There were thousands outside the ground holding what they thought were valid tickets but they couldn't get in. The stadium was already full. Fans invaded the field. The police charged them. There were fires. One of the stands collapsed. Then the fans rushed the VIP stands. Most of the players escaped by running to the pavilion and then getting on to the team coaches to get away from the stadium. But Wes Hall and Charlie Griffith ran out of the ground - they felt they were being chased. They were terrified but it was the officials the fans were after not the players. We saw Hall and Griffith running away and I got our coach to stop and pick them up. To this day Wes believes I saved his life! People were throwing bricks and bottles but despite the danger Conrad Hunte retrieved the West Indies flag from the pavilion - I thought that was one hell of a brave thing to do. He had so much pride for the flag and didn't want it lost or damaged. As for the fans while you can't condone what they did, you have to understand how they felt. They had been cheated. Tickets had been selling for massively inflated prices on the black market."

Fuelled by officials on the make and political unrest it was one of India cricket's blackest moments. Eventually the mob dispersed. Play was abandoned for the day and delicate negotiations on the following day, which was a rest day, ensured the match would be completed. "It was difficult for players. All we wanted to do was to play cricket. But all the time there was stuff going on the background which made everything more difficult."

Not that Engineer suffered too much on or off the field in England, certainly he had no complaints about the food. "I was wined and dined all over the place. Good wine, steaks. People invited me out and to their homes. England wanted me and I soon came to realise that I wanted to be there. I understood some of the boys having difficulties. But I got stuck into the egg and bacon and the ham salads just like I got stuck into the bowling." Engineer began with a brilliant 87 at Headingley, an innings in sharp relief to Boycott's double century marathon, and it cemented his image with the English public as a high-class entertainer, just what cricket needed.

After being whacked 3-0 by Ray Illingworth's side, India were beaten 4-0 in Australia the following winter but the scoreline is just a tad flattering to the Aussies. Set an 'impossible' 395 to win in the third Test at Brisbane they marched to 310-5 with M L Jaisimha, flown in for the game as a replacement for the injured Chandra, hitting a century. When his partnership with Chandu Borde came to an end, India stumbled to 355 all out. Also Pataudi missed the first Test with a hamstring strain and when he went to bat for the first time in the series, in the second game at Melbourne, India had collapsed to 25-5 on a spicy track. Having elected to bat Pataudi at least redeemed himself with a typically tigerish 75. India, though, left Australia in better fettle than when they had departed British shores the previous summer. They went immediately to New Zealand and pulled off a 3-1 win.

"It was the first time we had won a Test never mind a series abroad. New Zealand were not one of the aristocrats of Test cricket, I know, and at home we were expected to beat them but this was on their soil and so it was a piece of history."

Engineer was now India's regular opener. He had produced some decent innings in Australia, 89, 42, 37 without pulling up any trees but in New Zealand he helped Ajit Wadekar to clear a path to glory. Rusi Surti, the all rounder known as the 'poor man's Sobers' weighed in heavily along with excellent bowling from Nadkarni and Prasanna, whose reputation as an off spinner had spiralled throughout the winter.

"He was the finest off-spinner India produced but didn't play as much Test cricket as he should, partly through taking time off for his engineering studies but also because of the never ending political issues. Batsmen feared him and Pataudi always appreciated his value. He bowled a beautiful floater like Fred Titmus. It fell and left the right-hander."

Engineer took second spot in India's averages and third overall behind Wadekar and Graham Dowling. The pitches were not conducive to fast scoring but he was the quickest and he was also consistent going past 50 twice and past 40 three times.

India's ground breaking win came at Dunedin in February. Much of the credit deservedly went to Prasanna with 6-94 from 40 overs as New Zealand were bowled out for 208 in their second innings, leaving a target of 200 which India reached with five wickets to spare. However what sparked India into life was the second wicket stand of 79 between Engineer and Wadekar and a brave last wicket partnership between Desai, who ignored a blow from seamer Dick Motz which fractured his jaw, and Bedi. They put on 57 to give India a lead slender in runs but heavy in psychological value. Pataudi singled out Desai's bravery as the main factor behind that victory.

Engineer remembers it as a 'strange game'. "They were 200-2 on the first day but we stuck at it and restricted them to 350. We really pulled together on the field. And we won easily enough in the end even though only Wadekar and myself got past 50 in the whole match. For once we batted all the way down the order. Everyone contributed. We were pleased obviously we were. But there wasn't a big celebration. We shook hands. That was it. We dominated the series. They had one or two good players but we were by far the better team."

Beating New Zealand before thin crowds in thin weather did not have anything like the cachet of knocking West Indies, Australia or England off their perch but it was a start. Prasanna and Bedi were dovetailing neatly, Surti's all-round skills gave them more flexibility and the left-handed Wadekar was making big runs, although his century in the win at Wellington proved to be the only one of his Test career. There was one problem - Engineer's opening partner. Sardesai was out of the picture, Syed Abid Ali had taken over and had failed. Who next? India's selectors were able to put the dilemma on the back burner because the next Test was 18 months away, allowing Engineer to concentrate on his English career. When he and India returned to action in September 1969 the headache over the opening partnership was solved. Engineer was dropped to number eight! India launched the return series against New Zealand with Abid Ali and Chauhan facing the new ball.

The selectors justified this by pointing out the fact that Engineer had not been Lancashire's first choice opener in the championship. Yet, within six weeks, he was back at the top of the Indian order. "In my view it was not about form or ability. If I had been having a bad run or simply wasn't considered good enough I could have accepted it more easily. But one match I was in the tail-end against New Zealand, next I was opening against the Aussies. I was all for flexibility. I had no problems at all with switching the batting around according to the circumstances. But the way I was treated didn't make any sense at all. It had to be political. Personal. I can't think of any other explanation. But what could I do? I wanted to play, to represent my country. These were the people in power. They could make or break you."

India's performance against New Zealand in the three match home series of autumn 1969 provoked a barrage of criticism. Bedi and Prasanna earned victory in Bombay bowling them out cheaply on the last day but they lost heavily in Nagpur where they were accused of late night partying and were saved in Hyderabad by a thunderstorm. Injured, Engineer missed that game and so escaped some of the Press fury after they had slumped to 89 all out (after being 49-9) and 76-7. Fans rioted.

There were further disturbances in Bombay and Calcutta when Australia visited. Smoke drifted over the Brabourne Stadium and bottles thrown but play continued, India slipped to defeat and Pataudi came under pressure despite going close to a century. Engineer helped to pull things around a little with a sparkling 77 in a draw at Kanpur and Bedi and Prasanna teamed up again to earn them victory in Delhi, levelling the series. From there they should have gone on to win but the Aussies, captained by Bill Lawry and including Doug Walters and Ian Chappell were steely opponents, coming through a terrible Test at Eden Gardens where six people died and dozens injured in riots over tickets to win by 10 wickets. India were in bad books with their own supporters. Play was held up by stone throwing. They shouted abuse at Pataudi and attacked the team hotel.

In Madras Engineer missed a stumping chance. Reports say it was an easy one when Walters was on four - he went onto make a century and Australia won. "I can't remember that one," he says. "But I've never claimed I was perfect."

If India had arranged other Tests in the 1969-70 fixture list, then that error coupled with only one half century might have put Engineer's place in doubt. However he had pulled off a series of electrically charged stumpings in that series, Walters being one of his victims in Calcutta, and in general his 'keeping to the spinners helped Bedi, Prasanna and Venkat to claim all but 10 of the 72 Aussie wickets which fell. As a batsman he was not at his best but few Indians were that winter and Pataudi found it particularly difficult after his initial 95 in Bombay. More to the point, there was a huge gap in India's calendar. They were without a Test for over a year with a tour to the West Indies scheduled for early 1971 - time for Engineer to show that he remained one of the world's outstanding players and for Pataudi to polish his tarnished reputation with the public and maybe to evade any political manoeuvres, of which being India there were bound to be many. Both were to get a nasty surprise.

In an earlier chapter I said I would try to de-construct Engineer's bamboo and straw batting statistics for India and rebuild them with some bricks and mortar. Perhaps this is an appropriate moment so here goes (Farokh - put the kettle on and any, like him, bored stiff by stats please look away now). Here we are only reviewing Engineer's Test career and attempting to keep it within an Indian context.

Engineer played 46 Tests, 87 innings with three not outs giving him an average of 31.08. Modest? It puts him a fair way down India's batting table but of all those who appeared before or during his career, even those like Gavaskar and Venkat who finished well after him, only eight exceeded 40. Two were a little under 40, two were in the mid 30s. Then a group in the 30-32 region including Engineer. So perhaps a little better than modest but certainly not in the highest bracket. However....

What strikes me most is the number of positions he played in: 1, 2, 3, 4, 5, 6, 7, 8, 9, 10. He did not work his way up, or down, gradually as you might expect. Engineer was forced onto a trampoline sometimes by the events of specific matches but more often by erratic, illogical and/or politically inspired selection. He yo-yoed. No matter how he performed, good or bad, for half the time he was involved with Test cricket he never really knew where he might bat next.

There were a couple of comparatively settled periods, one at the outset of his career 1962-65. In his first 16 innings he usually appeared at the tail-end. Yes, he was inconsistent but he hit an important 65 at number 9 in India's 1962 win over England. In his next knock, at number 10, he made only 15 not out but helped the last two stands to add 40. He stayed at 10 for a

Test against West Indies, twice going to the crease with the innings virtually over and with little hope of making runs. Back at 9 he then slammed the Windies' attack for consecutive scores of 53 and 40, firstly putting on 94 with Nadkarni, and then helping two team-mates to add 64. Those two innings against Wes Hall, Lance Gibbs and Garry Sobers surely deserved some reward even though India slumped to a heavy defeat. Not on your life. Engineer stayed at 9 for the following Test and this time threw his wicket away, charging at Gibbs. It cost him his place.

When he fought his way back for the home series with New Zealand early in 1965 he started at 9 and hammered 90 in a record partnership with Nadkarni of 145 for the eighth wicket. This time the selectors acted accordingly, bumping him up to 3, and he responded with 10 and 45. And, obviously, for the next game he found himself at 8. Bizarrely, he was run out for 17 yet was India's second top scorer in a first innings debacle, 88 all out. The only other batsman in double figures was Chandu Borde. "Well done, Farokh," they said. "You can open in the second innings." He did so, failed to deliver and went back to number 7. Where he had another failure, was promptly ordered to open again … and had an even worse failure.

Engineer, it seemed, could not do right for wrong. He was willing to play anywhere without complaint. These early matches badly mauled his overall Test figures. In 19 innings and in seven different positions he made 420 runs at a meagre average of 22. I cannot find another batsman in India's top 30 from before and during his era who suffered so much in this way although many were switched around and his wicketkeeping rival and friend Budhi Kunderan played as low as 9 only two years after hitting 192 against England as an opener.

In 1967, 12 games into his Test career, Engineer stepped out of the pavilion at the Chepauk, smiled at the camera and launched his golden year. Hall and Griffith were mastered. Then he wowed English fans fed up with Geoff Boycott's grind 'em down approach. Finally he featured strongly in that first win abroad in New Zealand. Engineer played 24 successive innings in that spell all as opener scoring 865 runs at an average of 36 and never once shrinking back from his mission statement to destroy the opposition attack. This, I believe, is the true measure of his batting.

Accepted, there was only one century in that time - although he was to score another - and, granted, he never could quite grasp the notion that part of the job was to wear out the pacemen and take the shine off the new ball.

But here was an Indian opener, making good scores in expansive fashion, instilling confidence in his team-mates. It could not last. Not with India's selectors.

Dropped for political reasons he was recalled because they could not do without him. They pulled him up, pushed him down. Between September 1969 and January 1975, 44 innings, 22 as opener, the rest at 5, 6, and 7. Of those 22 against the new ball, the last nine were against a useful and varied West Indies attack of Andy Roberts, Vanburn Holder, Keith Boyce, Bernard Julien and Lance Gibbs when Engineer was 36 years-old and even his reflexes had slowed up. In his first knock of that series he was hurt, forcing him out of the second innings. As the series progressed there were some of the old flashes, two half centuries, but he ended with a pair at his beloved Bombay and knew that was it.

My conclusion is that as a batsman, Engineer was poorly used. With proper support and encouragement he would have served India better and would have finished with much superior figures, I am sure of it. But he was not the only player to suffer. And Indian cricket suffered far, far more than any individual.

CHAPTER 11

THE PAUCITY of English county cricket during the 1960s when attendances slumped by 80 per cent can be highlighted by any number of low scoring championship matches. As a loyal Lancastrian, Yorkshire's 23 all out against Hampshire at Middlesbrough in 1965 springs to my mind but to balance the books let's look at a game in which Farokh Engineer played during his debut season of 1968. Lancashire v Glamorgan, Old Trafford in August when the Welsh side won by an innings and 23 runs even though only three of their batsmen got into double figures! Only Engineer troubled them. Glamorgan's captain and opening bowler Ossie Wheatley once complained: "I don't mind Engineer charging me but I do wish he would wait until I started my run-up."

Engineer did not satisfy everyone all the time but the club had taken him to its heart. The committee's official report noted: "Although Farokh Engineer was disappointing with the bat his wicket-keeping was quite outstanding and, as anticipated, he proved to be a great asset to the side." And he was a crowd-pleaser. Which is exactly what crisis-torn English cricket needed at that stage.

Denis Compton was one of many who bemoaned the state of the game, particularly the lack of have a go batsmen. 'In my opinion there is nothing wrong with cricket; it is the attitude of so many first-class players that has gone awry. Cricket is still a wonderful game as played in the schools and at club level but so much big cricket is no longer the spectacle it used to be, and, in particular, the County Championship, which provided me with so much fun, no longer attracts huge crowds. Modern trends, like the family car and the thirst for excitement the whole time, now challenge cricket probably more than any other spectator sport. The safety-first outlook has bedevilled professional cricket far too long and like our traffic in the big cities the three-day game has come almost to a full stop.'

Being the player he was, Compton was desperate for cricket to provide entertainment. As a boy, Engineer had watched him play in India. "He was stationed there with the British Army during the war and naturally people wanted him to play. He was playing in a Ranji Trophy game at the Brabourne Stadium in Bombay when I saw him. My brother Darius used to take me there. We'd be in the East Stand where everyone was packed together like sardines and he'd sit me on his shoulders so I could see. Compo was fielding on the boundary and I shouted something to him. He had a pack of chewing gum and he threw a piece to me. I caught it of course! I kept that bit of gum for years."

The game Engineer referred to was the Ranji Trophy final between Holkar and Bombay, a 'timeless' match which lasted six days, drew capacity crowds and can best be described as 'wow!' Bombay scored 462 and 764 (Vijay Merchant 278) and Holkar needing a mere 867 to win managed a respectable 492. Compton, a PE instructor at a commando camp near Indore in the state of Madhya Pradesh, was playing for Holkar. A rich businessman Seth Hiralal had promised him: "Make a century and for every run after that I will give you 100 rupees." Compton made 249 not out in Holkar's forlorn victory bid earning a small fortune of around £1300 only for Hiralal to claim that the deal only referred to the first innings.

Holkar's captain C.K. Nayudu, one of India's all-time greats, had marathon bowling figures of 64.5-10-153-6 and 88-15-275-5. Mind you, Nayudu was only 49 years-old. He had stamina alright. He expected his players to be equally resilient, refusing them drinks intervals despite the heat although he made an exception with Compton. But perhaps the most jaw-dropping stat of an epic match belonged to *All India Radio's* commentator A.F.S. (Bobby) Talyarkhan who described each and every ball, being on duty for the whole 33 hours and refusing any help. "He did not like to share the mike," said a colleague.

Engineer remembers Talyarkhan with great affection. "I rated Bobby as by far the best commentator and journalist of his time. His command of the language was superb and his descriptive powers were better than any of the English. I used to enjoy listening to him and reading his articles in the *Times of India*. He used to end his daily column with the phrase 'Do you get me, Steve?' I never learned who Steve was."

Maybe Compton had Engineer's adventurous spirit in mind when he went into print to damn the over cautious approach of so many native

English batsmen. There was another way, a new direction and players like Lancashire's Indian star had the map. Engineer who had got to know Compton reminded him of the chewing gum incident. "We had a laugh about it. We were the first Brylcreem Boys in history to share a piece of Wrigley's."

One English player who loved to give the ball a biff was David Green, the Lancashire opener who had switched to Gloucestershire. "A bit of a helicopter," was how he described his style. Green was a rarity, an opener who preferred a run a ball 50 and time to complete the *Daily Telegraph* crossword before lunch rather than over-staying his welcome at the crease. He and Engineer might have made an interesting first wicket partnership but his Lancashire career was hampered by injury almost as much as the ability to speak his mind no matter the consequences. Asked why he had called the club chairman 'a prat' Green guffawed and replied: "I could have called him a lot worse."

Twelve months after leaving Old Trafford and after burning his Lancashire blazer on a pyre in his garden Green returned as a Gloucestershire player. It was August 1968 and he had already amassed over 2,000 first-class runs, an achievement to be acknowledged in *Wisden*'s Five Cricketers of the Year. Back in Manchester for a championship game he hit a quickfire 48 and sorted out the crossword before lunch but Engineer had the last laugh, putting on vital runs with Jack Bond as Lancashire earned a first innings lead and went on to win by four wickets.

It broke a month long series of unsatisfactory results, three draws and two defeats, and was reviewed as a significant step towards the club's resurgence. Only Middlesex claimed fewer bonus points than Lancashire's 26 but that win lifted Bond's team from the lower half of the table into the top six and over the last two fixtures they did enough to stay there.

Green said: "I was glad to leave Lancashire. I loved it down with Gloucestershire playing with Arthur Milton and John Mortimore. But I have to admit that game showed just how much Bondy had improved things. 'George' (Statham) had already packed up by then but they still had a strong attack with Ken Higgs, Ken Shuttleworth and Peter Lever. Most of all there was a real spirit about the side. They worked hard. I remember 'Rooky behind the stumps urging them on. He was very much at the centre of things. Yes, I think I would have enjoyed life a little more at Old Trafford if we had been in the same side."

The start of one sporting era coincided with the end of another. Half a mile up the road at the 'other' Old Trafford, Manchester United, Kings of Europe only a few months previously, were trounced 4-0 by Chelsea. Fights broke out between rival fans outside the ground. Chelsea supporters were rounded up and escorted by police to coaches or to the Warwick Road railway station. Matt Busby's ageing team was cracking up while Bond was laying the foundation stones of a modernised Lancashire.

Engineer felt on top of the world. In the space of 20 months he had conjured up one of Test cricket's most memorable innings, had figured prominently in India's first overseas series win in New Zealand and now was an instantly recognisable feature of a new look, go-ahead Lancashire outfit. "It could not have gone better. Everyone was pulling together. We lost so much play through the weather it would have been impossible to win the championship no matter how well we played. But you could feel something good was happening. I felt lucky to be playing with two brilliant captains, Jackie Bond and the Nawab of Pataudi."

Pataudi had his critics and suffered a fall from grace, politics and ego mostly to blame, only to rise again and he remains, one of cricket's outstanding personalities, a leader who pulled India towards a brighter horizon. Globally, Bond's name is less well known but no-one, not even Pataudi, could have been better liked and more respected than this quietly spoken man with the most appropriate of surnames. Team unity was Bond's theme.

Bond was nearly lost to Lancashire well before he was offered the captaincy. During the mid 1960s he was repeatedly dropped in mid-season but then brought back. There seemed no rhyme nor reason to it. A senior player with over 7000 runs in the bank he had already been mentioned as a possible future coach. True his batting had lacked something since having his wrist broken by Wes Hall in 1963 but his immense experience and hard graft were thought essential, at least by other senior players if not the selectors. At least twice he was on the brink of leaving, the second time in 1967 only to get a surprise call-up as 12th man for a game at Cheltenham. There was an ulterior motive for it. A sportsman's church service was to be held in the town on the Sunday, a rest day for the teams, and Lancashire had agreed to provide a player to read a lesson. Who better than Bond, a staunch Methodist? And so he was at hand to play when Geoff Pullar withdrew through injury. Bond stayed on and was soon asked to take over from Statham as captain, Divine intervention?

Many who played under Bond speak in reverential terms of his team ethic. How he led by example, always ready to sacrifice himself for the cause, how he encouraged, how he advised, how he never demanded anything from a player he was not prepared to attempt himself. Engineer said: "We would have a drink after play and go over things. Everyone could have their say but, even after a day when things had gone wrong, there was no-one shouting the odds. No blame game. He wasn't that type."

The captaincy had always troubled Lancashire. No-one had squeezed the best out of the players, not the strict hard as nails Washbrook nor the more laid-back Statham. Green had understudied Statham and was seen as a likely successor until he got into bad books with the committee. Engineer has nothing but praise for Bond: "Bondy was the finest captain I played under. We had a great rapport, a real understanding. If only he had been my bridge partner! His man management was first-class. He could motivate, encourage and inspire. There were no heavyweight or draconian measures. Of course there were vigorous discussions after a match but the argument was always constructive. We would have a beer and think of ways we might have performed better. Bondy never felt threatened by these debates - he wanted the same as the rest of us, to win and keep winning."

David Lloyd who had made his debut in 1965 but was still fighting for a regular place thought Bond was in some ways a father figure to the side. "His virtues were many," explained Bumble. "He was utterly unselfish and would use his wicket in whatever way the game dictated. If we needed to block out he would go in and do it, if we needed a sacrificial slogger he'd put himself forward. The team ethic burned strongly within him. And he obviously cared not just about results but about the people involved."

Bond was a solid churchman, a Methodist although - according to Lloyd - he 'cheerfully and regularly failed' in the shunning of alcohol. He was strict on discipline, setting the example, but he also gave players the freedom to express themselves on the pitch and to enjoy themselves off it - as long as they remembered they were professional sportsmen. His understanding of human nature and his 13 years experience in county cricket gelled into the perfect leadership material. He had witnessed one of the most dismal periods of Lancashire's history, knew where they had gone wrong and wanted desperately to put it right. And he had other advantages.

Bond was different, what Lancastrians would term a 'smashing bloke', a thoughtful, down to earth character with a depth of cricketing know-how who needed only a few months to mould together a side which was to take one-day cricket by storm over the following five years. It could be said he just got lucky. Lancashire had good players. Statham said farewell in August 1968, Green had left without a backward glance, Pullar was about to follow him to Gloucestershire and the off-spinner John Savage was nearing the end of his career. But Lancashire retained an attack to compare with any, Higgs, Lever, and Shuttleworth all of whom had played or would do for England. And Jack Simmons was ready to take over the off-spinner's role from Savage.

Lancashire also boasted some skilful batsmen, Harry Pilling, David Lloyd and Barry Wood among them with Clive Lloyd to come and a world-class keeper. Surely any captain worth his salt would have done well with such a squad? Was Bond really a cricketing magician or just someone who happened to be in the right place at the right time? Engineer leans to the former: "It was his man management. He was not one of the better players but he knew how to deal with people, how to get the maximum out of them when it counted. Just a word here and there. All along he urged players to be themselves. I helped him as much as I could in that first season. He rarely made a move without consulting me and on the pitch we had an almost telepathic understanding."

Yet Bond certainly benefited from the eruption of one-day cricket. When the 40 overs league started in 1969 Lancashire had a head start over their rivals without any input from their captain. David Lloyd explained: "We would have run through a brick wall for Jack but the fact is the Sunday League was right up our street because most of us had played hard, one day cricket in the leagues. So we took to it like ducks to water." But that does not explain why Lancashire had failed to make an impact in the Gillette Cup which had been going for some years. With Bond in charge Lancashire were transformed. He tightened up certain aspects of their game, notably the fielding, and made them much tougher to beat. Sunday afternoon cricket was right up their street.

Engineer remembers it with a sense of wonderment. "We did not consciously give any sort of priority to it but we all looked forward to the Sunday game. The atmosphere was amazing. You could be playing championship cricket all week, lousy weather, just a few hundred in the ground and while you were doing your best to win the match it could all get a bit humdrum. Then on Sunday there was this massive change. A real buzz about the place. Thousands of fans getting off the trains at the Warwick Road station and queuing up to get into the ground. Suddenly instead of a bit of handclapping from a few dozen spectators there was a huge roar from thousands. It was more a soccer type crowd. You'd have to be a Madame Tussaud's waxwork not to respond to that. United's ground was just up the road and on a Saturday afternoon you could hear the noise from them and know when United had scored but now it was happening in cricket. I'd smash a six. Clive would smash a six and 20,000 fans would be on their feet.

"There were big crowds everywhere but Old Trafford had a special feel about it. We were winning games straight away and everyone was talking and writing about us. Cricket dominated the back pages. The BBC televised one game live each week. After every match we were exhausted. We'd have a drink and some would hang around in the dressing room killing time 'til the fans had all gone. But even an hour or so after the game there would be dozens waiting for us, slapping us on the backs, wanting autographs. We were stars."

No-one really knew what to expect when the league opened in May 1969. Despite the cultural revolution which swept Britain in the 1960s, Sunday remained the Sabbath, a day of rest. Change was resisted by the Lord's Day Observance Society. You went to church, had lunch with the family, maybe a quick pint but it had to be quick because pubs were only allowed to open between noon and 2pm and then 7 and 10-30pm. Anyone found playing organised football or cricket, or even billiards, went on the Lord's Day Observance Society's 'Wanted for the crime of desecration' list. Towards the end of the decade the chains were loosened. Amateur Sunday football leagues spread quickly, there was some Sunday play in county championship games and the BBC televised Rothmans International Cavaliers games which drew good-sized gates although Mike Turner the Leicestershire secretary who was also heavily involved once received a letter of protest from a bishop starting: "Dear sinner..."

Engineer had revelled in the Cavaliers' fixtures. "They were very popular. We played most matches at seaside resorts. John Player must have looked at that - a perfect case of ambush marketing?"

However sceptics reckoned the new competition was a loser - that it was a Mickey Mouse tournament destined to flare and fizzle out in a couple of seasons. Even the initial ambiguous title 'Player's County League' as it was in 1969 caused furrowed brows. The following year it was changed to 'John

Player League'. The tobacco firm offered a list of prize-money possibilities including £1000 for the champion county and £50 for every win. But the biggest incentives were for individual displays - a share of £1000 for every six and a share of £1000 for each four wickets haul. The BBC, heavily involved in the venture, put £250 on the table for the fastest half century.

The early misgivings about the league's potential were similar to those expressed in the more traditional sectors of cricket, particularly the Press Box, when Twenty20 was introduced in England. I remember telling my Sports Editor: "It hasn't got a chance. A 20 overs thrash on a cold evening at Durham or Derbyshire. Who's going to turn up for that?" He replied: "Yeah, I suppose so. But they're talking about having jacuzzis and fireworks and dancing girls....do me a two page spread." The Sports Editor was a football nut who knew little about cricket but knew a lot more than me about marketing.

As with Twenty20 it did not take long to silence the Sunday doubters. Lancashire played the first game at Hove where, E.W. Swanton of the *Daily Telegraph* noted '..the sun shone on the lively scene if the wind blew shrewishly off sea.' He had kind words for Clive Lloyd's batting and fielding, 'leaping about with vast strides in the covers,' and the wicketkeeping of Engineer who 'sparkled behind the stumps (especially on the leg-side)' although he was acerbic about one feature. "All the hairstyles bar perhaps Higgs's would have severely tested the vocabulary of a sergeant major."

Cricketers, particularly the younger ones, were just as much followers of fashion as anyone and hair was getting longer. The short back and sides style favoured by the generation who had gone through a world war was 'square'. The Beatles were at top of the charts with *Get Back*, the Rolling Stones close behind with *Honkey Tonk Woman*, Bob Dylan was to play in front of 150,000 at the Isle of Wight Festival. Get with it Mr Swanton! All in all though cricket's most respected writer appeared to enjoy himself and, in that case, surely anyone could. The new tournament was a winner.

Engineer sizzled with anticipation at Sunday lunch-times. He loved it. Against Notts, albeit shorn of the services of Garry Sobers who was on tour with West Indies, he slammed 46 and stumped Barry Stead. Against Northants (at Peterborough) and Kent (Blackheath) he shared in quickfire stands for the first wicket of 71 and 45 with David Lloyd and against Somerset at Old Trafford he hit a six and five fours in his 43 before claiming three catches. "The most surprised victim being the young (Greg) Chappell who got a thick edge and was amazed by the agility of Engineer who flung himself yards to the left to hold the ball one handed,' wrote the *Daily Mail* correspondent.

"One of the strange things about Sunday cricket was that spectators were not allowed to pay to get admission into sports events," he recalls. "But the organisers got around that. They printed a programme with the scorecard on it. You bought one and that counted as the admission fee. Some of the matches were played at smaller grounds. We had one against Glamorgan at Southport when the place was absolutely crammed full. Hundreds outside unable to get in. BBC cameras were there. I went out and hit it so hard I was scattering spectators."

That game attracted over 10,000 fans, many of them on holiday at the seaside and seeing a 40 overs match for the first time, and Engineer initiated them into one-day cricket with a carefree innings of 78 not out, leading Lancashire to a nine wickets victory with plenty of time to spare. "It was one of the first matches on TV and I had many letters from people saying how much they had enjoyed it. I'm sure it gave the league a tremendous boost. People who had not followed cricket because they thought it dull suddenly realised there was a lot going on in a one day game. Perhaps this match, with its massive crowd, lots of attacking cricket, is where the Sunday League really took off."

Yet Engineer nearly missed it. "I was driving to the ground from Manchester. I had been to the ground before but it is not easy to find unless you know the area well. I stopped at a petrol station just to get some more directions but the attendant obviously had problems with my accent. At least that's my excuse. Anyway I found myself heading towards Birmingham or some place. I turned around and was lucky to see crowds of fans walking along the road so I more or less followed them. There was only a quarter of an hour to go before the start and I got there to find we had lost the toss and would be fielding so I had to be sharp getting changed. The lads had a laugh about it, they thought I would get lost on the way, but they wouldn't have been laughing if I had been any later. I suppose Harry Pilling would have had to put the gloves on. I'm just glad I made it."

Engineer was absent for a couple of league games at the back end of the season, first with a finger injury and then through having to return to India for their home Test series against New Zealand. Lancashire lost both matches although his understudy Keith Goodwin, apparently not resigned to ending his career in the second XI, took his chance well by holding on to six catches in the final match at Worcester. Unfortunately for him, Engineer could not be upstaged. In between his two absences he played in the crucial clash with Warwickshire at Nuneaton where they earned their 12th win and clinched the title. Typically he hammered 35 out of an opening stand of 37 with David Lloyd. And he had already stamped his authority on one-day cricket, combining with David Lloyd in a fruitful opening partnership throughout the summer.

With an average of 31 and third place in Lancashire's league batting chart Engineer overshadowed many of the other overseas run-makers including Clive Lloyd who linked up with Lancashire in mid-season following the West Indies tour of England, hit two half centuries and a clutch of sixes but lacked consistency. The diminutive Harry Pilling was Lancashire's highest scorer but the man who topped their league averages both with the bat and the ball was cricket's first one-day specialist John Sullivan. 'Little Harry' and 'Sully' - salt of the earth Lancastrians, this pair. Effective cricketers. Nothing showy. Pilling accumulated runs quietly but quickly. Sullivan, prepared to give sweat and blood and to sacrifice his own wicket if needed, was a captain's dream. Both were popular although neither really received due recognition except in the dressing-room and among the more experienced elements of the crowd. On Sundays the stands were full of a new breed of fan, younger, noisier, dressed in jeans and T-shirts with not a snowball in hell's chance of being allowed into the still ultra formal pavilion and what sparked them into life was the dynamism of a tall, gangly Guyanan and a cavalier Indian.

"Playing alongside Clive Lloyd was very special. I remember a conversation with Cyril Washbrook during my first season with Lancashire. The club were expecting Clive to join them the following summer but Cyril wanted my opinion and I had no hesitation. 'Mr Washbrook,' I said. 'He will be a fantastic player for Lancashire.' Washbrook replied: 'But Farokh, he wears glasses!' I said: 'Never mind the specs, just make sure we sign him.'"

CHAPTER 12

THOUGH, AS stated earlier, it is arguable for one to be 'born' to anything, it is difficult to knock back Farokh Engineer when he says "I was born to be a one-day player." All those who watched him agreed that he was a natural. "It suited me in every way. The speed of it. The big crowds. I only wish there had been more of it at international level during my time."

What a pity that Farokh Engineer never played top level one day cricket outside England. Although the limited overs style was an instant hit for the counties it was considered as an inferior product to Test matches and treated with suspicion and some disdain by the power-brokers of the international fraternity. And so by 1974 when Lancashire had already won five one-day trophies and were on their way to a sixth India - and most other nations - were still utter novices at the game.

"It was wonderful playing the one-day stuff for Lancashire but I only had a handful of matches for India. I don't understand why it took so long to catch on. It was obvious that it was the way to go. Lancashire had proved that. The game needed excitement and money. But I was in my seventh season at Old Trafford, six of those playing one-day cricket, by the time India had their first game."

One-day international cricket was born in 1971 as a mere afterthought, a makeshift game being arranged between England and Australia at Melbourne to give the crowd some entertainment after rain had forced the abandonment of the Test. Later the Aussie player Ashley Mallett admitted: "They called it the first one-day international which rather surprised me years later. I thought 'Gee, it's part of history. That game we thought was a bit of a joke.'"

Between then and the inaugural World Cup for the Prudential Trophy in 1975 there were only 17 ODIs world-wide and India featured in just two of them during the 1974 tour of England. Both were easily won by England, drawing on their vastly superior experience from their domestic game. Not that ODI cricket mattered much. The first World Cup in 1975 took some time to grab the public's attention. A week before it began in June the *Daily Telegraph* gave it less column inches than the Amateur Golf Championship. Slotted into a fortnight with only eight teams involved including Sri Lanka and East Africa it seemed hastily arranged, a desperate bid to inject much needed cash into cricket. India made a rapid exit losing the first two matches in the group and so Engineer's ODI record looks modest on paper, 5 matches, 4 innings, 114 runs, displaying little of his liking for and skill at the game although he earned India's first man of the match award with a quick half-century when they hammered East Africa in their last game.

"I was born too early for it I suppose," he says with a laugh. "I watch it now, the ODIs and the Twenty20s and really enjoy it. But nothing matches playing. And obviously so much has changed in the way the game is played. We played in whites with a red ball which stayed hard enough for most of the innings. We didn't have any helmets, nothing to stop us from being hit really. We were prepared to take the ball on the body if necessary and finish up with a few bruises. The ball often dominated the bat and you had to make a decision, either go for it like me or nudge it around like Harry Pilling, although Harry could play his shots. Not many sixes though. And the bat was totally different. To hit a six you had to time it absolutely right and put power behind it. The boundaries were long, not shortened like they are today. Top edged sixes were unknown on the bigger grounds. I imagine sometimes me and Clive Lloyd playing in the Indian Premier League. I think the fans would have loved it. We both could smack a ball out of the ground never mind over the rope. Clive and I would have been among the highest earners and I'm sure the Lancashire side of that era would have given any of the IPL teams a run for their money. We were that good."

Lloyd once hit a six at the Oval which flew over the stand, over the road and into a schoolyard. Brian Bearshaw, the *Manchester Evening News* cricket correspondent at the time, took the trouble to measure it and came up with a distance of over 200 yards. I saw Lloyd in a Gillette Cup match against Surrey at Old Trafford where, despite limping from knee trouble, he cracked an Intikhab Alam delivery into a wall between the pavilion and the old Press Box with such ferocity that it sprayed splinters of brick and mortar over a spectator. Engineer, too, had power but with both it was all about the timing.

When Engineer and Lloyd hit it off together in the middle the result was 'cyclonic batting' as it was in one of the 1969 Roses encounters when they battered Yorkshire for 140 runs in 130 minutes at Bramhall Lane, Sheffield - a championship match but everything Lancashire did underscored why they reached such heights in the one day game. Engineer hit 96, throwing his bat at everything in a manic attempt to wrest Yorkshire's grip on the game. Lloyd played second fiddle. Together they gave Lancashire a glimmer of hope although Engineer's chance of a glorious century disappeared when typically he lashed out at off-spinner Geoff Cope and gave a catch to mid-on.

"Cyril Washbrook congratulated me. He was old school, one of those who believed you should never hit a four before lunch in a Roses game but he also appreciated all-out attack when it was necessary."

Yorkshire's victory target of 65 in the last 19 overs seemed comfortable enough. But the team spirit engendered by Jack Bond came to the fore. They bowled and fielded as though their lives depended on it. Even so, at 64-3 with two overs left even Geoff Boycott would have put his mortgage on a Yorkshire win. However Lever, suffering a shoulder injury, sent down a maiden to Doug Padgett and Higgs who had sore shins produced an astonishing last over, dot, dot, wicket, dot, wicket, wicket. His first dismissal was Barrie Leadbeater lbw. Then Engineer pulled off a breathtaking stumping to get rid of Don Wilson and Harry Pilling held on at third man when Richard Hutton top-edged. Yorkshire finished on 64-6 with the scores level, the match drawn and the ground silent. Afterwards Bond, exhausted, slumped onto the dressing room bench and joked: "I think Alfred Hitchcock must follow us around."

The Roses thriller was an encore of a championship game six weeks earlier when Warwickshire needed three runs to win off the final over but failed to score any and lost two wickets in the process, Higgs shattering the stumps of Tom Cartwright and Eddie Hemmings to earn a draw.

Despite this refusal to lie down for anyone, Lancashire staggered along the 1969 championship trail winning only two matches and finishing third from bottom. Hampered by poor weather they were also ravaged by injuries, so much so that for one game they considered pulling Brian Statham out of retirement.

Higgs hailed from the Staffordshire town of Kidsgrove. The Nawab of Pataudi came from Madhya Pradesh where his princely state lay around the historic city of Bhopal. Once on a rainy day at Sussex's Hove ground they got into a cards session with other players. Higgs had a good hand. Pataudi thought his was better. "All in," said Higgs, pushing the rest of his chips into the centre of the table. Pataudi had already used all his but was determined to see out the game. "Right - I'll bet Bhopal," he said. Higgs won. He never got Bhopal but from then on his team-mates called him the Nawab of Kidsgrove.

A superb pace bowler as well as a decent poker player, Higgs was desperately unlucky to play only 15 Tests. He later played for Leicestershire, taking a hat-trick for them in a Benson and Hedges Cup final and was still troubling batsmen in his late 40s. He enjoyed a magnificent first summer under Bond's guidance, taking over 100 wickets, the first four of which came via Engineer catches when they lost at Canterbury in May. Engineer regarded him as a fine, boisterous player who did not take kindly to him standing up to the stumps. "I am an England opening bowler," complained Higgs with justifiable pride. "It doesn't look good when you do that."

"I had sometimes stood up to Statham as well," says Engineer. "I don't think he minded as much and he also knew that I could do it. But judging from his expression I don't think any other keeper had done it."

If Higgs was bullish he was also proud and sportsmanlike. Enraged when in one championship match David Steele of Northants refused to walk after edging a catch he ignored him when they bumped into each after the match on Manchester's Piccadilly station. They were due to catch the same train but Higgs waited for a later one. "He was one of the strangest people I ever met," Engineer reveals. "At times I could not understand his attitude towards the younger professionals. He was not the sort of man who won friends easily, something that would have bothered me but didn't faze him one bit."

Lancashire's injury problems in 1969 were aggravated by a series of facial blows. Although the TCCB were demanding better pitches, batting could still be a dangerous business. David Bailey, Graham Atkinson and Engineer were all hit in the face by deliveries which bounced unexpectedly. Engineer's nose was broken by Middlesex seamer Bob Herman at Old Trafford on a championship day when Harry Pilling was struck painfully on the left hand and Clive Lloyd was dazed by a no-ball which glanced off his head and sped to the boundary for four leg byes. Engineer was soon back in action but right through the summer Bond had to take a roll call of available players before each game. "Getting hurt was part and parcel of the game," says Engineer. "If you broke something you would probably be ruled out but if you had a strain or a pulled muscle or something you put your hand up and said: 'Count me in.' Lever, Higgs and Shuttleworth all had something wrong but they played. Not only played but bowled well. Shutt had problems with his run-up, kept over-stepping but he worked at it and got his rhythm eventually.

"Sometimes it was all hands to the pumps. That's the way it was in county cricket, when we were playing day after day and travelling long distances in between matches. Every county had the same problem but I think there was a difference at Old Trafford. The championship wasn't going too well for us but the Sunday League was. Everyone wanted so much to play. I missed a game with that injury and I hated it."

County cricket was not a game for 'softies'. They played hard on and off the pitch. Beer, women and fish and chips might all be on the menu for an away fixture with three nights in a decent hotel. Not everyone succumbed but temptation was all around. Lancashire partied with the best of them but, apart from unavoidable injuries, they remained the fittest side in the country. Engineer: "We were in action almost every day. It makes me smile now to hear about them having to play too much cricket and cutting down on the fixture list. We would start a championship game on a Saturday, work hard, go out and have a good time in the evening and report back to the ground at mid-day for the Sunday League match when we would give it everything. Then back to finish the championship game on the Monday and Tuesday.

"They might say that modern standards of play have improved with less cricket but is that right? Batsmen play more shots, it's true, thanks to Twenty20 cricket - there again they have far more protection than we had, much better pitches, and bats which can make a ball fly off an edge for six. But if you look at the way England's batsmen failed against India in the 2016 Test series I don't think you can say that batting has improved. India's spinners were good, very good. But the spinners I played with, Chandra, Bedi, Prasanna and Venkat were among the best the game has ever seen and were always difficult to cope with even on English pitches and on our tour in 1967 they took all the wickets for us. But England still had batsmen who could knuckle down and score runs. Boycott, obviously, and Ken Barrington come to mind. Both of them got dropped for slow scoring and you could understand that. Cricket has got to entertain but the point is they had the technique and concentration to stay in. While we were complete opposites I had the highest regard for him as a technically correct batsman - I had to go wide of the stumps to see the ball because he was always right behind it and blocked the view. England didn't have that in India last time and as a result they got absolutely hammered.

"Look at the physique of a modern cricketer. Biceps like Popeye the Sailor. They walk out to the middle swinging those massive bats. They look like lumberjacks. They can play all sorts of shots and score quick runs. And for someone like me that's great. But come the time when they have to bat it out to save a Test and all the muscles and all the biggest bats in the world aren't enough. They haven't got the technique. So when people say batting standards have improved I'm not sure. Maybe fielding standards are overall better. Some of the catches you see are astounding. Groundwork is top-class. But then I think back to some of the fielders I had around me with Lancashire and India. I've never seen anyone as good as Ekky Solkar."

Solkar made the forward short leg position his own taking 53 catches, many outstanding, some close to unbelievable, in 27 Tests. Tall, athletic and with similar fast forward reflexes to Engineer, he rarely took his eye off the ball even when a huge swing of the bat threatened to send it crashing into his skull. With Engineer dancing and diving behind the stumps India had the perfect double-edged foil for their spinners.

"There were many batsmen who could not believe they were out," says Engineer. "They might have nicked it down the legside and wondered why I was appealing. Then they would see the umpire's finger going up. Or it might have dropped towards the ground off bat and pad and they thought why was Solkar bothering to dive for it and then he would come up with it in both hands. He wasn't afraid. He didn't have any shin guards or helmet, nothing like that, but he never ducked out of the way if the batsman swung at it. There was one Test, Calcutta I think, when he pulled off such a sensational catch to get rid of Bill Lawry that Lawry actually presented him with his bat after the match.

"As for Lancashire I don't think there was a weak link in the fielding. Bondy demanded the highest standards. We changed the game. Previously fielders didn't bother too much about chasing balls to the rope. Yes, if they were 100 per cent confident of reaching it in time but if there was any doubt they would probably give it up, particularly seam bowlers who knew they would have to put in a hard stint with the ball. You didn't see fielders crashing into the advertising boards or doing relays. But generally they had good hands and good strong arms. And with Lancashire Bondy raised the bar for one-day cricket because he told us that he didn't want any of us to go back to the dressing room in clean whites. He wanted to see plenty of grass stains. He understood that one-day matches could be close-run things and there was a lot of value in saving runs in the field. He was way ahead of other captains. It gave us a big advantage in those first few years."

Close to the stumps Lancashire had three of the best catchers in the business, Engineer, Barry Wood and David Lloyd. Clive Lloyd 'The Big Cat' prowled the covers and, at his best before knee problems slowed him up, was rated as good as the legendary South African Colin Bland. David Hughes and Frank Hayes were among the speediest and safest around, Harry Pilling belied his size with a powerful throw. But every player hurled themselves around the ground until they were breathless.

The Lancashire squad was populated by stout hearts and strong minds. This was a set of honest, down to earth players prepared to speak their minds and therefore the dressing room was fertile ground for discord. However Bond's leadership and their coincidental success smothered any problems. David Lloyd who took over from him found life more difficult as did David Hughes over a decade later on.

Engineer: "We were a happy crowd. Bumble was always good for a laugh. He had a streak of comedy in him even then, a happy go lucky sort of character. Clive was easy going, I took no time at all to fit in. There were one or two more serious types. We called Shutt Rasputin because he could lose his rag very quickly and would rip his sweater out of the umpire's hands but we all blended into the mix.

"Little Harry Pilling was a really good cricketer, but more than that he was a good team man and a real character. He was one of the first people I met when I arrived at Lancashire from India and he greeted me with a traditional 'alreet lad!' I will never forget it, I didn't have a clue what he was saying! He should have played for England. We used to call him Mr Reliable in the dressing room because we knew that what ever happened at one end, he would be at the other steadily going along making runs, whatever the wicket. And he would never stop talking. I remember we were batting together at Lord's in a Gillette Cup final and we met in the middle of the pitch between overs and he started talking about the what he'd seen at the cinema."

A cheeky chappy was Harry. There is a nice story about him sitting next to a titled lady, bedecked with gems, at a posh cricketing dinner in London. He asked if he could have the name card on her plate explaining: "Ah'd like the missus to see what sort o' company Ah keep when Ah'm away from 'ome." On another occasion he was having a drink with a group of members in the Old Trafford pavilion after the close of play and asked one if he could pinch his wife's bottom. The man took it in good heart: "You'd better ask her," he said.

Pilling was four feet seven inches tall when he joined Lancashire aged 15 and five feet three inches when he left 18 years later. He could hit the ball hard and was unfazed by ugly fast bowlers over a foot taller but no-one expected him to be a star of one-day cricket. But he was. A canny, consistent accumulator of runs who shared in major stands with Engineer and Clive Lloyd and was the first in the country to notch 1,000 Sunday League runs.

A smile quickly followed by a grimace flashes across Engineer's face when Pilling's name crops up. "Once or twice he was used as an emergency 'keeper. There was one game at the Oval when Clive and I were delayed and we got to the ground late. The game had started and Harry was out there behind the stumps but he was having a terrible time of it because the new ball was flying around, wide of off, way down the legside and over his head. When I got out to the middle he ripped off the gloves and said: "Here, take these back - you can stick wicketkeeping up your arse."

"It was hard not be fond of Harry. Partly because of his lack of height but also because he was a cheerful type. It wasn't always wise to get too close to him though. His personal habits were sometimes not to my taste. His corner of the dressing room stank and he was always scratching at something. And there was one incident which Clive Lloyd and I will remember forever but which is better left for the moment…."

CHAPTER 13

SATURDAY, AUGUST Bank Holiday weekend 1970. Over half a million rock fans 'hippies and druggies' have flooded over to a small island off the south coast of England for the biggest 'gig' of all time. The third Isle of Wight Festival. Among the line-up, Leonard Cohen, The Who, The Doors, Jimi Hendrix. In the Press Box at the Old Trafford cricket ground is a small amiable group of cricket writers most of whose musical tastes are more inclined to Beethoven or Ella Fitzgerald. Over to our left, in the dressing-rooms Lancashire and Yorkshire players are getting ready for the first session of the Roses match. The radio is on, Brian Matthew's Saturday Club show with Elvis Presley crooning the current number one hit *The Wonder of You*. David Lloyd is trying to persuade Farokh Engineer to sing along a la Engelbert Humperdink.

The crowd is building up nicely. Mostly the traditional type of supporter. Jackets, some blazers even, and ties and Daily Telegraphs in the members' stand. Strolling onto the other terraces are mature blokes in short-sleeved shirts and flannels, copies of the Mail and Express tucked into their pockets. A small pod of younger fans, long hair, jeans and T-shirts saunter over the practice field which is used as a car park on match days.

One of my Press colleagues points to them saying: "There's your mates. Shouldn't you be with them? Or in the Isle of Wight?" One or two titter. But much as I love The Who etc the Isle of Wight Festival is small beer compared to the 'gig' I am about to enjoy that weekend. First, two and a quarter hours of Roses cricket starring Farokh Engineer and Clive Lloyd with Geoff Boycott as back-up, then a fish and chips lunch, then a quick scoot up Warwick Road for a football fiesta involving some of the world's top players - Bobby Charlton, Denis Law, George Best, Bobby Moore, Jimmy Greaves, Geoff Hurst - as United take on West Ham in the first division, then a sprint back to the cricket for the last hour of play. And, next day,

Lancashire's Sunday League finale when they meet Yorkshire in a bid to win the title for the second time. For a long-haired 'hippy' sports writer what could be better?

Barry Wood, on his way to another century against his native county, and Harry Pilling dominate the cricket morning and at two o'clock, stuffed with chips, I flash my pass at the Staff Door and make my way up to the Press Box at the football ground to watch, report and criticise my United heroes. It is a 1-1 draw with some outbreaks of fighting on the terraces. I tear back to the cricket ground to find Lancashire in command thanks to Wood's 144, half-centuries from Pilling and Clive Lloyd and an unbeaten 82 from our new golden boy Frank Hayes. (Hayes was also tagged England's new 'White Hope').

By 7pm the ground has more or less cleared but the railway station is still busy with happy but comparatively peaceful Lancashire supporters and some noisy remnants of the football crowd chanting 'United, United'. Engineer, who has had a few minutes of batting with Hayes before the close of play, comes out of the pavilion and offers me a lift home. He lives in Timperley. I live a further eight miles along the road.

I say: "Thanks Rooky. You could drop me off at Sale and I'll get the train from there." He takes my elbow. "No, no. I'll take you home," he insists. Typical of the man. (In recent times he has offered to give me various lifts, one of which was to a hotel 100 yards away. If I asked him to take me to India, via Europe, Iran, Afghanistan and Pakistan I am sure he would say: 'Hop in.') Eventually I persuade him to leave me in Sale. "Thanks, Rooky. Big day tomorrow." "Sure," he says. "Looking forward to it."

It turns out to be one of the biggest days in Lancashire's history. Engineer, Clive Lloyd, Jack Bond, Harry Pilling, all my favourites, would hold centre stage, Along with someone who loved the spotlight and deserved to be in it but who came to be regarded with grudging respect. Cedric Rhoades, the Lancashire chairman, was an energetic, go for it businessman who did much to resurrect the club's fortunes after leading the members' revolt in the mid 1960s. He held a wider view of cricket than most administrators. One idea was a big city league - almost 40 years before the first IPL game. Another, as he celebrated Lancashire's successes under Bond was to make Lancashire 'the Real Madrid of cricket'. (Actually he said 'I want Old Trafford to be the Real Madrid of cricket" and so I pointed out to him that that did not really make sense. He was about to pour me a glass of bubbly but stopped - he did not like to be corrected).

Rhoades knew how to manipulate the media, if not how to house them. Miraculously our wooden Press Box swaying high on top of the Ladies' Stand survived for 40 years until a fire in a kitchen below threatened to engulf it. Luckily it was a non-match day otherwise, in the absence of a fire escape, a dozen less than fit journos would have been forced to leap for safety out of the windows. While he was inspecting the damage the fire brigade chief asked Rhoades: "That shed is a serious fire risk - do any people use it?"

"No," snorted the chairman, adding contemptuously: "Not people. Only Press."

It was demolished and a new one (made of brick) erected on the other side of the ground and officially opened by John Arlott in 1987. A framed photograph of Neville Cardus was hung on the wall behind the seat which I used. I always had the feeling that Cardus was looking over my shoulder, smirking at my miserable attempts to write a few decent paragraphs.

Arlott and Cardus were among Farokh Engineer's most ardent admirers. Arlott tried hard to persuade him to sign for Hampshire, plying him with wine from one of the country's best stocked cellars. "He was a lovely man," said Engineer. "And the wine was extremely good." Arlott wrote of Engineer's spontaneity - 'he plays it as he does because it is his nature to enjoy the game and he sees no reason to conceal that enjoyment. His hooking and cutting are fierce; his cross-batted slash through the covers is vivid and his driving, especially from the off stump or outside it, through mid-on is a stroke of constantly effective violence. On the slightest provocation - or none at all - from a bowler he will give him the charge.'

What I liked most about Arlott's analysis was that it had nothing to do with cricketing technique. "Farokh Engineer," he added "finds both cricket and life fun; he laughs easily and his jokes are often very funny but he can be grave. His appeals are as loud as anyone's yet off the field he is quietly spoken. As a batsman or wicketkeeper he is aggressive, yet he is a man of consideration and courtesy. There has always been a quality of generosity about his cricket and his way of life." I think that sums it up although a Cardus comment is also apt: "We remember not the scores and the results in after years but those men who remain in our minds, in our imagination."

Jessie Lockwood, a lifelong and well known Lancashire supporter, had memories of Cardus - by then, Sir Neville - making his way to the Lancashire dressing-room before Lord's finals. "He would sit on the low garden wall reminiscing about old Lancashire players and enquiring about others like Eddie Paynter and Brian Statham," she said. "But he also enjoyed talking to the current team. He found the boys so full of life and personality, none more so than Farokh. I'm happy that Farokh gained immortality in the Cardus Book of Lancashire Greats."

Cardus was the Lancashire President in 1970 when Jack Bond's side retained the Sunday League and landed the Gillette Cup in the first one-day double. Rhoades called it "...one of the finest playing seasons in the history of the club, not just the fact of winning trophies, the most important manner was the attractive and entertaining manner in which the trophies were won." All agreed. Not yet the Real Madrid of cricket but, as Engineer said, certainly the Manchester United. Lancashire returned from their Gillette Cup final win over Sussex to be regaled at civic receptions as the new sporting champions of a football crazy city.

While not planning escape routes from their hazardous HQ, the entourage in the Old Trafford Press Box wrote epic poems about Lancashire's heroes. Engineer and Clive Lloyd were their favourites because each or both were likely to offer the best material for their match reports. Engineer's bat was a 'scimitar'. His headlong dive for a catch was reminiscent of 'Banks saving from Pele.' Lloyd's big hitting left more holes in the perimeter fence 'than there are in the government's economic policy' etc.

Both also made themselves available to reporters but in journalism's green and pleasant land of those times sports editors did not always demand 'quotes', being satisfied with a fact based report on the day's play, as long as it was well written with a good 'intro' on which they could base a headline. For the scribes from the popular papers it made it a lot easier if Engineer or Lloyd produced some fireworks. Arlott and Cardus of course did not concern themselves with looking for an 'angle' for their report. And they were never ordered to 'nip over to the dressing room and get some nannies' (rhyming slang: nanny goats=quotes) which, for some years, was my role working for an agency.

Usually I made a bee-line for the captain, if not to ask him for a comment then to get his permission to speak to another player. Bond was accommodating but sometimes, particularly after a tense, exhausting one-day game he would tell me to come back later. It was then that I searched for 'Rooky'. He never refused although he avoided anything remotely controversial. Never slagged anyone off. Never complained. He enjoyed the attention and talking about himself, still does, and usually he had something good and positive to talk about. I remember catching him only once on an off day. He had been needlessly run out for the second time within a few weeks and I asked him if there was a problem again with his footwear. "Colin," he said in a tired voice. "I understand you journalists have a job to do but..." I thought here was the moment where our relationship might founder. "But," he continued, "Come on, let's go and get a drink." At the bar Engineer proceeded me to give enough quotes to fill a book.

Lancashire came close to a treble in 1970 with a one-day double and third place in the championship giving the Press ample chance to sing their praises. One reporter, however, sounded a warning. Tom Longworth, who acted as Lancashire's 'independent' reviewer, asserted: "Time limited competitions in which Lancashire have proved themselves so adept during the past two summers are welcome and stimulating but the sometimes boisterous enthusiasm they create provides entertainment more for one-day excursionists rather than those who loyally pay annual subscriptions and prefer play to unfold itself with less speed and more dignity."

Longworth had obviously suffered an ear bashing from members nurtured on three day cricket. For some of them the new game was ok as an occasional respite from the championship but many others stayed away, put off not only by the rapid-fire format but also by loutish behaviour in the crowd. And all the critics among Lancashire's traditional support agreed that the championship remained the premier competition and should be the number one target each season. Publicly the club nodded its collective head. After all Lancashire had not won the championship outright since 1934, a stain on their record and one which grew ever larger until their long-awaited coronation in 2011. Every player wanted the championship. Yet on that August Bank Holiday weekend a Sunday afternoon game - or 'knockabout' as the League's critics disparaged it - turned English cricket on its head.

Here is how the *Daily Mail* described it: 'Lancashire did far more than win the Sunday League title yesterday. They did what they always vowed they would do and what most of us thought was no longer possible - to fill Old Trafford with 30,000 people so eager to watch their kind of cricket that they were prepared to scale the walls for the privilege.

'And when Harry Pilling nudged the single that carried them past Yorkshire's 165 with only three wickets down the crowd - skinheads and cricket purists alike - swarmed across the field. They gathered in front of the pavilion chanting the chants that they have learned on the football terraces and would not be silenced until skipper Jack Bond appeared on the balcony.'

I do not remember any 'skinheads' but some fans certainly had United scarves tied around their wrists. Twenty four hours earlier they had watched United draw with West Ham at the other Old Trafford. Then they had roared support for George Best and co. Now .....

Cricket would never be the same again, could not afford to be the same again. There is a photograph of Pilling pushing his way through the fans who had rushed onto the outfield after he had secured victory. Many are young men but there are one or two young women as well and that is significant, considering that women had been turning their backs on the county game. Four uniformed policemen are trying desperately to hold the fans back. In the members' stand there are bald heads and trilbies, one of which is raised in salute.

I had watched Lancashire since 1956, sitting on the turf behind the boundary rope at quiet, sedate championship games, marvelling at Statham's accuracy and occasionally joining in the polite applause emanating from the Members' Stand and, now I had witnessed something extraordinary. A cricket crowd as uninhibited as Engineer's batting. There was noise, an outburst of beer soaked rowdyism here and there, and a soccer type chant of 'Lancashire, Lancashire' which in subsequent years metamorphosed into 'Lancashire La La La', a witless drone which tortured the more reserved minority and 'Oh Lancy, Lancy, Lancy, Lancy, Lancy Lancy Lancashire' which was even more witless and irritating. Almost as bad as the constant replays of Jerusalem during the 2005 Ashes series. Almost.

In hindsight and certainly in comparison to the razzmatazz of modern one-day cricket, the Sunday League show of the 1970s was tame stuff. A total of around 180 was defendable. Anything more was a winner. Initially most teams played it as though it were merely a truncated championship game, the difference being it was all done and dusted in one afternoon between the pubs closing and opening again and sometimes the closing overs were nail-biters.

One-day crowds had grown through that summer. Five thousand for an early league match, then Somerset had to close the Taunton gates for the Gillette Cup semi with Lancashire, the first time they had done that since entertaining Bradman's Australians in 1948. There followed a record

Sunday gate of 10,000 at Liverpool's Aigburth ground where Lancashire beat Northants and where a naughty fan walked off with Clive Lloyd's bat only to be shamed into returning it. Lloyd used it to batter 46 and outshone that with a catch, diving full-length at mid-wicket to dismiss Jim Watts, which umpire Fred Jakeman described as 'the most amazing I have ever seen'.

The league decider against Yorkshire could not have better scripted and while reports gave the attendance variously at 26,000, 27,000 and 30,000, I guessed it nearer 35,000. Every inch of the stadium was filled. Fans clambered over the walls. Stewarding was negligible. It was surprising that no-one was badly hurt in the crush but there were plenty of bruised toes as the skinheads' Doc Martin clad feet trod on those of the cricket purists encased in sandals and brown suede Hush Puppies.

The wave of euphoria carried Lancashire through to the Gillette Cup final at Lord's six days later and swamped Sussex. Pilling and Engineer combined in an unbeaten stand of 72 to wrap it up and while Pilling collected the man of the match award from Alec Bedser, he was quick to give his partner due credit. "It was another great team performance," Pilling said. "I did alright I know but it was good to have Rooky at the other end. Getting the man of the match award was great because my mam and dad were in the crowd. They didn't get to places like London usually, they had holidays in Blackpool and Morecambe."

Clive Lloyd got out early in that game and glumly sat in the dressing room for a while, tears in his eyes, thinking he had blown it. But Pilling and Engineer calmly steered them home in fading light. "Harry was always a chatterbox out in the middle. At the climax of a match like that with everyone on the edge of their seats he'd start talking about what he saw at the pictures or something like that."

Lord's was at capacity. Which meant that by my estimate Lancashire had been watched by an aggregate of at least 65,000 fans in two back to back one-day games. Engineer was used to massive crowds in India. Noisy, excitable crowds too. But all this felt new even to him.

"In India we played Test cricket in front of 50,000 crowds regularly and they could get really worked up. But if Lancashire's one-day crowds were not quite that big they made up for it with the noise. They were our 12th man. You wanted to do well for them. I know that a lot of them were younger than in times gone by. Maybe they did not have the same sort of cricketing knowledge as the more established supporters. You could mistime a shot, get an edge and if it carried to the boundary it would probably get as big a roar as a superb cover drive.

"It was all so different from anything that any of us had experienced. There were trophies at stake. When we did the double in 1970 we had a special presentation back in Manchester and I remember Jack Bond giving me the two pieces of silverware to hold, one in each hand. It was a magical moment. And everywhere we went people stopped and wanted to shake our hands. Some of the Manchester United and Manchester City players were into cricket and we were friendly. United had won the European Cup in 1968, City won the league, the FA Cup and the European Cup-Winners Cup in the same years that we were winning everything and so we all came together to celebrate. Manchester was the capital of sport."

Certainly the city swelled with pride. Along with news of sectarian riots in Northern Ireland, race riots in London's Notting Hill, huge economic problems and the break-up of the Beatles, the yellow delivery vans of the *Manchester Evening News* carried souvenir issues of footballing and cricketing prowess. Those who lived and worked in Manchester and most other parts of England's north-west region could lord it over the rest of the country. Engineer, an adopted son, sighs: "Great days, great days." When he returned to India, following the 1970 Gillette Cup final, he got a shock. "I went home to make myself available for the tour of the West Indies but the chairman of selectors said to me: 'What can we select you on - the newspaper reports?'"

The chairman was the former batting star Vijay Merchant, a hard-headed businessman - although driven by a powerful sense of social justice - and a purposeful official who had been elected a couple of years later and was determined to leave his stamp on India's progress. The President was the immensely rich M.A. Chidambaram. According to Engineer: "They had personal prejudices which had a negative effect on Indian cricket particularly in the selection process although of course I accept totally that Merchant was one of the all-time batting greats. Chidambaram was a control freak and the other office bearers licked his feet. Merchant disliked flair and he must have disliked the flair and personality of myself and Pataudi and a few others."

Merchant wanted other players and possibly a change in the captaincy, straining his relationship with Pataudi. Although he had known little of it, Engineer was also under threat. "One or two of the selectors took a dim view of the fact that I had left India to play county cricket," he explains. "I reckoned it had helped me to improve my game a lot. But I was virtually asked to withdraw as a candidate for the touring party for reasons that have baffled me ever since. No doubt it was politically motivated. It was beautifully engineered by the powers that be.

"The fact is I had been secretly approached by a senior cricket board member about the possibility of me captaining the touring party to the West Indies after Pataudi had been unceremoniously sacked. I was flown to India from Manchester to help select the squad at which stage Merchant pointed out that I played for Lancashire - although I had not missed any of India's domestic games. He never liked me or Pataudi and he brought it up. He said I was not eligible to captain the team and I said 'What about playing?' He said I was not eligible to play either and I walked straight out of the committee room, went straight back to my room at the Cricket Club of India and took the first flight back. I was horrified by his tone. What a shame that a great cricketer like Merchant had allowed prejudices to override his judgement. I had admired him as one of the all time greats.

"I had a suspicion that it would happen. Merchant was there with Tarapore his pipe smoking henchman. He was secretary of the CCI. I was not one of their favourites. I kept wicket to Merchant as a kid. I was standing up to a medium pace bowler and I actually stumped him down the legside and his bat swung around in the follow up and hit me in the face. I was so proud of that."

Merchant whose Test career was restricted by World War 2 and ill-health, had founded the Bombay School of Batsmanship. Perhaps he sniffed at some of Engineer's displays which came out of a different manual. But the salient clue was his patriotism - he once protested against the British jailing of Mahatma Gandhi in the 1930s by refusing to go on a tour of England and he also persuaded John Arlott over issues relating to India's independence.

Engineer's replacement was Pochia Krishnamurthy, a tall, neat enough keeper from Hyderabad who had played lots of domestic cricket with South Zone but was uncapped at Test level. He was definitely not a Test class batsman while in the previous 12 months Engineer had put up some useful scores in a home series against the Aussies and had honed his experience against good fast bowling on the English circuit where he faced among others Keith Boyce (Essex) and Vanburn Holder (Worcestershire), two members of the Windies' attack. A useful 'net' you might think with a tour of the Windies at hand.

Engineer had suffered before at the selectors' hands, as had several of his contemporaries, and was to suffer again. But this slap in the face was a real stinger. The previous summer when, at the height of the apartheid controversy, the proposed South African tour was cancelled the Test and County Cricket Board arranged a stop-gap five match series between England and a Rest of the World XI. Engineer played in the first two games at Lord's and Trent Bridge, the only Indian among such luminaries as Garry Sobers, Clive Lloyd, Graeme Pollock, Rohan Kanhai, Mike Procter and Barry Richards. While he failed to impress with the bat, in the second match he had six catches and a stumping. But his actual performances were not really the point. How could he be regarded highly enough to be picked for the Rest of the World and then to lose his place with India to an inferior player?

If things had gone differently on that tour of the Caribbean, the selectors might have taken a hammering but, although Krishnamurthy embarrassed them to an extent by scoring just 33 runs in six knocks, they emerged smelling of roses. Merchant got his way in displacing Pataudi, Ajit Wadekar being promoted to captain, and they gave a chance to a new opening batsman from Bombay who was to take the world of cricket by storm.

After missing the first Test with a painful whitlow on his index finger debutant Sunil Gavaskar recovered to open for the remaining four matches and shocked Sobers' team and everyone else with the following sequence: 65, 67 not out, 116, 64 not out, 1, 117 not out, 124, 220. India won the second Test at Port of Spain and drew the rest, the first time they had toppled a side who so often had blitzed them in the past.

It was the second time that Engineer had been dropped without justification. Each time India had notched up a sensational triumph, first his replacement Indrajitsinjhi being involved in the historic 1964 win over Australia, then Krishnamurthy being among the players mobbed by jubilant Indian supporters in Trinidad when Gavaskar led them to their decisive seven wickets win. Engineer felt cheated.

"I was in my prime. I knew I would have contributed a lot in both those series. If the team had been picked on merit I would have been in. The truth is that Krishnamurthy played for South Zone and the politics came from that area. They wanted their own man in. That was the way of it in Indian cricket."

Engineer took solace from his recently acquired status in England and that winter while India were sorting themselves out for the Caribbean he played in another Rest of the World series in Pakistan along with such luminaries as Clive Lloyd, Colin Cowdrey, Mike Brearley, Kanhai and, ahem, Harry Pilling, and, ahem ahem, Keith Goodwin! A reet Lancashire hot-pot in Karachi. Pilling scored two half centuries. Goodwin grabbed some catches and a couple of stumpings, one to send back Zaheer Abbas. But while Engineer could wryly smile at his Lancashire understudy's success he inwardly raged at his sudden and unwarranted demotion from the Test scene.

"Gavaskar and I became batting partners for India and good pals. Like every Indian I was delighted with what he did in the Windies. It was sensational. He became known as the little master, by far the best batsman we have ever produced. I just wish I had been with him on that tour. It took time for me to get over it but I suppose I knew that I would be back. Krishamurthy was a flop with the bat. He only once got into double figures. They could not keep him in the team. In a way I felt vindicated. I would still be playing county cricket but they would have no choice but to put me back in the side."

CHAPTER 14

POTENTIAL IS a strange concept. If it indicates someone's reservoir of *perceived* untapped talent it also exists to give hope and/or to satisfy the expectations of others, often false hope and illogical expectations. When George Best found that wine women and song were preferable to playing football he was rounded on by the critics for throwing away his career and wasting his life. He had achieved great things on the pitch but surely he could have done more - he had failed to 'maximise' his potential.

There is the story of the waiter at one of London's top hotels who delivered caviar and champagne to Best's room and found him in bed with Miss World. "Tell me Mr Best," said the waiter. "Where did it all go wrong?" Farokh Engineer, who became firm friends with the Manchester United star, laughs every time he thinks of it. "I introduced him to Miss World if I remember correctly." Engineer, who judged a number of beauty contests, adds: "But I'm not taking the blame for anything else!"

I gnash my teeth when I hear bleats about Best's lack of dedication, loyalty, what he could have done if he had been more like Bobby Charlton. Best was Best. I saw him throughout his career, first from the Stretford End at Old Trafford and then from the Press Box. The most skilful, most exciting footballer of all. And he gave everything he had. There was no remaining 'potential'.

Engineer was similar. Those who claim that he could have done better, scored more runs or more consistently, will use in evidence a number of performances where he gritted it out for match-winning 20s and 30s. If he could do it on occasion why not at other times instead of trying to whack everything out of the ground? But he did not have that 'potential'. Engineer was Engineer.

"I had the ability to play more carefully, I know. But it's not just about ability, technique and so on. It's what's in you as a person. What you are."

I suppose it is like a computer programme without its relevant 'driver'. All the bits are there but it will not work. Engineer was born with immense talent but with a different driver than most other batsmen. Would it have changed him if he had received more official coaching as a schoolboy?

"No. They would have had to change my personality as well as my batting style. It would not have worked. I was a Cavalier not a Roundhead." More a swashbuckling pirate (a 'Persian Pirate' he was once labelled) than a Cavalier but his meaning is clear. Picture him now on a damp, grey Wednesday morning, the ball moving and seaming around, Lancashire 61-5. Engineer lunges, the bat arcs, second slip holds on and within minutes of taking guard he is walking back to the pavilion. One or two groans can be heard but there is also a twinkle of amusement. Even with a gross duck he has lightened up Old Trafford.

A former player revealed to me that the team never had false expectations of Engineer if only because they never knew what to expect. Perhaps Engineer never knew either. In England his mistakes and cheap dismissals were generally treated with sympathy even a chuckle. If nothing else he provided something to talk about, value for money. The media loved him because he was so approachable and friendly and on a dull day Engineer was always likely to provide them with something to write about. He got a good Press in England. He also had stability - there was never any danger of him losing his Lancashire place. Back in India where deceit and jealous whispers haunted the corridors of power it was a different scenario. Some influential men demanded more orthodoxy, sneering at his determination to entertain. In doing so they ignored the words of one of India's most important cricketers C.K. Nayudu, the first Indian to make an international impact.

C.K. (Cottari Kanakaiya - but in India initials are often preferred to full names) Nayudu came from Nagpur, a city called the bellybutton of India because of its central position. He was an exceptional player and in the 1920s was head-hunted by one of the country's cricket mad princes, Holkar who made Nayudu a captain in his army and put him in charge of his cricket team. When the MCC sent the first representative team ever to visit India in 1926 Nayudu played against them for the Hindus in front of 25000 spectators and hammered 153 with a world record 11 sixes. His century came off 33 scoring shots. Nayudu became a revered figure. In *A History of Indian Cricket* Mihir Bose states: "He had an almost messianic faith in cricket believing that it could be traced back to ancient Aryan scriptures." He could withstand pain. Once in a Ranji Trophy game he was hit in the mouth, breaking two teeth. He refused treatment and brushed the remains of the teeth off the pitch 'lest they caused any deviation.'

Twenty years later in 1946 Nayudu presented his view on how cricket should be played in the inaugural issue of *Indian Cricket* (again I am indebted to Bose for this quotation): "Our age is an age of business and cricket has not escaped the fatal touch of commercialism. There is a tendency to regard statistics as the best indication of a player's ability. This has led to the emergence of a school of stonewallers. Cricket must be played in harmony with its inherent genius with wild and free abandon. Let our players attack the bowlers and provide spectators with a feast of strokeplay. If cricket, like life, is full of uncertainties why make it a dull affair?"

Engineer, then eight years-old, obviously read this! Not only read it but digested it and carried out Nayudu's entreaty to the letter. Not many others did.

A white, stone statue of the tall, upright Nayudu, batting and executing a hook, stands in the gardens outside the Nehru stadium in Indore, next to the Vijay Balla which bears Engineer's name amongst others. When I first saw it I was busy looking for the spot where my ancestor Edmund Avery died in 1857 and, while the statue dominated the landscape, I did not recognise the batsman although it obviously represented a figure from pre-war days judging by the style of cap, pads and bat. Unable to find an inscription I asked a bunch of employees from the nearby Municipal Corporation buildings who were lounging around the gardens on their lunch break. A couple of them looked towards the statue, frowned and stayed silent. The third said: "Famous Indian player. Gavaskar."

"He's grown a bit," I said, smiling. He stared back hard, said: "Gavaskar most famous player," and walked away.

Nayudu took cricket by storm with his world record innings. Gavaskar created even greater shockwaves with his record breaking introduction to Test cricket in 1971 when he tore apart a transitional West Indies team in the Caribbean. Engineer missed that tour. It hurt him but he had another rewarding summer in England to look forward to. Already parading three pieces of silverware from the previous two seasons, Lancashire looked stronger than ever. Some fans were booking hotels in London for the Gillette Cup final before the first round was played.

Engineer claims: "We were the best team in the country. We had everything. A great captain, top batsmen, England pace bowlers, and two spinners Jack Simmons and David Hughes who had quickly formed a good partnership. And while other counties had been taking a leaf out of our book by improving their fielding we were still way out in front in that regard."

But Engineer was also set to regain his Test place. India were due for a three match series in England. Normally this was hardly a cause of great excitement but India's shock triumph over West Indies gave it a real edge. India presented a real challenge, no longer the whipping boys of Test cricket. They had just claimed a number of 'firsts' - winning a Test against Australia, winning a Test and then a series abroad in New Zealand and capping all that by toppling Garry Sobers and co in their own backyard. And, of course, everyone was itching to see the new batting ace, Gavaskar. Over the three years 1971-74 India played no-one else but England. Eleven Tests on the trot, six away, five at home. Part way through that phase they were successful and cocky enough to crown themselves as unofficial 'world champions'. Engineer had not been part of the celebrations in the West Indies but he made a decisive contribution in what followed.

In April 1971 he faced a hectic summer. Lancashire were down to play 24 three day championship games, 16 John Player League fixtures and, hopefully, five in the Gillette Cup - if they won it again. On top of that there would be three Tests. But cricketers were used to playing day in, day out, and rarely whinged about it. "There was nothing to moan about. It was a great way to earn a living. I really looked forward to that season. When we all got together at Old Trafford for some pre-season training we talked of retaining the Sunday League and the Gillette but not just that. We felt we had enough to go for the championship as well. Lancashire hadn't won it for years. A treble, now that was really something to go for. As for India it was another series where I had something to prove. I was confident. I had gained a lot of experience of English pitches, bowling, conditions in general. I was the most senior player in the squad and I was ready for the responsibility."

India had controversially changed captains for the Caribbean tour, sacking Pataudi and putting Ajit Wadekar in charge, a makeshift choice in some eyes but one which bore fruit. Wadekar, a 'good guy' in Engineer's estimation, was thoughtful and respected but perhaps not a natural leader in the manner of a Pataudi or an Engineer. As it turned the West Indies was the right place at the right time. Pataudi had endowed him with a talented, versatile squad. Gavaskar's early performances left the likes of Garry Sobers and Clive Lloyd open-mouthed in astonishment.

Wadekar's hand was strengthened by Engineer's return for the contest with Ray Illingworth's England while the three matches were slotted for the middle of the season when pitches would be drier and more conducive to spin. If India were finally to break England's stranglehold over them surely this was the moment.

I shared Engineer's optimism. The dream ticket was a Lancashire treble and an incident packed Test series, crammed with controversy if not good cricket. I was, after all, a youngish sports writer trying to make a name for myself! John Arlott, E.W. Swanton and the other purists could write long, poetic essays about a handsome off drive or a beautifully flighted off-spinner etc but what I wanted, really really wanted was for Engineer or Big Clive to smash sixes any old how, or a row about an lbw decision, or for Boycs to stage another go-slow and get the sack-like thousands of others who were suffering in the economic downturn. Unemployment had shot up to over 800,000. Our agency needed stories to sell, we could hear the dole queue's siren call.

Also a good summer of cricket might part some of the blackening clouds hanging over Britain. Industrial unrest, the bombs of the IRA and The Angry Brigade, the first attack of Thatcherism with the abolition of free school milk and the disappearance of real money. In place of pound shillings and pence our pockets now jingled with decimalisation. But do you know the worst of it? Arsenal had done the double and Chelsea had beaten Real Madrid to take the European Cup-Winners' Cup. Many sports loving Mancunians turned to drink. Or rather, turned even more to drink.

I sashayed down to the two Old Traffords searching for nuggets. United were on the look-out for a new manager but were staying tight-lipped about it. Lancashire had little out of the ordinary to offer. "What are you after?" demanded Bond. "Nothing going on here." Bond liked to keep things on the straight and narrow without interference either from the club committee or the Press. In fact Lancashire's dressing-room welcome for some members of the Press, particularly those with long, fluffy hair, flared trousers and wide checked shirts (not Arlott and Swanton) was hardly the warmest. More Siberian than Mancunian. I usually targeted David Lloyd, Harry Pilling or, of course, the Brylcreem Boy.

Engineer had spent most of the winter in England. By then he was good friends with United and City footballers and officials, so much so that Matt Busby had offered to become a godfather to his daughters Minnie and Tina. "I was honoured but I had to say no, thank you. Godparents are not part of our religion and culture. He was a great man and it was touching that he should want to do that."

Often Engineer linked up with George Best who was proving a handful for United, drinking, womanising and generally having a good time. He would have fitted in neatly to life as a county cricketer. "We had a lot in common. After all he was from Northern Ireland and I was from India." Engineer is talking as he sifts through a load of photographs. "Look, me and George...look, me and Indira Gandhi.." I must look surprised. Not at his high profile connections of which he has far too many for his own good (I'm just jealous) but at his link between Belfast and Bombay.

"Yes. We could talk all night. It was difficult because women were hanging off both arms but we managed to chat. A lot of the time we'd meet up at the Blinker's nightclub. Selwyn Demmy owned it. There was a VIP corner and George basically set up house there. Champagne, caviar, beautiful ladies. What more could a red-blooded male ask for? But he loved to talk about his family and his home and he asked me about mine. What was it like in Bombay? What sort of house did we have? Religions, everything. Family ties seemed to be important in Belfast, just as they were in India. He was fascinated by some of my stories about India. And he loved a good curry. We got on famously. Of course he was the golden boy. They were like moths to the flame. Girls thronging around him. He could take his pick. But I could hold my own in that respect. I wasn't there to pick up the crumbs if you know what I mean.

"Basically he was shy. We all know that now, but not many understood it at the time. He was drinking heavily. If I were playing the next day I'd have a few drinks but never too many and I made sure I was home in time for a decent night's sleep. George though would keep going, We might be at Blinkers and I'd be going out the door and look back and he'd be there, surrounded by women, glass in his hand, smiling. I knew he wouldn't get much sleep. But then next day he would go out and play a great game for United, dribbling past opponents, scoring goals. I don't know how he managed to do it. Sometimes though I would leave him in a pub, playing cards with an Irish landlord or someone. Once or twice I dragged him away and took him home, even put him to bed. He had this strange designer built house in Bramhall. It did not do him any good, living on his own. One of the United managers ordered him to live back at his old landlady's, somewhere in Davyhulme I think. I couldn't see that working. George Best knocking on the door at 3am with a blonde on his arm... He got into all sort of trouble and people say he wasted his career but he also happened to enjoy the other side of his life away from the football pitch."

I tell Engineer that Best once played in a cricket match at Lancashire's ground, a United XI v City XI for Ken Higgs' benefit. There is a photograph of him walking out to bat with Jack Crompton who trained both teams. "Did he really? I bet he was good. He was a natural sportsman. But we never talked about cricket. In fact we never talked much about football. It was more to do with women."

In the early 1970s footballers could get away with the odd night out and there was nothing wrong with a few pints on a Saturday night after the game. With county cricketers it was a bit different. They could play every day and most nights if they felt like it. They had tremendous stamina.

Engineer was 33 when the 1971 season started, not a veteran in cricketing terms, but very experienced, the oldest member of the India squad and the second oldest behind Bond at Old Trafford. He had days of glory behind him in Test cricket and under the Red Rose flag and there was a lot more to come. Lancashire had a powerful versatile squad with enough back-up to mount a three pronged challenge for honours. They went close but left it too late in the championship, four wins in the last six games pushing them into third place, they kept hold of the Gillette Cup and they threw away the Sunday League title when it was at their mercy.

Engineer: "It looked like it was going to be a repeat of 1970. Another one-day double. We were on fire. I think we won the last three championship games. It wasn't quite enough but we had the Gillette final against Kent to come, then the last League game with Glamorgan and we knew if we won that we'd keep the title. There didn't seem like anything could stop us. To top it all Clive Lloyd was to be married. That promised to be a bit of fun."

Lancashire beat Kent by 24 runs at Lord's to spark off another celebration. Bond flew through the air at extra cover to hold a jaw dropping catch which wrecked a magnificent attempt by Asif Iqbal to thwart them. Engineer poured bubbly over the captain as they stood on the balcony acknowledging the crowd. "It was one of the best catches I've ever seen," said Jack Simmons.

"I was bowling, I didn't get the line right and Iqbal clubbed it. I thought oh no, that's a four but then Bondy was tumbling over with the ball in his hand. It definitely won us the match." David Hughes joked….'he tripped over and took a stunning catch."

E.W. Swanton reported it like this: "Asif, avoiding Simmons's strong on-side field, made room to off-drive and hit the ball clean and hard, heading well wide of extra cover's right. Lancashire's captain hesitated a fraction of a second, then took off, and with a leap that Clive Lloyd would not have disdained, pulled the ball down one-handed as he fell. Bond's hesitation might have been explained by the extraordinary fact that his first instinct was, as he said afterwards, that it was a bump ball. In that case Kent could well lament that, with a man at long-off behind him, someone in his 40th year should have made so prodigious an effort to save a single."

Exciting though that game was it could never match the drama of the Old Trafford semi-final against Gloucestershire. Nothing ever could. After an hour's delay because of rain Lancashire were still batting and still well short of their target of 230 when the clock struck 8pm. Dusk was approaching and umpire Dickie Bird, a nervy figure at the best of times, was worried about the light. By 8.30pm it was difficult to see from one side of the ground to another. As darkness set in, the lights on the adjacent railway station shone out like beacons. Bird wanted to abandon and return to finish it the following day, but there were 25,000 in the ground growing ever more excited and his colleague Arthur Jepson and club officials feared a stampede. According to a chuckling Bond, Jepson told Bird to look up the sky and tell him what he could see. "Bloody moon," was the reply. "Well, if you can see something that's so far away there can't be a problem with the light," said Jepson. Hughes then hit 24 in one over off John Mortimore, 4,6,2,2,4,6, and Bond finished it off with a single. The clock stood at almost 8. 55pm. Hughes roared with laughter when he watched a video of the game some years afterwards. "I didn't realise at the time that the crowd had pushed the rope in about 20 yards!"

Engineer shakes his head in amazement as he talks about it. "You couldn't see what was happening. How we got it finished I'll never know. Yozzer was smashing it. Thousands of fans were sitting on the grass just behind the boundary rope making it difficult for the fielders. You couldn't tell what was happening to the ball. You could call it Lancashire's first ever floodlit match. But the floodlights were the lights on the railway station! We were just glad to finish it."

After the Gillette spectaculars, Lancashire intended to put the icing on the cake by completing a hat-trick of Sunday League successes. All they had to was to beat Glamorgan. It went horribly wrong. Over 30,000 spectators were primed to celebrate, thousands sitting on the grass and again making life impossible for fielders on the boundary. When Kevin Lyons tried to pull off a comfortable catch at deep mid-wicket he fell into the less than loving embrace of a brigade of Lancashire fans the ball disappearing and a 'four' given on the assumption it must have touched the rope. But needing a modest 144 for victory they collapsed from 43-1 to 109 all out. Someone muttered: "Probably hung over the lot of 'em. It was Clive's wedding yesterday."

Engineer denied any link and there was plenty of evidence to the contrary. They had bowled and fielded well enough, Lever and Simmons collecting three cheap wickets each, and despite Engineer's early exit they had a good enough start through David Lloyd and Ken Snellgrove. 'Just one of those things, perhaps a bit of over confidence' was how they explained it. The fans were stunned. Some barracked and slow hand-clapped the players who had earned the club four trophies.

In the Press Box there were dark mutterings. It had looked like an easy day, an early finish and the story written up well before the close. As wickets tumbled sheets of copy paper were torn up, hurled away in disgust, new 'intros' written. Newspaper coverage was unforgiving. The *Daily Telegraph*, normally restrained, roared: '...they folded, lay down and died'. When the shock subsided Lancashire were able to brush themselves down and look back on another fabulous season. Massive crowds, another trophy and a record profit of almost £22,000 after eight years of deficits and some thrilling cricket including a last ball one wicket championship win over Warwickshire. Millions of viewers had watched them and the Old Trafford gates for one-day games averaged more than 20,000 over the second half of the summer. In between the Lancashire showpieces Engineer cut himself a thick slice of Test match history in a famous victory which was to be inscribed in stone and in the hearts of all Indians.

"You dream about this sort of thing," said Engineer. "Six weeks of pure magic. I will never forget it."

CHAPTER 15

MRS INDIRA Gandhi was chuffed. Her armed forces had beaten off Pakistan in a thankfully short war over the independence of Bangladesh and her cricketers were world beaters. Indians had good reason to feel proud. It was December 1971 and, whether with gun and bullet or bat and ball India felt ready to take on anyone.

Four months earlier the Prime Minister had sent a telegram to Ajit Wadekar, captain of the cricket team: "The country is thrilled to hear of your exciting victory." India had just won a Test, and a series, in England for the first time. The old colonial masters beaten at their own game on their own soil. When the news of the historic victory at the Oval on August 24 reached the sub-continent the people went wild, lighting bonfires. Bombay, the birthplace of Indian cricket and Farokh Engineer's home town, partied through the night.

Engineer, one of India's linchpins throughout the series, had also celebrated in style after that match - with champagne and tandoori chicken. Then he dived into his car and drove back from London to his adopted Manchester. "I had another game to play," he explains, "for Lancashire against Derbyshire. I got back in the early hours of the morning. A few hours later I was walking out of the pavilion at Old Trafford. There was no question of me not playing. It was an important game. We still had a chance in the championship. I wasn't tired. And if I had been the Old Trafford crowd would have lifted me. They were fantastic. When I walked out to bat they gave me a standing ovation. I couldn't believe it really. An English crowd standing to salute an Indian - and for helping to beat England! It underlined to me just how sporting and generous the British were. There was a tear in my eye as I walked on to the pitch that day."

His India team-mates also had further cricketing engagements with three matches against county teams and one against T.N. Pearce's XI to round off their triumphant march around England but eventually they went home to a ticker-tape reception, fronted by Mrs Gandhi in the capital Delhi. Engineer stayed behind - he had business with Lancashire as they tried to pull off another one-day double. As he said earlier, a magical finale to 1971 where he played one memorable game after another all in front of huge crowds.

Back in July that summer India landed in England on the crest of a wave after their Sunil Gavaskar inspired success in the West Indies. England, led by Yorkshire's Ray Illingworth were also pretty pleased with themselves having brought the Ashes back from Australia. It promised to be some series. Almost a world championship. India retained several members of the squad which last toured England in 1967 - Engineer, Wadekar and the spinners Chandra, Bedi and Prasanna. But there were major differences - a new record breaking batsman in Gavaskar, a new captain in Wadekar, but most of all a new attitude.

Engineer: "We had been rolled over in 1967. That seemed to be the way for India in England. Not this time. The boys had done so well in the Windies. They were full of confidence, ready for a real battle. I was back in the side and was desperate to show that I should never have been left out and also I'd had four seasons in county cricket. I had learned a few things. I knew what to expect."

India showed their calibre in early matches against the counties and when the first Test started at Lord's England knew they could not take anything for granted. Except the weather. Cold and damp, it stayed that way for most of the tour, helping England's seam bowlers. If Illingworth was lucky with the toss India would find themselves fighting against the odds. He was lucky, winning it every time. But at Lord's, where Engineer added to the dampness by leaving on a tap and flooding the dressing room, they showed the tenacity which would serve them so well throughout the contest. Despite rain and bad light this superb clash whetted the appetite for the series, full of good cricket and remembered chiefly for the moment when a big, bad Englishman sent a little Indian flying and was kicked out of the side for bad sportsmanship, although it is unclear whether the 'disciplinary reasons' mentioned by the authorities referred to John Snow's controversial barging of Gavaskar on the pitch or to his terse 'get stuffed' message to said authorities in the Lord's pavilion. The incident occurred when Engineer called for a quick single as India chased a gettable target of 183 on the final day. Snow, the six feet plus bowler and Gavaskar the five feet five inches batsman collided and Gavaskar crashed to the ground. Luckily he was unhurt. As he brushed himself down Snow picked up his bat and tossed it to him. "I could sense the shocked silence in the MCC committee room," said Snow later. "I knew I was going to be in trouble."

Engineer was furious. "I went up to him and said something like 'What the hell do you think you are doing. Why don't you pick on someone your own size?' There is no doubt in my mind that he shoulder charged him. Snow had taken lots of wickets in the Ashes and he was getting frustrated at the way we were treating him. Especially Sunny because of his size. Snow was much taller and powerful. It was bad. Sunny could have been hurt because he went down heavily. I don't know what would have happened then. He was on his hands and knees almost crawling to the crease without his bat. Anyway Sunny did not make a fuss. It was just before lunch and when we were walking off at the interval Alec Bedser met Snow at the door and told him to apologise. Afterwards we just got on with the game. While we were at the crease we had a chance so we had to keep focused on the game, not on what had happened."

During lunch Snow was on his way to the Indian dressing-room to offer an apology but was pulled up short by Billy Griffith, the secretary of the Test and County Cricket Board who told him it 'was the one of the most disgusting things he had ever seen on a cricket field.' Snow's heated response settled it - he was dropped for the next Test at Old Trafford. Engineer and Gavaskar did their best to make Snow pay. When Engineer edged left arm spinner Norman Gifford behind they had slammed 66 in 50 minutes, his share being 35 off 40 balls. India's bid tailed off when Gavaskar also fell to Gifford and they had to hang on at 145-8. But what a taster for the second game at Old Trafford.

From a Lancastrian perspective Snow's ban was perfectly timed for it offered Peter Lever a comeback chance on his home ground. Lever had made his England debut in Australia at the age of 30 and had taken 7-83 against the Rest of the World at the Oval the previous summer. He was a cracking fast bowler who would have played more often had Brian Statham not been around and he promised to form a powerful new ball partnership with the very tall, very quick Price. Guess what - Manchester was wet and bleak. The pitch was indistinguishable from the rest of the square, like nothing most of the Indians had ever seen. Engineer, however, hardly gave it a second look. Lever just smiled.

"It was green," Engineer explained. "There had been a lot of rain. We knew we would have to bat well."

First though they had to bowl and Syed Abid Ali surprised everyone with a wonderful spell, three wickets in 10 balls turning back the top order. It seemed as though Illingworth's decision to bat had backfired but through gritted teeth he grafted a captain's century, helped by one of several questionable umpiring decisions, paving the way for Lever to show why in his early career he was rated as an all-rounder. At Lord's Snow had shocked India with the bat as well as with his shoulder, hitting 73 after England had stumbled to 183-7. At Old Trafford his replacement hammered an unbeaten 88 after they had slipped to 187-7. As the prospect of a hundred for 'our Plank' increased I got a mite too excited on the back row of the Press Box, roaring out my approval at one pulled four. I was told to calm down.

Lever, who followed that up with 5-70 from 26 overs, was disappointed with the way it finished saying: "If I'd have got 100 I'd have been on both honours boards and I only played one Test there. It was my own fault. The final guy to bat was John Price and I ran him out. I smacked one and someone fielded it really well. I tried to turn round, he tried to turn round but slipped on his backside."

Engineer: "Plank was out for a duck! I had him off an edge before he had scored but the umpire didn't give it although the snick must have been heard at the other Old Trafford. Plank turned around to me, smiled and winked. After that he batted very well. Illy should have been out similarly a little later. The decisions went against us."

A few days after the match, needing material for a newspaper feature on Lever, I asked Jack Bond what he thought of his innings. "I didn't see it," said Bond. "What's all the fuss about? He's always been able to hold a bat." Relaxing a little, Bond added: "Bit of a nuisance though. He's done that well they might pick him again for t'Oval and that means we'll be missing two players again." In fact Snow returned for the showdown. Unfortunately Lever suffered a finger injury which sidelined him for a while.

India survived that Test because of a Manchester monsoon which wrecked the last day but there was time for the 22 years-old Gavaskar to again show his mastery against red-hot pace. His 57 on that pitch against Lever, who bowled it full, and Price who banged it in short with terrific speed was easily worth a century in easier circumstances. Despite the chilly weather he batted without a sweater, his shirtsleeves rolled up. "It was the most satisfying innings - a turning point in my career."

Despite India's obvious improvement since their last visit four years previously, England were favourites for the third and deciding Test. Snow was back and itching to get at Gavaskar. But this was evolving into a bowlers' series and India's spinners were busily stacking up victims, filling England's batsmen with doubts. It deservedly goes down as Chandra's match, his 6-38 being described as 'astonishing'. He bowled with pace, precision and turned the ball viciously to bowl England out for 101 in the second innings but Engineer has good reason to stiffen with pride when he talks about it.

All fired up, Snow quickly sent back Gavaskar and then Illingworth's off-spin reduced India to 125-5 in reply to England's 355 still well short of avoiding the follow-on, when Engineer joined Ekky Solkar. They stopped the decline with a stand of 97. As they had also featured in five English dismissals they were, at that stage, India's star turns. Engineer's 59 was their top score throughout the whole match and a magnificent example of how he could grind it out when the chips were down. Saturday was grey - rain had washed out the Friday - and the ground was less than half-full. India had their backs to the wall in conditions they usually hated but which they were becoming accustomed to and England's attack was good and varied - pace from Snow and Price, troublesome seam from Richard Hutton and Basil D'Oliveira and spin from Illingworth and left armer 'Deadly' Derek Underwood. Even if England could not force a win, the prospect of an Indian victory looked as remote as sunshine.

Here, though, in the most unpromising of circumstances, Engineer steeled himself for an extraordinary performance which, in the great majority of reviews, has been over-shadowed by Chandra's bowling. No doubt at all that Chandra justified all the accolades which were showered upon him. World-class bowling won the match. But, well before that, India had to be saved and the man who rescued them was Engineer with sterling help from Solkar. Imprisoning all his natural instincts to attack, Engineer buckled down to chisel out an escape route, resisting not just England's frustrated bowlers but also the undying urge to blast his way out of trouble. For over two hours he stuck in there and when, late in the day, he did try to hook and skied Snow to Illingworth India were 230-7 and back in the game. Abid Ali and Venkat weighed in with useful runs to haul them to within 69 of England.

E.W. Swanton wrote: 'Engineer, for two vital hours, confronted England with just the right mixture of modified aggression'. John Arlott criticised Underwood for setting a defensive field, adding: "Engineer, of all people, made the highest score ever recorded in a Test in England without a boundary.....there was affection as well as congratulation in the applause that welcomed him in'.

Engineer points out: "Illingworth knew my batting and set the field accordingly. I didn't get a boundary but I found the gaps and was quite happy to take singles. It worked well. Yes, I had to be patient." Solkar also batted with resolution and skill. What a player to have in your side. He took two wickets in the first innings and put England under intense pressure in the second with his close-in catching. They said Chandra weaved a web of uncertainty for England but Solkar was the spiderman, lurking threateningly a few feet from the bat and moving with blinding speed to grab his victims. His full-length dive to send back Alan Knott for a single lived long in the memory. Chandra deceived John Edrich with his faster ball the 'Mill Reef' named after the racehorse and, with Solkar's aid, he also removed Keith Fletcher, both in the last over before lunch. Illingworth was so bewildered that he dollied a simple return catch to Chandra and England collapsed to 101 all out in 45.1 disastrous overs, their lowest ever total against India.

Engineer still marvels at Chandra's skill. "He had polio as a child and it left him with a withered right arm, only an inch thick in some places. But he converted this misfortune to make him into one of the greatest bowlers cricket has seen. He was very thin, always wore a long sleeved shirt and his wrist looked almost as if it was broken. His action was whippy, he bowled at real speed and he had everything - leggies, googlies, top spin with variations in bounce and pace. Time and time again he tried to bowl a leggie and it emerged as a googly almost without him realising. Batsmen could not read him. I could. But my reactions had to be split second, almost as if computerised. He couldn't bat for toffee, of course - had more Test wickets than runs. The Aussies presented him with a bat with a hole in the middle of it and he saw the funny side. A wonderful cricketer and a very unassuming man."

At the Oval, Chandra ran off through a phalanx of ecstatic fans, Engineer close behind. India needed 173 to clinch a place in their history books. Indian fans had brought an elephant, Bella, to the ground from Chessington zoo, parading her around the outfield to celebrate the Hindu festival of

Ganesh, the elephant god. Their prayers had been answered. But they still needed to bat well. Wadekar made a useful 45 but was needlessly run out. As he walked back towards the pavilion steps the affable BBC commentator Brian Johnston tried to grab a quick word with him but the captain refused, saying: "No English." When Johnston reminded him that they had spoken regularly throughout the tour - in English - Wadekar brushed him off, saying: "Hindi only," and promptly settled down in the dressing-room for a nap.

The *Daily Mail's* cricket writer Alex Bannister reported: "Like Montgomery before Alamein he had laid his plans in advance and retired to confident sleep." When a bleary-eyed Wadekar was finally woken up by his teammates, Ken Barrington came to the Indian dressing room, and said: "It's all over. The match is yours. They'll want you up there on the balcony." As he strode out, even the typically unperturbed man gave in to emotions, admitting: "I was moved to tears. It was the greatest day of my life".

Breathtakingly confident, Wadekar claimed he 'always knew' India would win. India were only 76-3 when he departed and while Dilip Sardesai and Gundappa Viswanath put on 48 Underwood was making inroads and tension was rising, if not within the players then on the stands which had been taken over by expectant colourfully dressed Indian supporters, some in turbans and saris lightening up the surroundings. Solkar fell cheaply this time. The run rate had slowed to less than two an over. Engineer joined Viswanath at 134-5, still 39 needed, and considering their lengthy tail, still vulnerable. Again he did what was necessary, playing carefully (after heaving and missing at his first ball!) but this time punishing anything loose. The sixth wicket pair took India to the brink.

Engineer: "Vishy went to a catch behind but we were so close by then. There were fans encroaching on the outfield ready to storm on. But after all the effort I didn't want anything to go wrong. I had to keep my emotions in check. Abid Ali came in, I went down the pitch to chat with him. Just to say: 'Look, we don't have to take any risks." He sort of nodded. Brian Luckhurst was bowling, left arm spin. Abid Ali went down the pitch to him and didn't connect. I couldn't believe it. So I had another word with him. The rest is history."

Abid Ali was a highly talented player who responded by cutting the next ball towards the boundary. Charging fans smothered it well before it got there. The umpires signalled a four and it was all over. Engineer, ecstatic, began to run back to the pavilion, realised his partner had disappeared, stopped and turned back to see where he was before being engulfed. Abid Ali had re-traced his steps, presumably to grab one of the stumps as a trophy. But one set had already gone, the umpire had uplifted the other and was using them to ward off souvenir hunters, including India's hero of the moment.

Engineer was a little miffed by it all: "Abid Ali got the glory and all he had done was to get the winning runs. I had been out there for nearly an hour making sure we wouldn't throw the chance away. But nothing could spoil the occasion. We had played like a team. Everyone chipped in and we had beaten England on their own soil. It was hard to define how much that meant to us." Illingworth who had joked about India playing in front of a home crowd said: "India have proved themselves to be a world class side."

Engineer topped India's batting averages - as his wicketkeeping pal Alan Knott did for England - in a strange slow scoring series played in poor weather. India won without anyone making a century. Indeed they recorded only eight half-centuries. Gavaskar claimed two of them but otherwise was dismissed cheaply and aggregated only six runs at the Oval. England had two centuries and nine 50s. India totalled 300 plus just once. England did it three times. The difference was Chandra's bowling on that last dramatic day at the Oval. Or was it?

Wisden noted: "Engineer's availability for the Test matches made the difference between defeat and victory. At the Oval he batted most sensibly during a difficult period in the first innings and his experience of playing in a tense situation - which most of his team-mates lacked - came in handy in the final stage of the battle for victory. Although it was a long time since he had kept to the Indian spinners - and taking Chandra needs a lot of practice - Engineer's performance behind the stumps was of the highest class."

Every Indian player contributed overall. Solkar, a tad behind Engineer in the runs chart, had six wickets and his catching drew sharp intakes of breath. Venkat had as many wickets as Chandra, 13. Bedi had 11. Wadekar captained well. Much more serious than Pataudi, perhaps more canny in some respects, he worked hard with Engineer and the manager, peanut scoffing Col Hemu Adhikeri to get players into a positive frame of mind.

The Oval Test came between the Gillette Cup semi and final. There was also a massive Sunday game in the offing against Glamorgan. "I was shaking my head in disbelief really," Engineer said. "India had made cricket history,

Mrs Gandhi herself was congratulating us. Lancashire were making cricket history. The Queen was the Lancashire club's patron - maybe we would get a telegram from her!"

Engineer returned to India during the winter of 1971-72. It was a good homecoming. India were proclaiming themselves as world champions after winning three away series on the trot in New Zealand, West Indies and England. Engineer was heavily involved in two of those successes. In England he had been chaired off the Oval pitch by ecstatic Indian fans and less than 24 hours later the English crowd at Old Trafford stood to acclaim him as he walked out of the pavilion with his Lancashire team-mates. His personal standing could not have been higher in either country. And India, as a team and as a nation, stood proudly on a pedestal.

CHAPTER 16

ONE OF the many intriguing features of the 1971 series was the comparison between two illustrious wicketkeepers Farokh Engineer and Alan Knott. Each had tremendous respect for the other. England and India expected much from them and neither disappointed. Engineer was India's top batsman, Knott was England's. They claimed 17 catches and two stumpings, aided and abetted in several run-outs and acted as right-hand men to captains Ajit Wadekar and Ray Illingworth.

England captain Ray Illingworth found it hard to split them. At various points of his career and afterwards he placed Knott as the best he had ever seen. But, referring to the 1971 tour, he said: "I had the pleasure of playing Test cricket against Farokh and I feel that India's emergence as a world-class side probably owed more to him than any other member of the side including their world-class spin bowlers. Apart from his wicket-keeping which I rate alongside Alan Knott (and anybody in county cricket knows how much I rate Knotty). He gave the Indian batting that bit of flair which was lacking if he didn't play." Generous praise from a bluff Yorkshireman who gave little away.

At Lord's Knott neatly stumped Engineer off the left arm spin of Norman Gifford just as Engineer and Gavaskar were hauling India into a match-winning position. But that was mundane stuff compared to the way Engineer stopped England, and John Edrich in particular, from constructing an unassailable lead. Batting was tough. England would be hot favourites if they could set India a target of 220 plus. In fact Illingworth would have been happy enough with anything over 200 and at 145-4, 136 ahead, they had a clear chance. Edrich was 62 and in control until he nicked Bishan Bedi.

Knott was at the other end. "John got a thick edge which saw the ball hit Farokh on the body and as it fell towards the ground he flicked it up into the air with his left foot (he's right-footed too) to take a truly unbelievable catch."

Engineer raises both eyebrows at that description. He thinks his old pal has not given him due recognition. "It was the best catch I ever took and I took a lot of good ones. We needed to do something about Edrich. He and Knott were building a stand which could take the game away from us. Bedi sent down a quicker ball and it pitched in the rough, clipped the shoulder of the bat and caught me on the shoulder. It flew high up into no-man's land. I went after it, realising I could not reach it with my hands so did a deliberate slide, kicked the ball up hoping it would go to a fielder. But there was no-one close enough so I did it again, another slide and another flick with my other foot, but again there was no-one else near enough to grab it and so then I just had to dive for it and it lodged in the tips of my glove. I ended up full-length on my front with my kit and face covered in mud. Edrich marched off muttering something that I could not possibly repeat."

At the end of the series Knott and Engineer shook hands warmly. Knott said of Engineer: "He can concentrate all day, is very fit as he proves by diving away to the legside to take great catches and, as with all his keeping, giving the impression that he is made of elastic.. he must go into the bracket of all-time great wicketkeepers."

Engineer is equally complimentary. "Knotty was technically brilliant. But I think it would be difficult to separate us in terms of what we brought to our respective teams. We set the bar. Knotty in the way he kept to Derek Underwood, particularly, and me in the way I combined with Chandra, Prasanna and Bedi. We had a lot of respect for each other. He loved talking about wicketkeeping and I enjoyed chatting with him. We had very different styles but were both very effective. I remember he was superstitious. He always touched the bails with his gloves when he came in to bat.

"All through that series we were competing hard against each other. He would pull off a great catch, then I would. He stumped me at Lord's. I stumped Brian Luckhurst at Old Trafford. He got lots of runs. So did I. At the Oval he got 90 in the first innings and a single in the second, 91 altogether. I got 59 and 28 not out, a total of 87. It was neck and neck all the time until that last day. I finished as a winner, he was the loser but I hold my hands up - Alan Knott was an all-time great. I think we would both say that wicketkeeping standards then were far higher than of now."

Knott's enthusiasm and talent was not fully exploited by England after he finished playing. He coached for 10 years but never on a full-time basis with the national squad and eventually retired to live on a Greek island.

Engineer's experience and desperate desire to put something back into cricket also fell on stony ground. Such waste.

Former England captain Keith Fletcher underlined how Knott's immaculate glovework set the standard for England's fielding - "I can't remember him missing a chance." As such he was not too impressed with M.S. Dhoni's work behind the stumps.

Engineer is at variance with that. "Fletcher had trouble remembering names so I can't accept his recollection that Knotty didn't miss a single chance. And anyway it's not always about being perfect. Other factors come into play. I cannot say I never missed a chance. There were many good days and a few bad days. But I believe I always set the highest standard for the way the team fielded. I was willing to dive for anything. Like the goalkeeper I once was. Other fielders followed my example. And I was always on my toes, ready for anything. Some wicketkeepers would not take risks in case of dropping the ball. I was prepared to take a risk with only the slightest chance. Most times I got it and it was a brilliant catch. Once or twice I missed it. It came with the territory. As far as Dhoni is concerned his record speaks for itself."

The eminent Indian author Raju Bharatan described Engineer's 1971 *tour de force* as 'the series of his lifetime'.

"Engineer, in heralding the spin revolution, was the wicketkeeper, first slip and leg slip rolled into one. It was on his agility and mobility as a stumper that our world-class fielding cordon came to revolve - Eknath Solkar omnipresent at forward short leg, Syed Abid Ali ready to snaffle anything even a centimetre in the air, Venkataraghavan closing his capacious hands on anything that flew between him and Engineer, Wadekar anticipating outstandingly at first slip and Gavaskar by his side rising well above his average catching ability in such predatory company."

Engineer's oft repeated shout 'Catch, Ekky!' echoed around England that summer. Another aspect of his keeping was raised by Illingworth who reckoned he saved 'hundreds of quick singles' by standing up to the seamers and swooping in front of the stumps to retrieve the ball.

As for Dhoni, Engineer wafts away any criticism. "He was an attacking batsman who took to wicketkeeping and worked hard to improve his skills. From the first time we met and I saw him play he reminded me so very much of my younger days. He had the same enthusiasm and attacking instincts as a batsman. All credit that as a young man made his mark playing cricket in

Jharkhand, a place, unfortunately, I've never visited. There must have been so few opportunities there (compared to what he had in Bombay).

"Supremely fit and extremely gifted with hand/eye/feet coordination he became a fine batsman-wicketkeeper. I've always considered Dhoni as an extraordinary all-round package. His captaincy and his bold approach to the game made him into one of the most popular Indian cricketers of all time. I've heard a lot of people and ex Test players saying Dhoni was lucky in many ways. Of course we have all needed Lady Luck some time or other but M.S. certainly grabbed his opportunities and with his man-management skills and shrewd captaincy he became the complete package. No wonder a film was made about his life. A fantastic cricketer and a good friend."

Whatever people thought of Engineer's wicketkeeping and batting he was certainly immensely popular. Even the most conservative observers were won over by his personal charm and cavalier approach on the pitch. After the Lord's Test of 1971 Ken Barrington told *Daily Mail* readers: "Farokh Engineer, brilliant wicketkeeper and batsman extraordinary, was for me the man of a memorable Test. He is a player of spirit, action and adventure. When he heard of a forecast of rain by mid-afternoon he volunteered to bat No. 4 and go for the bowling, Skipper Wadekar wisely agreed and Engineer, with his knowledge of English conditions and weekly experience of Sunday League for Lancashire, very nearly won the Test for India. Perhaps his final act of charging down the wicket was too impetuous, but at least he brought the game to life, and England were more than thankful to see him go." Now that's what you call a tribute. After a score of 35!

Barrington's eulogy highlighted the Engineer dilemma. Pat him on the back for having a valiant go when others would not dare, or kick him up the backside for magnificently creating an opportunity and then wasting it. The English, so sentimental at times, usually preferred to regard him in a positive light. Why? Partly, I suppose, because he lit a torch through the drabness. Engineer's career in England coincided with the change of black and white to colour TV, an apposite dovetailing. Another aspect is that Brits have always honoured a particular form of foolhardiness - that which is blessed with the romantic notion of courage. Engineer was The Forlorn Hope, a one man Charge of the Light Brigade.

The only time I saw him 'live' in a Test was the 1971 Manchester game. Rain ruined it and Peter Lever's all-round show of 88 not out and 5-70 was the highlight. Obviously I was pleased for him, but only pleased, nothing more. He was a top quality cricketer, honest as the day is long and a Lancastrian but when he sent back Engineer for 22 all I felt was disappointment. I had longed for a typical Engineer innings. No, not the type where he sashayed down the pitch to his first ball, swiped, missed and turned around to see the bails off and the keeper smoking a cigar. No, what I wanted, expected, was a salvo of attacking shots, a blaze of glory. That is how Engineer tugged at your emotions.

Although the last day was wiped out there was little respite from the daily diet of cricket, cricket and more cricket. Next day he was at Blackpool for Lancashire's championship game with Middlesex, also ruined by the weather and when that finished in a 'no result' he and the lads travelled down to Leicester for another three day extravaganza and on completion of that, while his team-mates took a well merited coupled of days off, Engineer drove to London to re-join India in time for their pre-Test net. Commitment? Take a peek at his diary for August 1971:

August

1:	*Lancs v Northants (JPL) at Bedford;*
2-3:	*Last two days of Roses match at Sheffield;*
4:	*Net practice at Old Trafford for Test match;*
5-10:	*(inc rest day): England v India, second Test;*
11-13:	*Lancs v Middlesex at Blackpool;*
14-17:	*(inc rest day): Lancs v Leicestershire at Leicester;*
18:	*Net practice at the Oval;*
19-24:	*(inc rest day): England v India, third Test;*
25-27:	*Lancs v Derbyshire at Old Trafford;*
28, 29,31:	*Lancs v Worcestershire at Old Trafford;*
30:	*Lancs v Worcestershire (JPL) at Old Trafford.*

Twenty four days of cricket out of 31, a mixture of Test, championship and Sunday League fixtures. Three rest days, two more with no play because of rain, and two practice days. In between lots of driving taking in six venues up and down the country. I put it to Engineer he was lucky to get in a few days when he could put his feet up, because of the weather and convenient gaps in the Sunday programme. "Not at all. I wanted to play. This was an exciting time. I didn't want it ever to stop. I was in action so much, hardly ever having time to put my feet up. But I didn't care. And anyway I never felt so tired that I didn't want to play."

Even taking his stamina and enthusiasm into account it was an exhausting schedule. Not that he was alone in having to switch from Test to championship or league mode in a flick of the eye. All the England players were in the same boat while the Indians had a series of three day games against county teams. Ray Illingworth, the England and Leicestershire captain, was involved in the three day match at Leicester against Lancashire and led them to a convincing win, a result which ultimately cost Bond's side the title.

Cricketers in England were used to playing and travelling almost non-stop but it could blunt performances. Engineer scored few runs for Lancashire between the Tests, a half-century against Yorkshire being the best. Do not think that his Lancashire colleagues had any sympathy for him. As one of their overseas players he was better paid - the fact that he had also to play for India was not their problem. Rather than congratulating him on his latest Test display they were more likely to have a light-hearted dig about his modest championship innings. County cricket, at least in its Northern bastions, was congenial enough but it was no place for softies or show ponies.

"I had to produce the goods for Lancashire. It was a side full of good players and if I'd have slackened off they would have let me know it. Peter Lever had played brilliantly at Old Trafford for England and Ken Shuttleworth was to play for them as well. Not so far into the future I found myself playing Test cricket against Barry Wood and Bumble. But I didn't feel under extra pressure. I was on a high. If I didn't score runs I would be taking catches and stumping batsmen. I always had something to give to the team. One day playing in front of a Test match crowd, the next at Bedford or Sheffield. It didn't make any difference to me, I loved it all."

The thought of Engineer motoring around the highways and byways of England to get from one round to another had David Lloyd and friends in stitches. Though he had been in the country for four years his navigation was always a source of ribaldry. "How he didn't end up in Edinburgh is a mystery," joked Bumble.

India did not have a series in the winter of 1971-72 and Engineer was able to concentrate on his other job in the textile business which he enjoyed thoroughly. Not the same kudos as that which cricket offered but a deep satisfaction. He was a good salesman, still is. Could have sold Margaret Thatcher a bag of coal. The Iron Lady had begun her march towards

Number 10, she was a Minister in Edward Heath's government and at the start of 1972 she looked askance at the industrial chaos which threatened the UK. Miners went on a seven weeks strike, there were power cuts, a three day working week in many factories, the unemployment figure topped one million for the first time, and a state of emergency was declared. On top of this, there was Bloody Sunday in Derry and a bomb which killed six soldiers in Aldershot. Dark days.

All in all I longed for lighter days and for Lancashire to give us something to smile about. The summer promised a new one-day competition, the Benson and Hedges Cup - and surely Lancashire would do well in that - and an Ashes series. We lit our candles and waited impatiently for Engineer, Big Clive and the lads to rescue us.

Something went wrong. Some days in the early part of the season felt colder than the winter just gone. Geoff Boycott hit a superb century in near Arctic conditions in the first Roses match at Headingley in late May when Engineer responded with 69 to save Lancashire after they slipped to 46-4. This was a careful Engineer innings with Richard Hutton, Chris Old and Tony Nicholson who finished with 7-49 always threatening with swing and movement off the pitch. He spent two and a half hours in reaching 50.

There was lots of rain. David Lloyd's dad kept a careful record of play lost to weather and he added it up to more than 70 hours that summer, dashing hopes of a championship challenge. The two main strike bowlers Lever and Shuttleworth struggled with injuries and subsequent loss of form, Engineer could not buy a run after that Roses knock, and other teams were now matching Lancashire's industry in the field. By mid-season they were bottom of the championship, out of the B and H, and without an earthly of the Sunday title. Lancashire's specialist batsmen propped them up. David Lloyd hit six of their 14 first-class centuries, Clive Lloyd three with two each for Barry Wood and Harry Pilling. Bond got the other, in his last championship match at Lord's.

The Gillette Cup offered salvation. A spectacular win over Somerset in the second round, watched by 12,000, was followed by a tightly fought victory at Bournemouth where Hampshire's South Africa ace Barry Richards hit 129. Even those tussles could not match the semi, another epic with Kent which attracted 21,000 to Old Trafford in mid August.

This was cricket at its best. Hard, relentless cricket with splendid batting against tight seam and spin attacks and fielding as good as any I have seen in the modern game. Barry Wood, refusing to chance his arm, was imprisoned in the opening stages with six feet eight inches tall Norman Graham and West Indian left-armer Bernard Julien giving him just one single in seven overs. Wood refused to panic and eventually helped David Lloyd to put on 59 for the first wicket. Which brought in five feet three inches Harry Pilling. "Norman were a good bloke," he said. "But he were a bloody skyscraper next to me. I got a crick in me neck talking to him." Pilling defied him, and Julien and Underwood to score 70. England's selectors continued to shun him. He did make one Test appearance, at the age of 17 when he went on as a sub for Brian Statham at Old Trafford. Colin Cowdrey patted him on the head afterwards - Harry was only five feet two inches at that point - and said he had done well. Pilling was more concerned about getting home in time for his tea before turning out to play an evening match for his club Staley.

Frank Hayes, beginning to make a name for himself, fell to a catch by Asif Iqbal which came close to excelling Bond's acrobatics to dismiss him at Lord's. Driving Underwood high and wide of long-off Hayes ran one and was going for another when he glanced over his shoulder to see Asif sprinting 20 yards at full tilt to clutching it at knee-height with outstretched hands. Because of a delayed start Kent spent over three continuous hours in the field but maintained their spirit and disciplined aggression. Then, with their reply at 34-2 and the light fading, Cowdrey and Mike Denness were asked if they wanted to call it a day. Anxious not to disappoint an enthralled crowd they said no. Umpire George Pope said afterwards: "I take my hat of to those two players." Even so a second day was necessary and while the attendance slipped to 5,000, the cricket remained as riveting and pulsating as before.

Engineer had suffered a nasty blow to the right eye. It swelled up and hampered his vision. He looked like a boxer at the end of a punishing fight. "Jack Bond asked me if I wanted to go off but the game was on a knife edge. How could I? It was painful, puffed up and not easy to keep wicket. But I just had to keep going. Apart from the Gillette it hadn't been the best of seasons. The Gillette was our only chance."

Truth is that he had suffered a dismal time with the bat. Atrocious weather was partly responsible, cutting down time in the middle. The team in general were struggling. From my admittedly poor vantage point in the Press Box I felt that for once he seemed unsure of himself. One low score followed another, the spark was missing.

The clash with Kent proved that he had not lost heart and that, no matter what his batting problems, he was still vital to Lancashire's progress. With the big-hitting Julien and Bob Woolmer at the crease Kent needed 43 off 11 overs. Not easy with Lancashire's fielding livewires on red alert but Julien had just smashed Simmons for two sixes in an over and looked dangerous. Bond and Engineer conferred. Adjustments were made. From that point on Kent failed to notch another boundary, the scoring rate drooped and Engineer's shouts and calls of encouragement grew louder and ever more confident.

"Lancashire drove Kent relentlessly below the required rate, the major part in this period being played by Engineer," said the *Daily Telegraph*. As they panicked David Hughes grabbed the last three wickets in 15 balls, one being Engineer's stumping of Derek Underwood, giving Lancashire a seven runs win and another Lord's final. Throughout the morning Engineer had to wipe blood from the cut above his eye and later it required stitches. Picking the man of the match from such a wonderful game was tricky. The umpires, in the absence of the official judge, handed it to Pilling although my choice was Hughes, always in the action, a match-winning all-round performance. Engineer was also a candidate, an Indian with British bulldog spirit.

Two days later Lancashire took on Worcestershire in a mid-table Sunday game at Old Trafford with little at stake. Engineer was out of action and I grabbed the chance to have a chat, asking him whether he would be ok for the Lord's showpiece in a fortnight's time. "Why not? Don't worry I'll be there. I'm not going to miss that." I gestured at his eye. "It looks a bit of a mess." But he just made a joke of it. "I'm a quick healer. Anyway the women will want to mother me. They love a wounded soldier."

Engineer was at Lord's of course. But with the eye still swollen and troubling him, his performance was not one for the scrapbook. Fortunately Lancashire had Clive Lloyd who brought Lord's to its feet with 126 including three sixes, sealing a four wickets win and a hat-trick of Gillette Cups. What a send-off for Bond. The captain's Old Trafford farewell came on September 10, the last league game, players and officials forming a guard of honour for him, fans cheering and clapping him all the way onto the pitch. He signed off by clouting a six.

"An emotional day," says Engineer. "A great man, a great captain. It was an honour to play with him."

CHAPTER 17

WHEN ENGLAND under the auspices of the MCC arranged a tour of the sub-continent in 1972-73, offering the chance to quickly avenge their 1971 setback, they sent out invitations to 42 players in the preceding August asking politely whether they would be available for selection. Several, including Ray Illingworth and Geoff Boycott, turned the opportunity down. Boycs explained that he needed the winter to fully get over a recent op on his spleen. The other no-shows basically said: 'No way.' Could you blame them? Four months in India, Ceylon (Sri Lanka) and Pakistan? A year earlier India and Pakistan had fought a short war over the independence of Bangladesh and in the minds of some players this was a tour fraught with danger. Terrorist groups all over the place, an outbreak of cholera in Bengal, stifling heat, lifeless pitches....you name it they didn't want it.

The replies hurried back to Lord's. Illingworth and M.J.K. Smith turned down the captaincy opening the way for a Welshman, Tony Lewis, and other 'Thank you but no thank you' responses from John Edrich, Richard Hutton, Peter Parfitt, Mike Smith and John Snow piled up on the desk of MCC secretary and tour manager Donald Carr. He could still turn out a decent enough side but nothing like full strength and India, understandably, were outraged.

It had happened several times before. Some England players did not relish the sub-continental conditions, both on and off the field. It was a seam bowler's graveyard for one thing and batsmen had problems playing their shots on slow, dusty wickets tailor-made for the Indian spinners. And you got sick in India, either from sunstroke or a dicey meal. All in all not worth the trouble. Best to have a quiet winter at home, put the feet up, have a nice Christmas with the family. Who is going to criticise you or pressurise you into changing your mind? No-one.

This time was different. India were the world's top team, judged by their hat-trick of series wins in New Zealand, West Indies and England. South Africa were out of contention because of the apartheid ban and the one missing scalp, Australia, had in turn been beaten by England. World champs had a right to expect that the opposition would send out their best players but again India had been snubbed.

Farokh Engineer was incensed. "There was no good reason to pull out of this tour. Had they no pride? Surely a professional player at the top level wants to test himself against the best - and at that time India were the best. We felt angry. It seemed that there were some people in England who would always look at India differently than other countries. They were negative and would talk about all the things that could go wrong, rather than looking it as a challenge. They should have looked at the good things, playing in front of 50,000 crowds for one and enjoying the genuine warmth of the Indian people. For me the positives heavily outweighed the negatives."

Lancashire's doughty opener Barry Wood, one of the 16 chosen to fly out to Bombay on November 30, looked forward to it. 'Sawdust' had made his Test debut in the August, taking on Dennis Lillee in the fifth Ashes Test at the Oval and impressing with his second innings 90, getting into line and being prepared to hook. Now he faced the world's best spinners on their own dusty soil. David Lloyd reckoned he should have gone instead.

The argument went like this: Wood, better against pace than spin - keep him in reserve for the Ashes tour the following winter. Lloyd - better against spin than pace, give him a baptism in India. England did it the other way around. Bumble's horses for courses theory seemed sensible enough but how could you drop a player after just one Test when he came close to a century? And, no matter who was bowling, Wood was a scrapper determined not to give his wicket away easily. Unfortunately Lloyd was proved right. Wood struggled. Bishan Bedi soon had his measure and dismissed him four times in the first three Tests after which Wood, with only 101 runs to his credit, was sidelined. In 1974 Lloyd did get to play against India and hit a record breaking double century only for Lillee, Jeff Thomson and a neck injury to curtail his Test career a few months later. Wood and Lloyd never played together for England and between them this fine opening pair made only 21 Test appearances.

While many agreed with Lloyd, Wood bounced into Delhi for the first Test on the back of a century against a modest Central Zone attack in Indore and immediately met up with Engineer. "He took me to some kind of fete," Wood said, "and plied me with coconut juice. That night I got dysentery and lost almost a stone in weight and it's fair to say that I never fully recovered for the rest of the tour. Obviously I did not blame Rooky. I subsequently learned that the juice was often topped up with water and that is probably what caused the problem."

Engineer snorts: "There was nothing wrong with what we drank. He must have had something else that disagreed with him."

Whatever the cause, for a fit as a flea player like Wood the debilitating effect of Delhi Belly was disastrous. He had a couple of days to get over it before the first Test in which he endured a total of four hours torment from the spinners, scoring a creditable 45 in the second knock, but was nowhere near his best during that tour whether or not he had the appropriate technique. He fielded brilliantly but given the chance to bowl at Delhi he came up against none other than Engineer. "I had figures of 6-0-36-0. He scored them all. It was the first and last time I bowled for England in a Test."

Wood's memory is wrong there. Actually his stint was 2-0-13-0 before Lewis pulled him off. With Engineer bounding down the pitch, bat raised, and his guts still nagging away at him it probably just felt like 0-36! Engineer explains: "However good a bowler Woody was in England - and he was extremely good in those conditions having taken Sobers' wicket a number of times - his type of bowling would have lit up the eyes of most Indian batsmen. In India for a bowler to have success he has to be really quick with the ball movement in the air and off the pitch and unfortunately Woody was neither."

Engineer hammered 63 but could not stop England from popping the Indian bubble. Lewis, rapidly establishing himself as an astute leader, was in charge of a mixed bunch alright, but somehow discovered a winning formula. While India continued to rely almost exclusively on Chandra, Bedi, Venkat and Prasanna, Lewis demanded stamina draining spells from his seamers, notably Geoff Arnold and Chris Old, and they responded magnificently. Later in the innings he had Derek Underwood, Norman Gifford and Pat Pocock to exploit any turn. Arnold had match figures of 9-91 at Delhi and not even Chandra's first innings 8-79, the best of his career, could sway it. Tony Greig was England's other major hit - India could not shift him. His unbeaten 68 earned a narrow lead and he was with Lewis in an unbroken stand of 101 when they clinched a six wickets victory on Christmas Day.

India recoiled in shock. This had not been in the stars. Not only had Chandra's very best not been enough, Sunil Gavaskar had flopped. So had Dilip Sardesai. Badly drained of confidence, lacking the support of Vijay Merchant who had been replaced as selectors' chairman, Sardesai called it a day, a disappointing end to a career which had climbed a formidable summit in the Caribbean two years earlier. While India re-grouped, England plotted a same again performance for Calcutta's Eden Gardens. This, though, was to be Engineer's match.

While the MCC had settled on a weakened (apparently) squad, the travelling English Press Corps was unusually at full strength. Those who had never visited the sub-continent were amazed by the sight of 70,000 fans cramming into Eden Gardens, providing a backdrop of colour and noise to the drama on centre stage. When Engineer was called out to bat just before tea on the opening day India had at first crawled (53-1 at lunch) and had then struggled to 100-5. Gavaskar and Ajit Wadekar, run out and complaining of feeling unwell, were among those back in the hut along with Salim Durani who fell cheaply on his recall to Test cricket.

Arnold, who had pulled out with illness, was not there but his replacement Chris Old, a 23 years-old Yorkshireman, was making it a debut to remember with some superb pace bowling. India, 1-0 down from Delhi, were in serious trouble. World champs? Eyebrows were raised. "Cometh the hour, cometh the man," laughs Engineer when he talks about that moment. "Who couldn't be inspired by something like that?"

Just as at Madras in 1967, Engineer marched out, sleeves rolled up and while I have not obtained any evidence and while he cannot remember, I bet he looked up at that packed Press Box and smiled. This was a script made for him. But his response was totally different from the gung-ho approach in Madras where, as an opener, his team still had the resources to recover if he flopped. In Calcutta he could not afford to take chances. He had a responsibility to salvage something from the wreckage, knowing there was one batsman, Syed Abid Ali to come before the woefully weak tail-end. Moreover, with Wadekar unwell, he was about to become India's acting captain. "Pressure? Yes, but I always responded to that sort of situation. I loved batting in front of those massive crowds."

Engineer produced a captain's innings, stifling the pace and swing of Old and his seam partner Bob Cottam, the tricky left arm of Underwood, and the off cutters of Greig. No-one else could cope with the variety and accuracy of

England's attack, backed up by immaculate fielding, particularly of Wood. Engineer stuck it out to the end of the first day with India 148-5, Ekky Solkar helping him to stem the collapse. On the next morning India added 62 with Engineer claiming 49 of them, protecting the vulnerable tail-enders along the way and finishing with 75 when he had a hoick at Underwood and was bowled after three hours 35 minutes at the crease.

India went on to win by 28 runs. A cliffhanger with 703 runs and 40 wickets. Drama all the way with Durani 's second innings 53, Chandra's nine victims, and a marvellous all-round display by the 6 feet 6 inches tall Greig all filling Mr Swanton's notebook. But, not for the first time, Engineer's batting was the crux of a decisive Indian win. And, not for the first time, I believe his contribution to be under rewarded. When Pataudi was brought back for the third Test in Madras and hit 73 India went wild. Here was their 'Tiger', their great champion slaying the opposition once more and wasn't it wonderful? Grown men had tears in their eyes, women swooned. The Press lapped it up. India won that match too. Number one - yes!

Pataudi's romantic comeback was certain to grab the headlines. 'Coming in to a royal and tumultuous welcome...' reported *Wisden*, he went on the attack, reached 50 with a six and made 73 helping India to set a platform for another win. Was it as good, as defining as Engineer's 75 at Calcutta? Surely not. Engineer did it with little help, clicking off his attacking default mode to construct a patient rescue act. Pataudi did not switch styles. He was his old self, picking the right balls to punish. Two sixes and 10 fours encouraged *Wisden* to sell his innings as a 'glittering array of strokes' but there were long, quiet spells in a stay of three hours 50 minutes.

If Pataudi's was a great performance then what was Engineer's? I suggest that it was at least as good and at least as important yet he did not receive anything like the applause. Engineer took some consolation from the accolades bestowed on him for his captaincy at Calcutta where he led the side for parts of the game and for all the final act when India foiled England from reaching a target of 192.

"It wasn't unusual for me to act as captain. I was the senior player and I had a good rapport with the boys. Not only that I had a lot of experience and I knew how to work with the spinners, helping them to set fields. I had done that anyway in my work as a wicketkeeper. You need respect as a captain. I feel I had that, both in the way I played my cricket and the way I tried to encourage other people.

"I certainly remember that Calcutta game. If England had gone 2-0 up in the series I think all hell would have broken loose and they had a real chance. Tony Greig was making a real difference for them. They needed 192 with plenty of time and they went into the final day at 105-4. They had been 17-4 early on but Greig and Denness stopped them collapsing completely and were still together. Greig was scoring lots of runs already in the series, the pitch was turning a bit but not viciously and before play started that final morning we learned that Wadekar had suddenly become unwell and could not take the field. I was handed the captaincy.

"We had our spinners but with Greig still there England looked favourites. I thought the only way we could win was to launch an all-out attack, surround them with fielders and let Chandra at them. I wanted to force them to take chances, which they did and they paid the price. Everything went my way. Bowling changes, fielding changes, they all turned out right. England started to panic. Chandra had Greig lbw, Alan Knott caught at mid-wicket and Denness lbw in a spell of 3-5. That was it really. Bedi weighed in with a couple, Their last wicket pair added some runs but I always felt confident we would do it and Bedi finished it.

"Chandra's magic was crucial. But I like to think that my tactics won the game. I enjoyed those few hours. It was a momentous day, a wonderful victory. We levelled the series and went on to win it and that cemented our position as the best team in the world. Of course Wadekar suddenly got better. The record books will show that he had won another Test as captain but that's record books for you."

After Pataudi's triumphant return in Madras, Wadekar went on the defensive in the last two matches to ensure India kept their lead. The fifth and last Test on a good Bombay pitch presented Engineer with an opportunity to finish the series on a high note in front of his home crowd and he grabbed it with both hands, striking his second century and helping Wadekar pile on 192 for the second wicket.

"It was the last official Test on the hallowed turf of the Brabourne Stadium - I praise the work of Raj Singh Dungarpur and other presidents and committees who have maintained the highest standards." says Engineer who loves that ground. "The home of the elite Cricket Club of India with its magnificent clubhouse. Most of the bedrooms or suites overlook one of the most picturesque and finest grounds in the world - it was rumoured that the great Sir Frank Worrell would rest in his suite before going out to bat. It was an honour just to play there, to score a century in a Test there was very special.

"When I got out and was heading back the late Mr J.R.D. Tata, head of the TATA conglomerate, came down the steps of the governor's pavilion to give me a big hug and congratulate me. I had to apologise as I was sweating profusely and spoiling his white safari suit. He followed me into the dressing-room and handed me a glass of water, a nice thing for him to do. Then when I was sitting down with a cold towel over my head I felt somebody trying to unbuckle my pads - it was him! One of the world's most powerful businessmen. It was a humbling experience. I was embarrassed but it showed the humility of the man. He asked me to lunch with him at Bombay House."

Greig made sure that India kept working for the draw with a magnificent century of his own. The tall South African born all-rounder certainly made an impression in India, not always a good one. In Madras he confronted umpire Ahmad Mansa with a volley of abuse, forcing tour manager Donald Carr to issue an apology. But Engineer wiped out any hopes England might have harboured, following up his century with 66 in the second innings when he shared in a big opening stand with Gavaskar.

Engineer headed the batting averages for that series with a total of 415 at 41.5, the second series in succession against England that he averaged over 40. Most of the time he batted at 7, sometimes with the side in the mire, and when at Bombay he was allowed to open he stole the show with some uninhibited driving and pulling. Add on his leadership at Calcutta and you might say he had a decent winter.

As the highest scoring batsman on either side, Engineer won a full-sized silver bat from an Indian jeweller. "I beat Greig to the prize. I enjoyed doing that. Anyway when I flew back to England I thought I had better declare it at customs and I told one of the officers that I had something unusual to show them. 'It wouldn't be a silver cricket bat would it?' he said. Apparently he had read about it in a newspaper."

A second prize presented to Engineer was a scooter. "It was no good to me because I was flying back to England the next day. Someone came up to me saying we had been to school together. I didn't recognise him but I asked him if he wanted a brand new scooter. He was dumbfounded but he took it away grinning all over his face."

Farokh with Fred Trueman, Colin Cowdrey, Sir John Major and Godfrey Evans.

Lord's Taverners Dinner.
Standing: Colin Cowdrey, Fred Trueman, Trevor Bailey, Tom Graveney, Farokh Engineer.
Seated: Sir Len Hutton, Denis Compton, Godfrey Evans, Keith Miller, Alec Bedser.

Farokh with two of India's greatest batsman Sunil Gavaskar and Sachin Tendulkar.

Farokh with megastar Shah Rukh Khan.

With Salman Khan - "Whose mum makes the best biryani".

In Dubai with Andrew 'Freddie' Flintoff and Geoff Baker.

Partying in Barbados with Wes Hall and Garry Sobers.

With Jeffrey Archer,
Sir John Major and
Freddie Trueman.

Lunching with
Sir Michael
Parkinson.

In the garden with some of his trophies.

Cricket in the snow in Switzerland with Tiger Pataudi, wife Begum Sharmila Tagora and wife Julie. Below: Farokh's greatest inspiration, brother Darius.

Dilip Vengsarkar, Sachin Tendulkar and Yuvraj Singh.

Sky studio with Charles Colville and Darren Gough.

Gillette cup winners with Clive and David Lloyd.

Two of Farokh's heroes, Fred Trueman and Brian Statham.

With World XI opening partner Barry Richards and Piers Morgan.

Being felicitated at Lord's

Entering No. 10 Downing Street.

Above and below: With great friend Dilip Vengsarkar.
Three consecutive 100s at Lord's - "Great achievement buddy".

FOTOCORP

PTI

Two Lords

With his upturned collar, long sideburns and swashbuckling ways, Farokh Engineer was the cricketer everyone swooned after. The dependable 'Colonel', of course, had other charms. The two met on the a 90th birthday bash for Queen Elizabeth in Mumbai.

Above: Champagne with Sachin Tendulkar and Anupam Kher in Mumbai. Left: Virat Kohli in Trinidad presenting Farokh with the bat with which he scored a double century in a previous Test in the West Indies.

Above: No Prasanna, but the rest of the Indian spin quartet are here. Farokh with Chandrasekhar, Venkataraghavan and Bedi.

Below: With M.S. Dhoni, a fellow Indian wicketkeeper/batsman.

Above: With Pele in Mauritius.

Below: With "the Greatest Sportsman ever" Mohammed Ali after he presented Farokh with his book. It took twenty minutes for him to write a special personal message and he even threw a jovial punch to complete a most memorable evening.

Farokh with dear friend Jeffrey Archer at one of his fabulous parties.

At Manchester Bridge Club with partner Jeff Morris. They were MCC Bridge Champions in the Long Room at Lord's.

With wife Julie.

With his four daughters Minnie, Tina, Roxanne and Scarlett with baby Zia in Tina's tummy

A proud grandfather showing off one and only grand daughter Zia.

For all his runs and motivating captaincy, the moment I cherish from the 1972-73 series is Engineer's stumping of Knott off Chandra at a crucial stage of the Calcutta match. Film footage shows Knott taking a controlled step forward, missing an attempt to paddle the ball to leg but keeping his back foot in safety and then...what was that?! A flash of movement and a huge appeal. For what? Not a catch, Knott obviously did not make contact. A stumping - how?! when Knott's back foot has not moved from the crease and the ball was going well down the legside. But Engineer is screaming for it and it's given. Knott, still down on one knee, stares at the square leg umpire. Then twists his neck to look behind him. You cannot see his face at that moment but you can assume it is one of utter disbelief. Knott has lifted his foot fractionally, just enough to let an ant squeeze under it. Just enough to fall into the spider's web. Knott was batting well. His dismissal helped to give India a narrow but vital lead and, it could be argued, changed the course of the series.

"I'd set an attacking field, Chandra was bowling in the right area and it was difficult to score. Knott got impatient and tried to swipe a ball down the legside. His back foot lifted just an inch or two but that was enough for me. It changed the entire complexion of the game."

Engineer had cause to believe that the good times would just roll on and on. Lancashire were gearing up for another trophy hunt. New players were coming through to augment the squad which had already conquered English cricket and before his exit Jack Bond had nominated a replacement captain who shared many of his ethics, thought just as deeply about the game, excelled in the field and was a good enough batsman to feel that one day he would play for England.

For me, David Lloyd had one extra quality - he said what he felt. Manna from heaven for us scribes. Only once did he fail to respond to my irrelevant, irreverent and irresponsible interrogations. That was when Ken Higgs, playing late in his career for Leicestershire, and Jack Birkenshaw thwarted Lancashire of an easy win with a defiant last wicket stand. Diving into the morose dressing-room to demand an explanation from the skipper I said rather accusingly: "What went wrong?" Frowning, Bumble said: "What can I say?" A voice from the back shouted: "Tell him to piss off!"

Lloyd's first season, without the services of Clive Lloyd who was touring England with the West Indies, went ok but, for the first time since 1968, Old Trafford was a trophy free zone. The bad weather of earlier years became worse, quickly wrecking their championship dream and four Sunday League matches were abandoned, leading to a successful campaign to change the points system - two for a washed out game instead of one. They suffered their first Gillette Cup defeat since 1969 when going down to Middlesex in the quarter-finals.

Through it all Engineer gave Lloyd solid support. He liked keeping to Peter Lee, the barrel-chested seamer signed from Northants. "We called him Leapy. He would bowl and bowl long spells and he took bagfuls of wickets. Over 100 that season. Bumble called him a dream bowler. He couldn't get the ball off him sometimes." Against Yorkshire Lee bowled unchanged for two hours after which he had taken 5-7. He took 8-53, four of them having their stumps uprooted, against Sussex and 8-80, including a spell of 7-15 in 45 balls against Notts whose batting line-up included 19 years-old Wayne Larkins and the 'promising Randall'. Lee twice claimed over 100 first-class wickets in a season. He never played for England.

From Engineer there were ever more brilliant catches, eight in the match with Notts, and some hearty knocks crowned by his first county century in two years when he belted Surrey for an unbeaten 128 and he was Lancashire's highest scorer on Sundays. Other compensations for Lancashire were the emergence of Frank Hayes as England's new Golden Boy, the all-round strengths of David Hughes and the continuing good form of Wood, Harry Pilling and Lloyd himself. They missed Big Clive, of course. That, and the rain, were the major factors in Lancashire's reduction.

Engineer recounted one particular incident which gave him immense pleasure. "We were playing Warwickshire at their place and John Jameson gave us one hell of a battering. He was a powerful batsman, it was a good wicket and he had just been picked for the winter tour of the West Indies. But Leapy got his 100th wicket when I took an edge from Norman McVicker. And then I dished out some punishment of my own when we batted. Lance Gibbs was bowling. I remember going down the track to him and middling one. It landed on the pavilion roof."

If that is reminiscent of a certain event in Madras six years before then this one was well documented by reporters. 'Engineer treated Gibbs with disdain,' said one.

CHAPTER 18

CRICKET CAPTAINCY has been described as an art, a science, a philosophy. I asked Brian Statham about it: Typically there was a long pause and a sigh before the answer came: "You have to know a bit about the game," he said. And lapsed back into silence. "George (Statham) was a great bloke but he couldn't captain a rowing boat," said Peter Lever, affectionately. Essentially Statham led by example, although he did not necessarily put in extra effort, he just bowled like he always did and that was example enough to anyone. I asked David Green who led Lancashire occasionally and might have succeeded Statham had it not been for his predilection for telling committee members exactly what he thought of them. "You have to stick up for the lads," said Green who once quarrelled with the selection committee over the dropping of Geoff Pullar, though Statham advised him to go with their decision and not cause trouble. Green got his way, Pullar played and scored a century at the Oval. Green, however, would not have made an effective permanent skipper - the responsibility would have burdened him.

Cyril Washbrook, Lancashire's first professional captain, granted me a rare interview in 1991. He did not talk freely to anyone never mind the Press. The first time I ever spoke to him, about 20 years earlier, I made the dreadful error of calling him 'Cyril'. He gave me a glare which left a sprinkling of frost on my sleeve, ordered me to address him properly in future, turned his back and walked away. This time I had to apply in writing, via his solicitor son, and although he agreed to meet he insisted on formality, so I put on my best bib and tucker and said: "Mr Washbrook, how would you describe yourself as a captain?"

"A total bastard," said (Mr) Washbrook. Several of his team would have agreed. No-one could have led more by example in discipline and fortitude but man management was not his strongest suit. "Young man," he told me, tapping my chest with a thick forefinger. "You have to be a total bastard otherwise no-one respects you."

Lancashire had terrible problems over their captaincy. One after another had tried and failed before they pulled Jack Bond back from the verge of retirement. And several others struggled after him. Like Mike Brearley he could not always justify his place purely as a batsman but he possessed the ingredients which raised Lancashire from a decent side into the most successful in the club's history.

Engineer and others have talked in detail about his qualities, his tactical astuteness, his organisation, his ability to get the best out of players and weld them into a team of winners. But he was a one-off. David Hughes led Lancashire into their second era of 'One Day Kings' at the start of the 1990s but suffered dressing-room strife which resulted in him dropping himself on the eve of the 1991 Benson and Hedges Cup final in favour of an extra batsman. Lancashire were well beaten. Under Mike Watkinson Lancashire enjoyed a series of Lord's finals but he too could not claim anything like the support Bond had.

In my time as a cricket writer there were others who commanded respect for their talent and team ethic, for example Frank Hayes, Neil Fairbrother and John Crawley but as captains they won only one major trophy between them. Hayes and Fairbrother could not stop the responsibility affecting their form. Crawley's reign ended contentiously after a row with the committee. It all underlines that captaincy is a complex subject. Art, science, philosophy - perhaps a mix of all three with lots of other components chucked in. Luck, if you believe in that. The coincidence of circumstances where things that you cannot control all come to play in your favour, for just an instant or maybe over a few years. Even then success is not guaranteed. You have to best control what is within your control. Bond did that.

India had many issues over their captaincy. But where, in the grey chilly realism of north-west England success and popularity were usually gauged by an inventory of the trophy cabinet, in the warmer hued romanticism of the sub-continent the empty-handed could still be revered. Defeat could be a cause for celebration if you went down gallantly. Pataudi, for example, 'was always associated with glorious losses rather than glorious wins' (*Mihir Bose, A History of Indian Cricket*). Pataudi was that kind of player. Engineer thought him a heroic captain, as did most of India most of the time he was in charge, yet there were personal flaws and team defeats. In Ajit Wadekar's time India climbed to the summit but after a horrible tour of England when India did not go down waving the flag he was kicked out unceremoniously. Engineer's view of him is more circumspect than of Pataudi, especially when dealing with Wadekar's untimely illness at Calcutta in 1972.

So, accepting that only rarely do we find the perfect captain, what were Farokh Engineer's chances? He never captained Lancashire. With India he only took over when Wadekar or Pataudi went off the field. Yet in Wadekar's self imposed absence at Calcutta he showed enterprise and guts as India grabbed a breathtaking win. As Bose stated '...it was noticeable what a difference his bright, engaging approach made.'

Obviously then, in India's next tour - England 1974 - Engineer would be the prime candidate for the vice-captaincy under Wadekar. Not so. Politics and mischief again. Venkataraghavan was chosen as Wadekar's lieutenant even though he was not guaranteed a place in the three from four spinners equation. As arguments raged Wadekar, possibly feeling unsure of himself and following a row over pay with Bishan Bedi, posted himself as unfit with a finger injury for the first Test at Old Trafford. He wanted to withdraw but the prospect of Venkat taking over, and therefore keeping Prasanna out of the line-up, provoked open rebellion. In the end both Wadekar and Venkat played and both had shockers. It was the overture to the tour from hell.

Why Engineer was shunned is impossible to say. Even he cannot pinpoint the reason. "Just the usual - politics." As it happened he was hampered by an ankle injury which was to blight his whole summer but he played and was prepared as ever to take on the vice-captaincy. Somebody up there did not like Engineer. Previously it was Vijay Merchant who railed against Engineer's decision to play county cricket. There is little doubt that he considered it a kind of desertion. Now India had a new selectors' chairman, C.D. Gopinath from Madras. Engineer was from Bombay. Venkat was from Madras. Enough said. Well perhaps not enough actually.

Leaving aside selectors' prejudices, did Engineer have what it takes to be a good captain? I think so. It would have been a roller-coaster reign but never short of entertainment with embarrassing defeats interspersed by wonderful victories. He proved at Calcutta that he could cleverly manage the spinners and lift the side as a whole. One weakness was his sensitivity to a bad Press and dressing-room mutterings if things went wrong. Maybe he would not have lasted that long, perhaps a couple of series. But he was definitely worth a go. In fact, for him, one match would have been enough to fulfil his dream of leading his country.

His one real chance came in the winter of 1974-75 when the West Indies toured India. Wadekar had gone, Pataudi was back in the driving seat again but after a terrible thrashing in the first match at Bangalore he pulled out of the second clash at Delhi with a finger injury. The alternative was Sunil Gavaskar but he too was on the injury list, hurt playing in a Ranji Trophy game for Bombay. Who next? Engineer seemed an obvious candidate but no-one knew what was happening. On the eve of the match there were frantic phone calls between selectors. The chairman, Gopinath, was held up in Madras and said he would not get to Delhi until the morning. That evening at a pre-match reception a vice president of the board, Ram Prakash Mehra introduced to all and sundry the new captain of Indian - Farokh Engineer.

Engineer draws a breath here. The manner of that announcement and the events of the next 24 hours still hurt.

"He had consulted other officials from Delhi. They thought that a decision had to be made, that they could not wait. There was too much uncertainty," Engineer said. "We had suffered a massive defeat in the first game, there was a lot of bickering going on and we needed someone to take the lead. It was wonderful to hear me being called onto the platform as the captain of India. There were reporters there and next morning there were stories about it in the newspapers.

"What made it even more special was that my good pal Clive Lloyd was the captain of the West Indies. We had roomed together on Lancashire trips and had shared so many good times. We were both adopted Lancastrians. Now we would be going out onto an Indian pitch to toss up in a Test match. It could not have been better. But at the ground that morning I could sense there was something very wrong. Players congratulated me but the atmosphere was tense. Then the manager Raj Singh Dugapur came up to me and said very quietly: 'Something sinister is going on behind our backs'.

"Even so no-one could have foreseen what was going to happen. Suddenly Venkat arrived in our dressing-room and presented a note from the heirarchy - Gopinath and his chum M.A. Chidambaram, the Board President who also, surprise, surprise, from Madras - saying that he was to captain India. This was literally seconds before Clive and I were to go out onto the pitch for the toss. We had our blazers on and a coin in hand.

"Rumour had it that they had chartered a plane from Madras to get Venky to the ground just in time. I don't believe this could have happened anywhere else in the cricketing world. It was a deceitful masterstroke. There was no apology to me. What made it worse was that Chandra who had taken a total of six wickets in the previous Test had to be dropped to accommodate Venky.

"Clive appeared and said something to me about the toss. I told him what had happened. He couldn't believe it. I felt like shit to be honest. There was nothing I could do but go out and show them something. Clive had told the West Indies boys all about it. Andy Roberts was bowling. He was fast and dangerous but I pulled and hooked and he shouted: 'Why are you taking it out on me man?' It was so funny. Everyone laughed including me. It broke the tension, made me feel a lot better. I didn't get many in the first innings but I played well in the second, got 70 or so, easily our highest score of the whole match. Venkat didn't do much to justify his new position. Viv Richards and the others clattered him and we lost by an innings. I don't blame and have never blamed Venky at all. It was not his doing. He was merely a pawn in a vicious circle.

"I knew then that I would never captain India officially. I would have to be content with what I had done all along, lead them in the field alongside Pataudi and Wadekar. I would never get the same credit as them, just personal satisfaction."

On the face of it Gopinath's regional bias denied Engineer the captaincy. The chairman was raging when he learned that the Bombay man had been chosen without consulting him. Engineer was never considered for the captaincy of Lancashire. Fair enough. He was getting on a bit by the time Jack Bond packed in and David Lloyd, bright, young and good - a smashing lad altogether - was a well judged successor. After that though perhaps Lancashire's own brand of regional bias set in. Clive Lloyd should have been appointed. By the mid 1970s he was leading the West Indies into a record breaking run of success. But he did not get the county job until 1981, 15 years after his Test debut, 12 years into his Old Trafford career. Crazy. His word, not mine, although I agreed forcibly when we talked about it some years ago.

"I wanted it," he said. "It could have been good. I would have brought in top players from the West Indies. Why I didn't get it I don't know for sure. I just hope there were no ulterior motives."

"Touch of racism?" I asked.

"I wouldn't like to think so," he replied. "But they knew I wanted it."

Part of Lancashire's reasoning was that Lloyd would miss too much county cricket because of international commitments. There was some substance in this. But some at Old Trafford also wanted a 'home-grown' captain. Struggling as they did from the mid 1970s on, it seemed bizarre that they waited until Lloyd was 37 years-old before handing him the reins. It was far too late and the captaincy continued to befuddle Lancashire.

Engineer never really recovered from the blow which Gopinath delivered at Delhi. He played only three more Tests and even now over 40 years later his face creases in frustration. "It was a real kick in the guts. So underhand. And humiliating. My picture was in the newspapers as captain of India. People would have been still reading the story when Venky went out for the toss. They must have wondered what the hell was going on. I do not believe I had done anything to deserve treatment like that. But that was Indian cricket. You can laugh about some of the things went on I suppose. But not if you were a victim of it. The politics and power games that went on were disgraceful, the worst of their kind. People who knew little or nothing about our game were only out to further their own cause, their own power and of course their own bank balances. It was rotten to the core, not just in my time but before and since. Selectors and managers acted like dictators. Everyone was scared of opposing them for fear of being kicked out. There have been exceptions but Indian cricket was full of these people."

Critics of Engineer, certainly the many admirers of Vijay Merchant, may claim that he was the author of his own misfortune by tying himself so tightly to England. Other countries and other sports have demanded that their stars stay at home. Engineer retorts: "I was never asked about it. I joined Lancashire in 1968 and they continued to pick me for India. There was never any problem with me playing in England. And, as we played England more than most, it was the experience of playing in English conditions which helped me to do so well on the 1971 tour. There was no consistency at all. It was all about politics. A few officials have held it against me for making my home in England even though I have always been very proud to be an Indian."

Even Pataudi suffered in Engineer's opinion. "We were both flamboyant characters and some of them in authority preferred people who kept quiet and did not disturb anything. Pataudi liked a practical joke. We were in the Windies once, on one of the smaller islands and a hurricane had been forecast. Pat and I went down to hotel reception and rang every room pretending to the receptionists, warning the players that the hurricane was coming and they had to come down to the lobby immediately, bringing anything breakable with them. They all appeared, some in their underpants, carrying all manner of little objects, bottles and things."

Pataudi also had a link with England. Was it coincidence that both he and Engineer suffered such problems? Engineer does not think so. "In Pat's case it was about politics, power. I came to England and stayed. In my view that doesn't make me any less an Indian but obviously others have thought differently."

As for Wadekar by the summer of 1974 he was garlanded with the title of the most successful captain in Indian history with four wins and only one defeat in 14 Tests, recording two series wins over England and one over West Indies. His autobiography with a foreword from Merchant was selling well. Yet within a few months he was very much yesterday's man.

Jack Bond's official connection with Lancashire also ended in acrimony. After retiring as Lancashire's captain he worked with Notts at Trent Bridge for a season before moving to the Isle of Man. He returned to Old Trafford as coach, with Peter Lever as his assistant, in 1983. Lever had retired in 1976 and so I was intrigued when, one evening after the end of a championship match, I spotted him working out in the nets on the practice field. Bond tersely refused to enlighten me. Next morning 'Plank' was named in an injury-hit side for a NatWest Trophy (formerly Gillette Cup) tie with Somerset. Aged 42 he bowled a very tight spell, an appropriate footnote to a long career.

Bond and Lever were still in their coaching positions in 1986 by when John Abrahams' stint had ended and Clive Lloyd was back for a brief second spell despite struggling with injury. He missed a lot of cricket and when Lancashire slipped to a NatWest Trophy final defeat by Sussex, Bond and Lever were instantly sacked by chairman Cedric Rhoades. The subsequent row came to a head at the members' AGM in December.

Bond rang me the day before. told me to make sure I was there and 'paying attention and not messing about as usual' and that I would hear a question of the chairman. The answer, he said. might or might not provoke a storm. I liked a good old set-up. Anyway when Rhoades threw the meeting open a member stood up and asked him whether Lloyd had been appointed captain on Bond's recommendation. Rhoades said yes. Afterwards Bond collared me and accused Rhoades of deceit. "I did not recommend Clive," he stated firmly. It was a decent story, ending with Rhoades resignation after almost 20 years in control. "I have given my life to this club," he said, close to tears. Few had sympathy for him.

As for Engineer's captaincy ambitions he said: "I would have enjoyed being a captain but it wasn't to be and I had to accept it. One of the greatest disappointments of all. I would have brought the best out in me because I loved a challenge. It would have made me more determined than ever to succeed and make the team succeed.

"I certainly would have liked to be a captain in English cricket. Very few in my days in county cricket attacked. It was a very defensive mind-set. Tony Greig was a good captain. I saw him set attacking fields to some ordinary bowlers at Sussex and he understood that psychology is an important part of the game. He was very aggressive, sometimes went too far and sometimes talked a better game than he played but he was a strong leader. I also didn't like the way he abused the trust placed in him when he became Kerry Packer's recruiting agent.

"But getting back to captains.. .there were others like Norman Gifford at Worcestershire and obviously Ray Illingworth who understood cricket. David Lloyd came in for some criticism at times but he was a better captain than some people realised. He was a good batsman and he thought deeply about the game. But it was difficult for him to follow in Jacky's footsteps. Bond was the finest captain I played under. What made him so special? A touch of gold dust."

CHAPTER 19

SPRING 1974. Manchester. India were on their way. So were the Irish Republican Army. Luckily they never met but....

The *Manchester Evening News* Sports Editor wanted a piece on Farokh Engineer for the *Pink Final* edition. A 500 words page lead - 'so make it sing' was the instruction. I jogged along Deansgate, past the City Hall where a year earlier rain had stopped play in a world championship snooker match (believe me), jumped onto one of the electric trains which buzzed between the city and its outskirts and alighted at Warwick Road, then a drab, pitiless station glorified by every Lancashire and United fan for its proximity to both grounds.

Luckily, Engineer was just emerging from the dressing room. He had spent most of the winter recovering from a troublesome ankle injury and was waiting to link up with his Indian team mates when they flew out from Bombay.

As usual he was as helpful as could be, revealing that he would be 100 per cent fit for the tour and was licking his lips at the thought of taking on England in the first Test 'just out there', pointing through the pavilion window to the Old Trafford pitch where head groundsman Bert Flack and his staff were working.

"It would be great if you got a hundred here," I said, hoping he would agree and then I could make the page lead 'sing' - Engineer pledges Old Trafford century or words to that effect. He did not take the bait. For once his swashbuckling had a little less swash about it. I pushed him about his fitness. The doctors had sorted out his injury, torn ligaments and he would be fine. He had rung the Board of Control to assure them.

I returned to my agency's office, typed out my article on a black, heavy metal Imperial machine and phoned it over the MEN's copy room. A few minutes later the agency boss Peter, all pinstripe suit and cigarette ash, strode into the office and said: "If you've finished with the cricket, old boy, get over to the magistrates court and see Stan. He's got something on the IRA girls."

As well as covering sport our agency worked on crime so we were deep into the Provisional IRA bombing campaign in the North-West. Stan was my senior colleague. The 'IRA girls' were the Gillespie sisters who worked at Manchester Royal Infirmary, had a part-time job making bombs and had been arrested after an explosion at their home in Fallowfield. Another operative had decided to light a cigarette while stirring the 'mix' in a large bowl, an incident which sparked off a myriad 'Irish' jokes. Shortly after that, one Saturday night in April, an unknown Irishman walked into the wide open underground car park of the Manchester City Magistrates Court where we worked throughout the week, exploded a bomb, strolled back to his pub, told his mates about it and persuaded them to go back to the court precinct to view his work. There was massive damage with 12 people hurt.

India were due to arrive in Manchester within two months. The Lancashire chairman Cedric Rhoades shrugged off the thought of any danger but it was frighteningly easy to make and plant bombs. They were going off all over the place. Police were concerned that the Provos might target more public buildings and even sports stadia. Despite Rhoades' attitude, there was in fact a concern over the Old Trafford Test but the police, not wanting to add to the ill-ease, did not want to go public on it and I decided not to mention it to Engineer when I interviewed him. He had enough worries about his ankle - despite his assurances he did not seem too confident about it. And there were other things.

India's visit could not have been more badly timed, nor more badly arranged. Britain was in a state of emergency, chilled by continuing economic and social turmoil and political upheaval. A *Daily Mail* editorial tried to put a positive spin on it by declaring 'it is a chance for husbands and wives to experiment with their sex lives while the children are doing a five days week at school'. Prime Minister Ted Heath, unable to cope, put his trust in the chief of the civil service Sir William Armstrong who warned us of the Red Army and the approach of Armageddon before being hauled off to a psychiatric ward. "I thought he was acting oddly the last time I saw him," murmured Heath. To crown it all United were diving towards the second division and City lost the League Cup final.

What else could go wrong? For India, plenty. The tour in the first half of the summer had England's heavy brigade of seamers champing at the bit. England, on cool, damp days with green tinged pitches was no place to be either for an Indian batsman or a spinner. Chandra, Bedi, Prasanna and Venkat were additionally hampered before bowling a ball by the fact that their own Board had agreed an experimental law restricting the number of legside fielders to five. And, despite all his success, Ajit Wadekar felt so undermined by internal divisions that he asked Pataudi to join the squad only to be turned down.

If there could be such a thing as a cricketing Armageddon then India were heading towards it.

England waited expectantly to avenge their recent defeats but they, too, had issues over selection and the burgeoning disharmony between Geoff Boycott and the captain Mike Denness. One ray of optimism was the weather. Manchester, the City of Rain, was in a drought. Between mid February and June, the start of the Old Trafford Test, there were only four days of rain. But dear old Manchester refused to let anyone down. Suddenly, the day before the match, the weather went bitter and stayed like that for the whole game, heavy showers constantly forcing the players off and a cold breeze encouraging the slips to keep their hands stuffed into their pockets until the last moment.

Fans spurned it. A total of 21,000 - much lower than some of Lancashire's recent Sunday games - watched England win by 113 runs. The stay away thousands missed a truly masterful Sunil Gavaskar century, but India flopped to a combination of England's seamers, Bob Willis, Chris Old and Mike Hendrick, the shackling of their spinners, and the cautious attitude of Wadekar who shunned a victory target of 296 in six hours. Admittedly it was a huge challenge.

One of our detective friends had warned us to stay alert for suspicious looking characters and packages. The Fallowfield mishap had not put the IRA off. Bomb scares were becoming part of everyday life. I took his advice seriously. Each morning I got into the Press Box early and checked for anything out of the ordinary. A parcel, maybe. Or maybe a scruffy hold-all. Nothing big, it would not have taken much to blow the ageing 'shed' into smithereens. It leaked copiously. It rattled when late in the day the breeze got up and whistled through the cracks. Parts of the ground looked empty and desolate. I was glad when the match was over.

"Well at least you got Boycs," I said later. Engineer smiled. His tumbling catch when Boycott edged Ekky Solkar in the second innings effectively led to the opener's self imposed exile from Test cricket. Out of touch, Boycott struggled against Solkar's innocuous medium pace putting himself under severe pressure for the rest of the series. When his rift with Denness came more into the open he pulled out of the Lord's game and stayed away for almost three years giving David Lloyd an unexpected but deserved chance.

To make your Test debut at Lord's is every player's ambition and not even the library atmosphere of the England dressing-room, populated as it was by a number of quiet, introspective and experienced characters could put him off. Lloyd did well enough and he quickly formed alliances with the younger bowlers which 'livened the place up'. India's dressing room was funereal. Not even Engineer could lift the black curtain which had descended.

"It was a disaster. England scored over 600 (629 with three centuries and 48 for Lloyd). There were problems from the start and Chandra hurt his thumb after bowling only a few overs. He could not bowl again and that was a massive setback. Sunny and I did our best. We really tried to put their bowlers under pressure. We put on well over 100 and I got most of them. A couple of others got a few but it was hopeless. We had to follow on over 300 behind and then they shot us out in no time."

India had two overs on the Saturday evening without losing a wicket. When play resumed on the Monday England needed only a further 15 overs to demolish them for 42, earning an innings and 285 runs victory and wiping out their embarrassment of 1971. Later the jokers termed it the Tour of 42. Wadekar had completely lost his way. During England's massive first innings he tried time and time again to persuade Bedi to bowl a tighter line and restrict Denis Amiss. Bedi kept tossing it up and, although *Wisden* praised him for a long, excellent spell, Amiss marched to 188. Denness and Tony Greig also notched easy centuries. As well as being a magnificent bowler Bedi was also a combative character who had already caused a stink over players' wages. Well before the end it was obvious that Wadekar's authority was shattered.

Engineer: "Bedi was one of the greatest left-arm spinners. Such an easy, smooth action and he was not afraid to be hit. He kept on flighting that ball. In that particular game he simply bowled like he always did. I remember at Old Trafford that Boycott asked Bedi to bowl at him in the nets. Bedi told him: 'What's the point? You're never in long enough for me to bowl at you.'"

India stumbled from one shambles to another. After Lord's their opener Sudhir Naik was arrested for shoplifting two pairs of socks from Marks and Spencer. Naik protested his innocence but was persuaded to admit it by the tour management apparently on the grounds of expediency rather than justice. The incident made them late for a reception at the home of the Indian High Commissioner who felt insulted and threw a wobbly. Later he apologised for losing his temper, but the incident did not go down well and the Indian newspapers put the players in the wrong, placing a further question mark against Wadekar. Meanwhile Naik was in a deep, dark place, almost suicidal, having to return home labeled as a thief. Gavaskar, who roomed with him, helped him through it.

The last Test was on the flattest pitch imaginable at Edgbaston. Surely whoever won the toss would make a mountain of runs. Wadekar called correctly for the first time in the series but play was washed out on the first day and conditions again offered help to the seamers, particularly the experienced Geoff Arnold, who was causing havoc when Engineer walked out facing another crisis with India 81-4. At Lord's Engineer was the only batsman with a real cause for complaint in the second innings collapse, wrongly given lbw to Arnold. "I got a big edge on that ball," he explained. "How it could be given out I don't know. So I had an extra cause to do well at Edgbaston. For me there was always hope no matter how bad things appeared."

Wickets continued to fall at the other end. Engineer played well for an unbeaten 64 out of 84 added while he was in the middle. David Lloyd patted him on the back. A few minutes later Lloyd was opening for England. He stayed for the rest of the day and then throughout the next, piling up 214 not out. "I thought he would get a few runs on that pitch but not a double century," says Engineer. "He could have got a lot more but they declared with only two wickets down." India struggled again in their second innings although Naik demonstrated incredible mental toughness with his 77 and England completed the whitewash with another innings success, Lloyd becoming only the fourth player in Test history to be on the field for the whole match. "They beat us by an innings and lost only two wickets in the entire game," recalls Engineer. "It was a terrible time. Everyone wanted to get away but we still had two one-dayers to play. We lost them too."

Some of the Indians pondered how to avoid the mauling which awaited them back in Bombay. Wadekar and his wife went for a month's holiday in Europe, Engineer, Bedi (Northants) and Venkat (Derbyshire) stayed in England to play for their counties. Prasanna, the senior player, led the rest back to a barrage of abuse. Their bonuses were withheld, a committee of inquiry set up and Wadekar was hounded out of the game altogether. Engineer did not entirely escape criticism, one report claiming he had been 'impeded by a pre-season ankle injury.'

While he came good with the bat at Lord's and Edgbaston with 183 runs from four knocks, including the unlucky lbw, India's fractured team spirit, coupled with the conditions and fielding restrictions, eroded the bond between keeper, spinners and close-in catchers which had served them so well. Eventually they all suffered.

All the off the field problems made it a difficult tour for manager Col Hemu Adhikeri but Engineer smiles every time he thinks of him. "On an earlier tour there was a reception at Buckingham Palace. He had a passion for peanuts, flicking them into his mouth from all directions and he had grabbed a couple of handfuls from trays when the Queen suddenly made her entrance. She tried to shake hands with him but his were filled with peanuts. He tried to get out of it with 'namaste', the Indian greeting where you press the palms of your hands together and bow slightly, but as he did so the nuts trickled down his arms. I believe one or two lodged in the Queen's shoe."

As the 1974 squad limped forlornly out of England, the Provos continued their all-out bombing onslaught on the British mainland. One of the agency's police sources told us that one of the top Provos was operating in Manchester but other 'freelances' were on the loose, making it difficult to stop incendiary devices being left in city centre stores. He insisted that police were desperately worried about the potential threat to the cricket and football stadia. Violent crime was increasing, gangs had become more 'professional' and guns were more easily obtainable and in mid-summer the newly formed Greater Manchester Constabulary were trying to figure out ways of combating the football hooligans who would soon be wreaking their havoc. Apart from that, and the occasional whisper of 'revolution', life went along as normal if you could cope with the 'unacceptable face of capitalism' as Ted Heath termed it. With inflation at 18 per cent the pretentious French restaurant in Manchester's Midland Hotel decided to charge £1 for a plate of snails. 'Ridiculous' cried TV's Bamber Gascoigne as he stormed out.

Not many of the Indians would have voted for a night out at the 'French'. Not on wages of 50 rupees a day as Engineer constantly and no doubt, annoyingly, likes to remind current players - though, of course, 50 rupees in his day was worth far more than in recent times.

Gratefully Engineer returned to Manchester and county duties. The thought itched at him that his Test career was nearing its end. He was 36 and Syed Kirmani was waiting in the wings. But, back at Old Trafford, his position was secure although a young keeper, John Lyon, was being groomed and had filled in while Engineer was on Test duty. His return to Lancashire action was greeted as ever with smiles from the office staff and dressing-room banter over how England had trashed India. Gentle stuff like 'What a load of crap. Bumble beat you on his own'. They could see he was hurting.

Clive Lloyd had taken over the Lancashire captaincy in the absence of David Lloyd. It pained him to hand back the authority. He had no problem with Bumble, only with the committee. His thinking was that as captain he could have persuaded top West Indian players to sign for the club at a time when Lancashire most needed new blood. Bond's side had lost its supremacy in one-day cricket, key players like Engineer and Peter Lever were getting older, and Lloyd could see trouble ahead.

Engineer said: "Clive sometimes looked a bit glum but he was a fun-loving guy, a party animal like and we had some great laughs. We roomed together. We had so much in common and of course he was one of the world's greatest players. People still talk about his batting. I first saw him when West Indies toured India and realised immediately that he had a great eye. When he got going it was his timing as much as his power that allowed him to hit the ball out of the ground. But I remember his fielding. He patrolled the covers and he was like a panther. They called him The Cat. There was one Lord's final when he gave such an incredible display, stopping everything on the off side. It was as though we had an extra fielder there. Later on he had a lot of trouble with his knees and that affected him. Clive could also provide a few useful overs so all in all Lancashire got a tremendous talent when they signed him.

"We combined so well on and off the field and have stayed very good friends. In recent years he has been involved in trying to get West Indies cricket back on the right track and I wish him well because the world of cricket needs the Windies. He should have been captain of Lancashire earlier than he was. When he was captaining West Indies people said all he had to do was to throw the ball to one of their fast bowlers and they would do the job for him but I don't agree with that. Clive had more about him as a captain than that."

The parties which Engineer, Big Clive and others enjoyed were, how shall I put it?.....lively affairs. When a former player heard I was writing a book with Engineer he queried: "Will it be about everything?"

"Well, as much as can be fitted in," he was told. "But not everything," he replied, eyebrows stretching. "Good God, not everything." Lancashire's players partied hard as they did at every county. Even for fans and, alright, yes, even for the Press, the social aspect of this wonderful game was so important. Wine, women and song provided the backing for the sound of leather on willow although for proper Northerners, and their adopted sons, it was more beer than wine and more women than songs.

Clive Lloyd was Lancashire's captain when they met Warwickshire at Edgbaston. He hit 114 with 16 boundaries, sharing in a big stand with Engineer who escaped an early run-out chance and suffered a hamstring strain which kept him out of several matches. On his return he struggled for form and the season ended on a miserable anti-climax with a Gillette Cup defeat by Kent which straggled into the reserve day because of rain and remains one of the worst Lord's finals of all time.

Not everything at Old Trafford smelled of roses anymore. Lancashire's one-day supremacy was under severe threat, while they had stayed unbeaten in the 1974 championship they had won only five of 20 matches and were no nearer to landing the championship (as time wore on the County Championship became known in the North-West as The Elusive Championship in similar vein to Fermat's Last Theorem). And, if you listened carefully, you could hear whispers of discontent over the committee's handling of players' contracts.

After a dismal summer, the winter promised much for some Lancastrians. David Lloyd and Peter Lever were off Down Under for the ill-fated Ashes tour, and Engineer and Clive Lloyd were soon to be playing and partying again during the West Indies' tour of India. In Manchester the explosions continued. The Gillespie sisters were jailed. Reporters at our agency received death threats. And everywhere Abba relentlessly sang *Waterloo*.

CHAPTER 20

FAROKH ENGINEER'S 'Waterloo' came in the West Indies tour of India where the fates, as well as the selectors, seemed to conspire against him. At the end of the winter he pulled the plug on his Test career, admitting: "I was devastated."

It could have been a glorious finale but at Delhi he had the captaincy ripped from his grasp just as he was about to toss the coin with his pal Clive Lloyd and then on his home patch of Bombay, when India had a chance to draw the series after losing the first two Tests, he suffered the indignity of a 'pair'.

"Bernard Julien got me both times. Bernard Julien of all people....I had smacked him around when he was playing for Kent. I could hardly believe it. We lost the match and the series 3-2. I felt so low. It was a terrible way to go but it was the final blow. I could not get out of my mind what had happened at Delhi over the captaincy and now this at Bombay - I had given my all for India but it was the end."

There were times during that dramatic series when Engineer looked as good as ever. West Indies, rebuilt by Lloyd, looked capable of marching to a 5-0 win but India, led once more by Pataudi, battled back despite the absence of the injured Sunil Gavaskar for three of the matches. From India's point of view, Vishwanath was the star with a century at Calcutta and an unbeaten 97 at Madras - one of the best Test innings of all time - pulling them level. But as they moved on to Bombay and the new Wankhede Stadium for the decider, a game extended to six days to ensure a result to the series, Engineer could fairly claim to have played his part in restoring India's chances.

At Delhi he shrugged off the captaincy controversy to swipe 75 and at Calcutta his 61 helped Vishy to add 76 at a crucial stage. Then at Madras he combined with Prasanna to send back Viv Richards and Lloyd within a few minutes, reducing the Windies to 65-4.

"Vishy quite rightly got all the praise for his century at Eden Gardens. He was magnificent. But would we have won the match if I hadn't stuck there with him? I doubt it. We had lost a couple of wickets and we had to make a big total in that second innings, otherwise we had no chance because they had a great batting line-up. Viv Richards had just got a big century at Delhi. So I got my head down. I was there for half a day and didn't even hit a boundary. Even though it went against the grain I could play like that for the team if I thought it absolutely necessary. I had to do it that way when we beat England at the Oval." *Wisden* concurred: "..even his (Viswanath's) vigil could not have sustained India had Engineer not cast himself in an unusual dour role'.

But all through that series Engineer suffered one blow after another, particularly blows to his pride. Two weeks later at Delhi came the kick in the teeth over the captaincy and at Madras he was controversially given out, caught at slip by Gordon Greenidge who later agreed with photographic evidence that he had grounded it and publicly apologised. "I genuinely thought it was a fair catch," he said.

Engineer knew it was not but, after standing his ground, he saw the umpire's finger go up. Maybe someone was trying to tell him something. There were question marks over his future, he was 35 and while he had friends in high places one of them was not the current chairman of selectors. And yet he was still well capable of a match-winning innings. Going to Bombay he had 222 runs under his belt at an average of 32 and considering his wrongful dismissal at Madras, he had cause to approach the decider with confidence. Sadly it went badly wrong. Clive Lloyd won the toss for the first time and celebrated with a little knock of 242 not out. Engineer got a duck in both innings, the second with a mistimed hook at Julien and the Windies did not need the sixth day to wrap up a massive win and take the series.

"Obviously it was not what I would have wanted. Especially it being in Bombay my home town. It was hard, humiliating. I'd had a great career in Test cricket. I'd smashed some of the best fast bowlers, Wes Hall, Charlie Griffith, and to get out twice like that to Julien was heartbreaking. He was a good all-rounder but not in the class of many West Indies pacemen. He did little in that series except bring my career to a close. It wasn't just that obviously. There had been a lot going on and I'd had more than enough. It was just the final straw I suppose."

Engineer's roller-coaster Test career had stretched over 15 years and 46 matches. He had one last hurrah with India, the first World Cup in England in 1975 but that ended in derision when Gavaskar messed things up at Lord's with his infamous go-slow marathon, scoring 36 not out off India's 60 overs. England had battered 334 on a sunny day watched by 16000 and India finished with a paltry 132-3 in reply, Gavaskar ignoring the boos and shouts and even a pitch invasion by frustrated Indian fans to get on with it.

"It was difficult to understand, even Sunny could not explain properly. I'm sure he did not go out to deliberately play like that. He got bogged down and couldn't get out of it. It is easy to say that a batsman in that situation should simply throw his wicket away for the good of the team but any batsman worth his salt have it in their blood not to chuck it away. They guard their wicket jealously every time they go to the crease, especially someone like Sunny, and so it's almost impossible for them to do something which is entirely alien, not just to them personally but to good batsmanship in general. He must have been praying that they would get him out but he was dropped a couple of times. The more it went on the worse it got for him."

India bowed out of the World Cup early which at least allowed Engineer to return to county duty. Lancashire were pleased to see him. Skipper David Lloyd said: "When he was unavailable it left us looking for two replacements, a wicketkeeper and a batsman. It made life difficult sometimes."

Lloyd had reason to believe that Lancashire would capture the championship for the first time since 1934 despite a bizarre spell in which a snowstorm had disrupted their game with Derbyshire at Buxton and three players, Barry Wood, Peter Lever and Frank Hayes had been suspended by the club's committee over a contracts row which led to the first known players' strike in English cricket.

As the overseas players, with different terms and conditions, Engineer and Clive Lloyd were not involved in the dispute which had rumbled on for almost a year and which came to a head at Buxton where, on the eve of the championship game, the club secretary Jimmy James held a meeting with players at their hotel. James tried to pacify them, insisting that the issue would be sorted out quickly. However when Wood, Lever and Hayes returned from World Cup duty with England they found that no progress had been made and withdrew from the championship return with Derbyshire at Old Trafford, citing minor injuries. Wood was banned for six matches, Lever and Hayes for two each. Lancashire, who had enjoyed outstanding wins in the first half of the season, were without all three when they lost heavily to Kent, a result which was to prove decisive, and the much admired Red Rose team spirit suffered accordingly. "We finished fourth that season but we could have won it," groaned the captain.

Engineer had a slightly different view. "What I remember from 1975 is some incredible weather, some fantastic matches and another trophy. I don't think anyone could say it was an unsuccessful season. I know the club desperately wanted the championship but we kept going and won the Gillette Cup again.

"I've never known anything like the blizzard that we had at Buxton. It had been really hot on the first day and Clive had been smashing the ball out of the ground. One or two of their players fell ill and Bob Taylor was working hard to keep them together. Then on the second day we got to the ground and it was covered in snow. We were into June by then. A freak snowstorm. Dickie Bird was the umpire. He called it off for the day. A reporter asked me if I'd seen snow before and I said 'We don't get much in Bombay'. Everyone was laughing and playing around in it. We had a snowball fight. Very funny. We got the game finished on the third day by bowling Derbyshire out twice. The sun had come out again and the pitch was steaming. The ball was jumping about and Ashley Harvey-Walker took his false teeth out handed them to Dickie Bird for safekeeping."

1975 was the summer of the Calypso King, Clive Lloyd. He kept hammering brilliant centuries, one at Lord's to win the World Cup and his 73 earned him the man of the match award when Lancashire comfortably beat Middlesex to win the Gillette Cup for the fourth time. By then Indira Gandhi's state of emergency was getting into full swing in India with its mandatory sterilisation programme and other dreadful goings-on and Britain was again in ferment with right wing and left wing conflagrations, football hooliganism and bombings. Police were searching for Lord Lucan, named as murderer of his children's nanny, and for a man who had started to savagely kill women in Yorkshire. The Free George Davis campaigners had vandalised the Headingley pitch, causing the Ashes Test to be abandoned. Violence and protest dominated the news. But a day at the cricket could ease the pain.

Watching Lloyd and Engineer that season was a delight. It remained hot and sunny and, while the West Indian six hitter hogged the limelight, the Indian extrovert continued to entertain as only he could. Neither was holding a bat when they linked up to wreck Gloucestershire in the Gillette

Cup semi at Old Trafford, Engineer whipping off the bails theatrically when danger man Mike Procter stepped out to take a swing at Lloyd's bowling.

Lancashire hardly broke sweat to dispose of Middlesex in a disappointingly one-sided final, capturing the Gillette Cup for a fourth time and while Big Clive again dominated the Lord's stage it was heartening to see a couple of younger players make their mark. Bob Ratcliffe, of whom Engineer had high hopes, took 3-25 with his clever medium pace and left-handed opener Andy Kennedy hit a half-century. Engineer liked Ratcliffe, believing he could tramp in the footsteps of Tom Cartwright whom he rated as the best bowler of all on a typically seaming English pitch. Although he became a familiar figure in the Red Rose side over the next few years, Ratcliffe failed to fulfill early expectations. Neither did Kennedy nor the all-rounder Bernard Reidy - although he had more to live up to than, having been compared to Clive Lloyd, as much for his 'Afro' hair-do as his boisterous left-handed batting. Hope of these players, and one or two others, forming the nucleus of a successful new team went badly adrift.

"We were a hard act to follow," explains Engineer. "An impossible act to follow."

The loss of Clive Lloyd who was touring England as the West Indies captain in 1976 proved a major blow to Lancashire. Ken Shuttleworth was also missing with injury and they crumbled in the heat and dust of a record breaking summer which felt more like India than England. The game which summed it up for me came at the height of the heatwave at Grace Road when after big centuries from Kennedy and Pilling they forced Leicestershire to follow on 187 behind and had them under the collar at 121-8 with half a day left. But somehow they could not force victory. Jack Birkenshaw and Peter Booth put on 73 and then Ken Higgs, of all people, gritted it out with Booth to lead them to 223-9 when a violent thunderstorm waterlogged any lingering hopes.

In the dressing-room David Lloyd tried to rally the troops. "Right lads, we've got to forget about this - we've got Middlesex in the Gillette Cup tomorrow. I want you at the ground at 9 o'clock." Which elicited a moan from Jack Simmons: "Nine o'clock? How can I get there at that time all the way from Great Harwood."

"Bloody hell, Jack," Bumble fired back. "We're playing at Old Trafford not Lord's." The thing is - no-one laughed. Except me. And I was promptly given my travel instructions.

Shortly after the Grace Road farce John Sullivan played his last championship game against Warwickshire at Blackpool. Engineer always felt that 'Sully' did not have the technique for first-class cricket but came into his own in the Sunday League and cups. "He was one of the hardest hitters in the game. I never saw anyone hit sixes with such fluency - even Clive respected the way he hit the ball. As a bowler he was under estimated. I don't think he realised himself which way he was swinging the ball and he was one of those bowlers who brought out the best in yours truly."

Lancashire lost that match and struggled for the rest of the season. They brought in a string of little known players including left-arm spinner Bob Arrowsmith who launched a brief career with a hatful of wickets in his first three games but could only manage three wins and slumped to second from bottom of the championship, a reminder of dark days we thought had long gone. Peter Lever's finale in first-class cricket came in a heavy Roses defeat although no-one realised it until he announced his retirement during the winter.

Engineer marked his benefit season with some fine performances. Over 600 runs in the Sunday League and almost 1,000 at first-class level including 96 against Middlesex at Lord's. Unfortunately his dream of signing off with a Gillette Cup triumph came to nothing when Northants beat them in the final. My mind returns to that August morning when Engineer is driving me to Buxton for the game with Derbyshire and we are chatting about whether he could play on for another year or so. His elbow lies on the window sill, the wheel steered by thumb and forefinger. His face is pensive.

"Cricket and my family has been my life. It's hard to give something up that you love so much. But I suppose the time comes for everyone and I can look back and tell myself that I've had a great career. Lots of good memories. Lots of friends. I was part of something good, something that will be remembered by others for a long time."

Anais Nin, the French author said: "We don't see things as they are, we see them as we are." I think Farokh Engineer is an exemplar of that theory. Now, all these years after his triumphs in Madras, Delhi, Bombay, Calcutta, London and Manchester, he tends to view his career and life in Bollywood style and sometimes I try to throw a spoke into his rapidly revolving wheels.

"Farokh - you are the cricketing cavalier but there must be a darker side." At the time he is chuckling away at a story of Harry Pilling's jock strap but when he gets to grips with the question he deals with it seriously.

"Of course. Not a dark side really but the reverse side of the coin. Well, I've always admitted that I'm extremely sensitive - believe it or not! People who have seen me play or spent an hour or so with me having a drink will think I'm a happy go lucky sort of guy, full of confidence, someone who loves life. And I am. But I can be hurt, badly hurt. Not that I would want to show it publicly. Of course not. But I have been known to sulk if I haven't got my own way, or if I've been criticised without reason. Unjustified criticism is very hard to take."

Despite his natural charm and sociability, it is not difficult to imagine Engineer getting the hump over perceived mistreatment. But, while occasionally dismissive, he remains an engaging character and I look forward to our get-togethers at his Cheshire home despite the efforts of his daughter Scarlett's pet Lola to ravage my ankle. ("Oh, it's a Shiatsu dog is it Farokh ?- I thought it was a Tasmanian Devil"). There is always coffee. He throws a packet of biscuits at me - "Help yourself" or cuts up a cake "Have some more..." And he is always giving of himself. No question goes unheeded. If at times the answers drift off into the realms of Indian mythology, I don't mind. Like Anais Nin said....After all he is a raconteur, not a statistician.

Approaching his ninth decade Engineer exudes energy and brightness. As we chat he is either making or taking calls on his phone, to arrange this or that, a game at the Manchester Bridge Club maybe, or persuading Tony in London to fix a room at his hotel for one of his old India team-mates, or sorting out a ticket for an ODI in Mumbai. I can hear people laughing at the other end of the line. Lola, imprisoned in an adjacent room, is yapping loudly. "Shut up; thanks buddy see you in Mumbai; now Colin you were saying...." All three issues dealt with quicker than it took him to whip off the bails. But there is no doubt that Engineer's pride is as deep as a desert well and as easy to sully. One pinch of salty criticism can be enough so it is to his credit that he is prepared now to have a go at a bit of critical self-analysis.

"I'm quite short tempered, even childish or churlish if things don't go my way. Obviously I'm not perfect. Is anyone? One thing I do believe in is an eye for an eye. To get one's own back especially when one is let down badly. And I can tell you now I have often trusted people and have been let down. Time and time again. It is something I cannot abide and it is where I have gone terribly wrong on quite a few occasions. I have made lots of mistakes.

Lots. But I have always tried to learn from them. I have never knowingly abused someone's trust. It is the way I was brought up. Our religion says Dushmatta, Dujucta, Dujuvaresta. Good thoughts, good words, good deeds. To be able to trust is essential."

Bishan Bedi once felt the lash of Engineer's tongue. Bedi revealed: "I must confess my first meeting with Farokh was not terribly endearing. I vividly remember my abrupt induction into the Indian team at Calcutta against the West Indies in 1967. I was indeed lost in the atmosphere of it all. By accident I walked into a room where amongst other stars was F.M. Engineer. I promise you he thought I was an autograph gate-crasher and I don't really blame him for that. If it wasn't for Budhi Kunderan with whom I had already played an ugly incident would have been on the cards. Fortunately my subsequent association with Farokh has been very nice and enjoyable."

There was little or no conflict in England where the mood was more relaxed although it is possible he dwelt on it when his Lancashire team-mates sometimes ribbed him about his batting technique. Generally though it was light-hearted banter which he could give back when necessary. He knew and they knew how valuable he was to the team. He also had the media on side and so public criticism was muted by euphemisms, 'impetuous' instead of 'reckless', 'cavalier' rather than 'crazy'. What he did not appreciate were the slights and muttered criticisms which stalked him in India where the pressures of Test cricket and of staying on the right side of certain powerful figures sometimes proved impossible.

Highly sensitive, a tad sulky....was he spoiled as a child? "No, not spoiled. In fact when we had a roast or whatever my mum would give the best piece to Darius as the elder and I used to have the second best piece. Then Dad would have the third best and mum would have what was left. She was a very self sacrificing lady - she just wanted the best for her children. I could demand perhaps and I could sulk but mum was a strong character. All I got was love, support and encouragement."

Engineer accepts that Minnie, in life and in death, has been the driving force behind everything he has achieved.

"My greatest loss was my mother's death at a pretty young age. It devastated me. Luckily I had Darius and my dad, the whole family. They would always be very close to my heart for all the support they gave me but I reckon this was what made me more determined to succeed. I wanted to make something of myself and reward everything she did, and they did, for me. I think of them each and every day and worship them in my daily prayers. I want to express my humble gratitude to my Ahura Mazda God, mother Minnie, dad Manecksha and brother Darius to whom I owe everything."

One of Yorkshire's most famous sons, Michael Parkinson said that if Engineer seemed a 'paragon of all virtues, then let me point out the weakness in the pedigree. He was born in Bombay and played at Old Trafford. If he'd have been born in Bradford and played at Headingley he would indeed have been perfect.' Tongue in cheek stuff from the TV presenter who has been a close friend for many years and Engineer laughs: "There is more than one weakness....I'm no angel and have never ever pretended to be one. Flings with women? Of course. Especially with Bollywood actresses too numerous to mention."

If the first cut is the deepest then it is little wonder that instinctively he puts hand on heart when he talks of his mum. His memory and love of her has piloted him through life, comforting him in times of stress, urging him on to new objectives. "She is always in my mind and, yes, I've wanted to prove myself to her as well as to myself. I wish she could have seen me play for India. She never did and I just wish she had."

CHAPTER 21

YOU COULD fill a book with Engineer tributes. Praise for this, applause for that, accolades and bouquets aplenty. This book already has enough so I won't bother you with too many more details of what Sir Don Bradman thought of him or how Professor Christian Barnard found him such refreshing company on a long flight, or why a cavalcade of other ex sportsmen and famous characters past and present rated him so highly, whether out on the pitch or at the dinner table.

But a brief selection would not be amiss....

Richie Benaud: "Farokh was rated the best wicketkeeper-batsman in the world and was naturally first choice in the Rest of the World XI that toured Australia in 1971-72 and as if to prove a point he slammed a typical Engineer century against Western Australia who had been boasting about their new find - a rather quickish bowler by the name of Dennis Lillee!"

I prefer this one by Fred Trueman. "He would rather risk the odd dropped catch so that he might bring off a superb legside stumping - and there is no better sight than that in cricket. As for batting just half an hour of vintage Engineer is better than three hours of boredom and I can name a few of those at Test level." I wonder who he was referring to.

Bishan Bedi offered: "Farokh was a 'gallery' man, always an entertainer. always aware of crowd appeal and always willing to oblige a responsive crowd. But if ever there was a natural wicketkeeper it was Farokh because I never really saw him working at his keeping like Alan Knott did for example. It must have been pure and simple instinctive ball sense which stood him in good stead throughout his career. And, no matter, how hard or long the day had been he was never one to miss out on the funny side of the game. He was a renowned leg puller."

Sifting through the Press cuttings of Farokh Engineer's career, including my own, I come across the names of many cricket writers who at times were entranced, sometimes bewildered, by his ability to shrug aside perceived wisdom in constructing an innings. The sheer audacity - or recklessness depending on your sense of perspective - sent Neville Cardus into raptures. If a little less flowery, John Arlott and others still glorified him. For me, however, the most eloquent article on Engineer was written by a dyed in the wool Lancashire fan who, in the manner of a proper journalist, refused to allow sentiment and friendship to blur objectivity. Michael Henderson also had a keen eye for the detail and here is his beguiling account of Engineer at his very best.

****

'Farokh Engineer didn't have a great career, but it was colourful enough to leave a lasting impression.

July 19, 1971 was the first Monday of the summer holidays. It was also the second day of the county championship match between Derbyshire and Lancashire at Buxton. And it turned out to be the only time I saw my cricketing hero, Farokh Engineer, score a century: 141 runs, all told. Runs that I can see now, some of them at least, in my mind's eye.

Engineer became my hero in the summer of 1967, the year I took an interest in cricket. I was already a football fan by then. For three seasons, I had been a regular at Burnden Park, the old home of Bolton Wanderers, and when Francis Lee moved to Manchester City in October 1967, I moved with him, though I retain a soft spot for the Trotters.

Although my father loved cricket, it was only when I went to prep school in April 1967 that cricket began to play a part in my life. As soon as I saw stumps pitched, I was hooked. At once, I began to read books about the sport in the library and started to play the game. Foremarke Hall had – still has – a wonderful ground, and the school had teachers who were prepared to hand on their love of cricket. When it rained, the geography teacher, Mr Hoare, used to read to us from England, Their England, which served as an introduction to the folklore of the game.

My father eventually took me to Old Trafford later in that summer of 1967, for championship matches against Middlesex and Derbyshire, and a Gillette Cup tie against Somerset. I recall being impressed by Clive Radley's forward defensive stroke, and T.J.P. Eyre's spirited fast-

medium bowling – and the fact that his "syrup" fell off in delivery stride. My mother's uncle, Harry Birtwistle, was a member of the Lancashire committee, so I was able to gather the autographs of most of the leading players of the day. Whenever visiting teams came to Manchester, he passed the book around and the players obliged.

Lancashire weren't much cop that season. I wasn't to know it at the time but players like Bob Barber, Peter Marner and 'Noddy' Pullar had recently left, or been booted out, and their successors struggled. Brian Statham was coming to the end of his great career, and Ken Higgs and Peter Lever were going strong, but it was a rag-bag side awaiting renewal. And one of the players responsible for that renewal was F.M. Engineer, Farokh Manecksha Engineer, the Parsee from Bombay, who joined the club in 1968 and stayed for nine summers.

English crowds saw him first in 1967, as a member of the Indian side that played three Tests. He also played for the Rothman Cavaliers, an international pick-up side, whose Sunday games were occasionally televised by BBC2. The camera loved Engineer. He was a handsome man who smiled a lot, his wicketkeeping was smart, and he was a natural striker of the ball when he got in. I loved a lot of cricketers in those days. Tom Graveney, Alan Knott, Derek Underwood and John Snow were my English favourites, and Garry Sobers made a big impression when I saw him bat for Nottinghamshire at Southport. Yet Engineer stood out. You only have one genuine hero in any sport. Mine were Franny Lee and Farokh Engineer. That much will never change.

Lancashire had originally tried to sign Sobers, who was without question the greatest player in the world. It was only when he chose to be Nottinghamshire's overseas player that the club moved for Engineer and Clive Lloyd, the brilliant young Guyanese batsman who came to Old Trafford in 1969. Between them they transformed Lancashire from palsied old step-takers to the supreme one-day team of their time. Winners of the first two John Player League competitions in 1969 and 1970, they won three consecutive Gillette Cups from 1970. They had a decent three-day side, too, though they were never quite strong enough to win the championship.

"Hubert" Lloyd was a great batsman. Let nobody tell you otherwise. In his pomp, he was also a magnificent fielder at cover point. Engineer was, well, exotic. He had a graceful, almost feline walk, and his glovework had the touch of an artist. He seemed incapable of doing anything ugly. But he didn't make the runs he should have done. John Arlott said that Engineer had a range of stroke that many heavier run-scorers envied and, fan that I was, I felt almost betrayed when he failed to turn lovely 20s and 30s into centuries. Until that day of days at Buxton.

Getting to Buxton from Rochdale was an arduous business. It still is. You pass through Shaw, Oldham, Ashton-Under-Lyne and Mottram-in-Longdendale, bypass Glossop and in those days had to drive through Hayfield and Chapel-en-le-Frith before dropping into the spa town from Dove Holes, one of the most benighted villages in the kingdom. An unlovely journey of 40 miles could take nearly two hours some days. And when we reached the ground on that July day, my father and I, our mood was not improved as Lancashire, responding to Derbyshire's score of 300 for 6 declared, lost half their wickets for 90. This was a fine Lancashire team: Barry Wood and David Lloyd, Harry Pilling, and Clive Lloyd at the height of his vertiginous talent. Yet Derbyshire were running through them.

It could have got a lot worse. Engineer and Jack Bond, the captain, were both missed early on. I don't remember which fielder reprieved Engineer but I recall that Bond was missed by Bob Taylor, that impeccable wicketkeeper who simply didn't miss catches. But down the ball went, to the disappointment of Alan Ward, the Derbyshire opening bowler who was, when the mood took him, very sharp indeed. Ward was originally selected for the tour of Australia the previous winter but had to come home, paving the way for Bob Willis to start his Test career. Fast and gifted, Ward should have been a contender. In the end his career withered on the vine and he is best known now for the day in 1973 when Brian Bolus, the Derbyshire captain, ordered him from the field at Chesterfield after he had refused to bowl.

What do I see now, at this distance? I see Ward running in down the slope from the pavilion end and Engineer pivoting to pull him into the rhododendron bushes at midwicket. However fast Ward bowled, however short he pitched it, Engineer kept on swivelling and pulling. He and Bond put on 168 for the sixth wicket to turn the game round, and send an unhappy bowler to the outfield where he stewed in contemplative misery.

At long last my hero had done something worthy of my loyalty! Hitherto Engineer had made only one century for Lancashire, at Swansea in 1969. After Buxton he was to make only two more, so it could be said that I caught him at his best. And that is how I like to remember him, meeting Ward's pace with a boldness that was quite special in those days. It was a boldness that served Lancashire well in the John Player League, the 40-over competition that was such a big hit when it was introduced in 1969. Engineer went in first and gave the ball a terrific whack. They played in front of big crowds, too. The Sunday fixture with Yorkshire in 1970 was the only time I failed to get into Old Trafford, because the gates were locked an hour before the start of play.

What a summer it was, 1971. The pop charts hummed with marvellous singles. It was the year of 'Just My Imagination' by the Temptations, 'Heaven Must Have Sent You' by the Elgins, and that bouncy number 'I'm Gonna Run Away From You' by Tami Lynn. Coming up behind those belters was Carole King's 'It's Too Late', followed by another five-star classic, 'I'm Still Waiting' by Diana Ross. And when summer gave way to autumn, Rod Stewart topped the charts with 'Maggie May'. It was also the summer – ahem! – of 'Chirpy Chirpy Cheep Cheep', which was No. 1 on the day that Engineer made his century but it was banished the following week by T Rex and 'Get It On'.

> *Days lost, I know not how,*
> *I shall retrieve them now,*
> *Now I shall keep the vow*
> *I never kept before.*

In those days players didn't get many favours from the fixture list or from coaches eager to 'rest' them for more pressing engagements. From Buxton, Engineer went straight to Lord's where, after one day's rest, he was pitched into the first Test as India's wicketkeeper-batsman. The match, remembered for Snow's spat with Sunil Gavaskar, was drawn but India took the series when they won by four wickets at The Oval. Who was at the crease when Abid Ali struck the winning runs? Engineer, of course. I have to confess, I wanted India to win that Test. I wanted everybody to know that my hero was a cricketer of substance.

There were two more remarkable days that summer for Lancastrians.

The first came on July 28, the day after the Lord's Test, and nine days after the Buxton century. The Gillette Cup semi-final between Lancashire and Gloucestershire, which ended in darkness as the clock ticked round to 9pm, has entered the annals on account of the 24 runs David Hughes plundered from John Mortimore's final over. What people do not always remember is how well Mike Procter batted that day, and how fast he bowled.

Had Peter Lever not dismissed Procter for 65, just as he was beginning to break free, Gloucestershire would have won that match. It was Engineer who took the catch, down the legside, though it was not for another three decades that I heard – from Lever himself – that Engineer had scooped the ball off the floor. The story went that, when it was put to him the ball had bounced, Engineer replied 'only once!' It's a good job we don't know everything about our heroes when we are young and impressionable.

The final treat from the dish of delights came at Lord's in early September when Lancashire beat Kent in the Gillette Cup final. Again they had to remove a batsman in the form of his life. It took Jack Bond's stupendous one-handed diving catch at extra cover to get rid of Asif Iqbal, the elegant Pakistani batsman, who was making the game look like child's play. That was the highest point of Engineer's English career. Lancashire were to win yet another Gillette Cup in 1975 but they were never so formidable as they were under Bond's captaincy in 1971.

My heroes retired within weeks of each other. After scoring two goals for Derby County at Ipswich in April 1976, Lee brought down the curtain on his 16-year career. That autumn, Engineer walked away from Old Trafford after Lancashire had lost the Gillette Cup final to Northamptonshire. Lancashire were in decline, and it took a decade of ordinary cricket before there was any kind of revival, notwithstanding a Benson and Hedges triumph in 1984. There were some grim days, so grim that I often stayed away from the ground that had played such an important part in my childhood.

Engineer's was a colourful career, not a great one. He scored only 13 centuries in first-class cricket, two of them in Tests, yet, as Arlott said, he left a more vivid impression on those who saw him than many players with more impressive records. There were some superb overseas players in county cricket in those days – Procter and Zaheer Abbas at

Gloucestershire, Clive Rice and Richard Hadlee at Trent Bridge, Eddie Barlow at Derbyshire, Rohan Kanhai and Lance Gibbs at Warwickshire, Asif Iqbal and John Shepherd at Kent, players who gave their all. Then came their successors: Viv Richards, Joel Garner, Malcolm Marshall, Courtney Walsh, Ken McEwan. And we can never forget the purest batsman of them all, Barry Richards. In one of those memorable Gillette contests, at Bournemouth in 1972, Richards made a century against Lancashire and then got out. "He could have made as many as he wanted," David Lloyd said later.

'Rooky' did not scale those peaks. He was 30 when he arrived at Old Trafford, so he was a late starter in county cricket. You could say that of Sobers too, though he was a man apart. Yet Engineer had a more profound effect on Lancashire cricket than the fabled Garry did at Trent Bridge. With his wicketkeeping, he sent an electric current through the field, and Lancashire's improved fielding lay at the heart of their revival under Bond's captaincy. When Lloyd joined the club in 1969, they were capable of beating all-comers, and they did.

They have switched the pitch round at Old Trafford, so it now runs north to south. To at least one mind, though, the pavilion still stands at cover. I grew up watching cricket from a position over mid-off, where the Ladies' Stand was built later. There were thermos flasks for the old-timers, cans of shandy for the boys, appalling hamburgers at the "refreshment stall" beneath the stand, and the scorecards always carried adverts for Truman's Steel. In my childhood Lancashire were usually 60 for 3, with Harry Pilling 15 not out. We wouldn't have to wait long to see Farokh Engineer. Perhaps one day he would give us the innings we knew was in him.

At Buxton we witnessed those three hours of rapture, three hours that will see me out.

> Past touch and sight and sound
> Not further to be found,
> How hopeless underground
> Falls the remorseful day."

****

Henderson's article revived many memories for me as well as being a matchless description of Engineer's performance in that sepia tinged setting. Engineer, however, strenuously denies Peter Lever's account of the Procter catch. "I never scooped the ball off the ground. It was only centimetres off the ground but it was a clean catch. The story about the ball only bouncing once developed when David Lloyd in his inimitable fashion joked about it after the match."

Although I had started reporting on Lancashire well before 1971 I was not at Buxton that day and, obviously, I missed something special. For reasons already expressed I differ from Henderson in that I believe Engineer did have a great career but I asked his permission to include this essay which he wrote for *The Nightwatchman* because he is a Lancashire supporter through and through, he is a critic of the utmost integrity and because, well... if you have read it, you will know why.

Buxton was a lovely place for cricket, except when it snowed. As well as his century there Engineer was once close to hitting the fastest televised 50 in a Sunday match, a feat which would have earned a big bonus for the team, only to be run out by Ken Snellgrove. "He got a terrible ear bashing from the lads. It went down in dressing room folklore as the Buxton Blast."

I saw two Lancashire matches there, the famous one of 1975, the other in 1976 when Engineer gave me a lift from Manchester and talked of his decision to retire. Late August, the heatwave over. Although the sun had baked England to a crust there were clouds of disenchantment over the club. The most successful team in their post-war history was breaking up and although they had fought their way into another Gillette Cup final they had struggled throughout the championship campaign.

Lancashire should have won that Buxton game in comfort after forcing Derbyshire to follow on 151 runs behind. But in the second innings they were worked over by Eddie Barlow with the bat and Geoff Miller with the ball and needing 202 for victory were bowled out for 186. Engineer, opening with Barry Wood, hit the top score of 48. When in the next game against Middlesex Engineer came close to a pulsating century at Lord's it seemed to me that he still had what it took and that Lancashire could well do with him for at least another season. But his reasoning was clear. He had business ambitions, his benefit season would reward him handsomely and anyway he had done it all. What was the point of hanging on? Perhaps there was also a romantic notion - that he would go out on the highest note by helping Lancashire to win the Gillette Cup again. The final with Northants was coming up. One last hurrah to crown a bejewelled career.

Sadly it did not end that way. John Dye, the left arm seamer, bowled Engineer without a run on the board, Barry Wood was forced off with a broken finger and although David Hughes slammed 26 in Bishan Bedi's last over Lancashire's total of 195-7 was not enough, Northants openers Roy Virgin and Peter Willey killed the game with a century partnership for the first wicket.

Lancashire's line-up for that inglorious finale included three players of 35 or over, Engineer (38), Peter Lever and Jack Simmons (both 35) with five others over or very close to 30. Only two John Abrahams and Bob Ratcliffe, both 24, could say time was on their side. David Lloyd admitted: "The fact was that the young, vibrant bunch of blokes who had come together under Jack Bond almost a decade earlier were now getting long in the tooth.... the athletic fielding that first made us such a force in the one-day came no longer came easily to us and nor was it our exclusive domain any more."

Bumble claimed that things had gone against them in the Lord's final. He lost an important toss and they had to bat first in less than ideal conditions, they lost Wood early in the game, and they were without Clive Lloyd. Even so it was obvious that Lancashire were no longer the 'Kings', as well as sliding to defeat in the final they finished second from bottom in the John Player League which, said Lloyd, 'had started its life almost as a Lancashire benefit tournament'. He added: "But it was the championship form that most concerned the members and committee. We'd had our chances to nail the elusive title and not been quite good enough (they finished second and third under Bond); now we were down among the deadbeats."

Lancashire had two championship fixtures after Lord's, both at Old Trafford and both failing to set up Engineer with a suitable farewell. Yorkshire easily won the Roses match thanks to Geoff Boycott's second innings century although Engineer dismissed him in the first with a superb catch off paceman Peter Lee. "It was always good to get Boycott and I enjoyed that moment." But the sense of anti-climax after Lord's, the under-achievement of the season in general and worries over the future pervaded the fag-end of that season.

Lancashire's decline was felt even more keenly when Essex came to Manchester to end the season in early September. Engineer's curtain call. Of course it rained. Engineer tried hard to make it a farewell to remember with three catches after Essex had won the toss and in the closing stages of the first day he went out to bat. The applause was heart-felt. Watching from the Press Box I prayed that he would see the day out and start fresh the next morning, perhaps crack a half century before lunch and stroll back to the pavilion with an ovation ringing in his ears. It was gloomy, the new ball moving around and difficult to play, and he essayed a booming drive to be caught. The crowd sighed but clapped him back believing no doubt that there was still plenty of time left in the game for him to produce a spark of magic. The weather wrecked that hope. No play possible on the second day and only 70 overs on the third during which Engineer spent most of the time in the dressing-room admiring an entertaining century by Frank Hayes. Lancashire declared to allow him a few closing overs behind the stumps and at least he was involved in the one wicket to fall, flicking the bails off to run out Ken McEwan.

There were handshakes from the players, the members' stand stood to attention and a few fans ran onto the outfield, patting his back. The dressing room was subdued at least in the context of a group of players who knew how to party. "I've had a great career," he said, sitting on the bench half dressed. "What more could I have wanted?"

Perhaps a couple of things. But Engineer was always and still is determined to extract the positives.

Engineer did not stop playing when he called time on his Test and county career and continued to get fun out of cricket, appearing for MCC, Lord's Taverners and for invitation sides all over the world. There were escapades with Fred Trueman, Tim Rice and the Rolling Stones - Mick Jagger being a cricket fan - and laughs with Brian Close on a game safari in Kenya. He turned out for a couple of league teams, sometimes bowling his tricky leg-spin - "I could turn it more than Robin Hobbs (Essex and England)" - and where he first came across a promising young player named Atherton.

He also turned eagerly to business life, exporting textiles, and continues to revel in it despite losing a fortune in the collapse of the Bank of Credit and Commerce. He blends it with a never ending round of public engagements but he would have liked a greater role within cricket and feels badly let down by the International Cricket Conference. "They promised to use me as a match referee and that they would send the details to me. I waited and the call never came. Eventually I rang them and found that they had appointed Chris Broad instead. Just another example of the way cricket is run. There are lots of former players who have very little to do with the organisation of the game and I find that sad and hard to understand. The ICC and the Board of Control in India had a lot in common - more negatives than positives. I feel justified in criticising some ex office bearers but of course there are others in India who have done a fantastic job particularly in relation to players' wages and benefits. Unfortunately there is still a lot of favouritism and bias."

However while fans are obviously interested in the way their particular sport is organised and while they are outraged at the inefficiency and corruption of governing bodies, all they really want is to support their team, watch a good game, hopefully see a great individual performance. Sponsors and others have a wider perspective but for most supporters it is all about the players and what they do on the pitch. To be honest, if Engineer had become a billionaire and had simultaneously taken complete control of the cricketing world, I would still, like Michael Henderson, remember him best for the way he played the game with that unbridled joy which could, if only briefly, let you forget the world's ills.

Henderson's Engineer day was at Buxton. Mine was at Southport in 1967 when I saw him for the first time.

I recalled the occasion in an article for a 1992 book which never saw the light of day because the publishers went broke and perhaps I can wipe the dust off it now.

****

'It was the day when the front pages of every British newspaper were filled with horror. Mainly terrible pictures of a broken up, burned out aircraft. "OVER 70 DEAD IN AIR DISASTER' said one headline. G-ALHG, a holiday charter flight returning from Palma had run out of fuel over Stockport the previous day and had dived into the town centre. The miracle was that the death tally was not much higher. The plane with 84 people aboard crashed onto a piece of waste land and with it being a Sunday morning not many folk were around. Those who were rushed to the rescue as flames engulfed the plane and they pulled out 12 badly injured survivors. There were horrifying stories of passengers, alive but trapped in collapsed seats, being burned to death.

Life goes on, I was just starting a week's holiday and I was determined to have my day at the pretty little Southport ground where there would be white marquees, candy striped deckchairs, warm beer, drippy ice cream and where Brian Statham would demolish the Indians who, it had been proved before, had no idea of how to cope with fast bowling. At least that is what I thought. I knew little of Farokh Engineer in those days, had seen a few grainy black and white pictures but little to truly identify him as the 'star' he now was back in India.

I had been up at 6am helping my fishmonger pal to crate up plaice, mackerel and trout after which we slaked our thirst with a couple of bottles of Double Diamond. I needed a couple of trains to reach Southport and when I got to the ground in Trafalgar Road, Birkdale, Lancashire had resumed their second innings with Barry Wood and David Green facing the spinners Chandrasekhar and Prasanna with Bedi waiting for his turn. A decent enough crowd for but finding a seat on the railway side was easy, particularly so as I exuded a heady cocktail scent of fish and beer.

The cricket was generally slow although the Indian wicketkeeper tried hard to enliven proceedings. Big shouts for lbws and bat-pad chances, stretching upwards on tip-toes, gloves reaching for the sky. "Bloody hell, I wish he'd shut up," murmured a bloke sitting upwind of me. The Lancashire fans were not used to that sort of behaviour. Me? I liked this player. He looked like Engelbert Humperdink, dark, swarthily handsome. Engelbert had been high in the Top 20 for six weeks and as he had been born in Madras I suppose he had a right to play for India!

"Look out!" The early start that day had left me sleepy. I was jerked fully awake by an alarmed shout and a shove on the shoulder from a kind spectator who reckoned I was in danger of a viciously bouncing ball which thudded against the fence behind us. Now I was on full alert. Lancashire had declared to set India a target of 200 in around three hours, impossible really with Statham and Ken Higgs on the loose, but already there were useful runs on the board and Engineer had most of them. I watched aghast as he continued to pull and drive my hero Statham to the boundary, forcing spectators to take evasive action as the ball ricocheted upwards off the board. Statham lasted five overs before taking himself off. I had never seen him suffer such punishment.

In the first innings he had dismissed Engineer with a return catch before he had really got going but this was different. Engineer's timing was impeccable. It was only when off-spinner John Savage took over that things returned to normal. Engineer had hammered 38 when he was lbw, the first of four more victims for Savage who had already overshadowed the Indian spinners in the first innings.

Thirty eight runs - what is so great about that? You have to be steeped in cricket history to appreciate why the fans that day went home happy. Though India batted out for a draw they had seen something different. Low scoring matches were 10 a penny. Pitches were poorly prepared, uncovered and often affected by the weather. Front-line batsmen had to fight for survival with a no risks strategy. There were some exceptions but fast scoring at the head of an innings was usually reserved for high days and holidays. Super fast was extraordinary. And, against Statham, unheard of. Engineer walked back to the Southport pavilion with applause ringing in his ears thinking: 'I could be big in English cricket.'

As for me, I trailed back to Southport's main station, a fair walk back to the town centre where I bought a left-over copy of the weekend's sports edition, the Pink, which carried lots of cricket news and features but still a couple of soccer pages in which Sir Matt Busby talked of Manchester United's ambition to emulate Celtic and win the European Cup. I cannot remember but I like to think that on the train I nodded off again and dreamed of the two Old Traffords, George Best, Bobby Charlton, and Denis Law leading United's bid for glory and F. M. Engineer smashing sixes for Lancashire.'

INDEX

Miller, Geoff 195
Miller, Keith 15
Milton, Arthur 100
More, Kiran 42
Morecambe 122
Mortimore, John 100, 134, 193
Motz, Dick 62, 93
Mukherjee, Sujit 39-40
Murray, John 50
Murzban, Behram 46

Nadkarni, Rameshchandra Gangaram 'Bapu' 59, 61-2, 92, 96
Nagpur 94, 128
Naik, Sudhir 175
Nayudu, C.K. 99, 128-9
Nehru cricket stadium 69, 129
Nehru, Jawarhal 27
Nelson C.C. 81
New Zealand 62-3, 66, 92-4, 96, 101, 106, 130, 144, 155
Nicholson, Tony 151
Nightwatchman, The (book) 195
Northants C.C.C. 22, 105, 111, 122, 149, 162, 176, 184, 193, 196
Northern Ireland 123, 132
Nottinghamshire C.C.C. 43, 74, 81, 105, 162, 169, 190
Nuneaton 107

Old, Chris 151
Old Trafford 13, 18, 21-6, 43, 45-6, 53-4, 66, 74, 77, 80-5, 87-8, 98, 100-1, 104-5, 108-9, 111-2, 115-7, 119-21, 127-8, 130-1, 133-6, 138-9, 144, 146, 149-53, 161, 165, 167-9, 171-4, 177-8, 181, 183, 187, 189-90, 192-4, 196, 200
O'Neill, Norman 57
Oval, The 109, 115, 136-9, 141, 143-4, 146, 149, 155, 163, 180, 192

Padma Shri (award) 15
Padgett, Doug 110
Pakistan 15, 21, 34, 47, 66, 81, 117, 126, 136, 154, 193
Parfitt, Peter 154
Parkinson, Michael 187

Parsees 26, 28-30
Partition of India 28-9
Pataudi, Nawab of 7, 17-9, 51-2, 56, 60, 65, 75-6, 90, 92-5, 101, 110-1, 123-5, 130-1, 143, 158-9, 164-9, 173, 179
Paynter, Eddie 82, 119
Pearce's XI, T.N. 136
Pilling, Harry 10, 24-5, 84, 86, 103, 106-7, 109-11, 114-5, 117, 120-2, 126, 131, 151-3, 162, 183-4, 191, 194
Pocock, Pat 156
Podar College of Commerce and Economics 34
Pollock, Graeme 125
Pope, George 152
Port of Spain, Trinidad 23, 55, 125
Powell, Enoch 73-4
Prabhu, K.N. 67
Prasanna, Erapalli 15-6, 40, 68, 90, 92-5, 112, 137, 146, 156, 165, 173, 176, 179, 199
Price, John 138-40
Procter, Mike 125, 183, 193, 195
Pullar, Geoff 26, 45, 49-50, 78, 101, 103, 163, 190

Queen, H.M. The 11-2, 144, 176
Queensland 12
Quick, Norman 83

Radley, Clive 189
Railways club 46
Rajasthan 29, 49
Ramachandra, M.G. 64
Ramadhin, Sonny 36
Ranji Trophy 42, 61, 99, 129, 166
Ratcliffe, Bob 183, 196
Rawtenstall C.C. 73
Real Madrid F.C. 23, 117, 119, 131
Reid, John 62
Reidy, Bernard 183
Rest of the World XI 15, 86, 125-6, 138, 188
Rhoades, Cedric 23-4, 72, 117-9, 169-70, 172
Rice, Clive 194
Rice, Tim 197
Richards, Barry 125, 151, 194
Richards, Viv 167, 179-80, 194
Roberts, Andy 97, 167
Rodrigues, Willie 36

Strolls & Walks
from
Midland Villages

by Irene Boston & John Roberts

****

WALKWAYS
J S Roberts
8 Hillside Close, Bartley Green
Birmingham
B32 4LT   0121 550 3158
****

Strolls & Walks from
Midland Villages
(Staffordshire Shropshire & Worcestershire)

by Irene Boston & John Roberts

ISBN   0 947708 34 0

First Published 1997

The Authors

IRENE BOSTON was born over 30 years ago in London, but always felt herself a country girl in exile. Building a career in advertising, then managing a business college she regularly escaped to Cumbria, Exmoor and the Sussex Downs. Interest in photography, churches and local history developed from a love of the countryside.

Fleeing the rat race in 1990, Irene married and settled in Stratford upon Avon. She devotes half her time to a proper job and the rest to supplying walking, countryside and photographic magazines with articles and photos. She has also written a book of Warwickshire walks. Any spare time is spent on a host of other hobbies including birdwatching, theatre, and natural history.

JOHN ROBERTS is yonks older than that and was born on the Wirral. His early playgrounds were the Cheshire woods and lanes, but natural idleness delayed any real walking until he moved to the Midlands.

Over the last 25 years he has managed to shuffle round a fair bit, and write many books of walks. Even worse than advertising, John worked in insurance, and served time as a Loss Adjuster, before a spell of lecturing. He is now a full time writer and publisher with his Walkways and QuercuS imprints.

Upper Pool, Badger Dingle

(i)

Contents

In the West

This third book in the *Strolls & Walks* series features villages to the west of the West Midlands conurbation.

They are spread over some 35 miles of Staffordshire, Shropshire and Worcestershire. In the north near Oaken and Brewood is a level, gentle landscape of fields, hedgerows and
isolated farms. Further south, round hills form the richly
wooded countryside near Enville and Kinver. At Highley
and Rock there are steep valleys hidden in long, wooded
dingles, while to the east Salwarpe lies in a wet, willowy
valley. The ground is generally sandy and drains quickly,
so there may be some mud but it does not hang about.

Memorable scenes from the walks include the canal and tree
lined driveway near Brewood, the Severn Valley near Highley
and a sudden, secret valley near Worfield. The villages are
all delightfully different; Shrawley strewn about haphazard-
ly, Claverley a compact gem of timber framed cottages and
ancient pubs, Badger a tiny cluster of houses and ponds. Brewood has the form and presence of a small town that never
quite made it. They all have their own tangled histories, fine
old houses and traditional pubs. Some had thriving industr-
ies, such as Belbroughton's edged tool trade, the iron mills
of Kinver, and Highley's collieries, and we have traced some
of the remains. The churches are breathtaking; visit St Cassian's at Chaddesley Corbett, All Saint's, Claverley with its
magnificent mediaeval wall paintings, and the church of Sts
Peter and Paul at Rock which is the biggest Norman church
in Worcestershire.

Our Midland Villages hold much of the history of the region
and are richly rewarding places to visit set in lovely countryside.

Using the Directions

The walking directions are separate from description and comment, quite terse, and set in short, numbered paragraphs in a clear and open typeface. These and less obvious features have been adopted for Walkways books after much thought and experience. They aim to give information in easily found and remembered blocks of convenient size, bearing in mind that you will be reading them on the move.

Distances in *yards* or *miles* are to give you a rough idea how far to walk. You do not need to measure because you will be given something to look out for, such as a stile or the old mill. If we say "go 1/2 mile", you will not start to worry if you cannot see the old mill, or whatever, after 200 yards. We use yards where you will know how far we mean, but few people know what 600 yards looks like, so for longer distances we turn to fractions of a mile. Walkways will turn happily to metres and Kms when we feel that enough people have some grasp of what they are.

Distances in *paces* are given to be counted out if you need to. These are infrequent and only for a few yards at a time. Paces vary but you can allow for being tall or short. People carry a pace with them, but not usually a measuring tape.

We have largely avoided abbreviations but certain phrases recur. From time to time you will see *"half right"* or left, meaning a half turn, or about 45 degrees. Therefore *"bear"* right or left means a narrower angle than a half turn, or just tending away from straight ahead. A *"road"* has a tarmac surface and is usually big enough for white lines down the middle. *"Lanes"* are tarmaced but smaller. *"Drives"* are like lanes but are not public. *"Tracks"* are wide enough for a four wheeled vehicle, even a small one; they may have an earth, or stone surface. A *"path"* may have any surface, from mud to tarmac, but is only pedestrian width.

The maps are sketches to an approximate scale of 2.5ins/1 mile (4cms/1km). The black arrows on them point north, but you had guessed that, hadn't you? The meanings of the symbols are mainly obvious but we show some below. The maps show paragraph numbers from the directions.

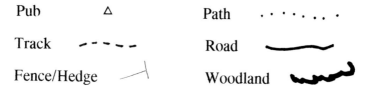

Pub △	Path · · · · · · · ·
Track - - - - -	Road
Fence/Hedge	Woodland

You will be able to find the villages on a road atlas and so find the start of your walk or stroll. From our directions and maps you should find your way very well, but some people carry Ordnance Survey maps. They will help you find starting points more easily, and might be useful in case you want to leave the route for an urgent haircut, or something. For each village we note the number of the OS Landranger map (1:50,000 - 1.25ins/1 mile or 2cms/1 km) and the more detailed Pathfinder (1:25,000 - 2.5ins/1 mile or 4cms/1 km).

Rights of Way & Obstructions

These walks are all on public Rights of Way or in places where the public is permitted to walk. They may be Footpaths, Bridleways or Byways (usually green lanes or tracks) with some stretches of ordinary road. Your rights as pedestrian are the same on all, you are entitled to follow the track or cross the land. The fact that it is "private" (most land is) is quite irrelevant.

Occupiers of land are legally obliged not to obstruct paths, it is an offence, but sometimes they do. Paths should not be ploughed up nor have crops growing over them, nor should you meet barbed wire fences. You are entitled to cross or remove any such obstacles, doing as little damage as you reasonably can. You may diverge to pass the obstacle so long as you go no further than necessary and do not enter someone else's land.

These notes appear in all Walkways books but you are not likely to meet problems on these walks. If you do, please report them immediately, as mentioned in the next section.

Amendment Service

The countryside changes all the time. You could meet new tracks, stiles and barns; hedges vanish, trees fall down and paths may be diverted. To keep directions as up to date as possible Walkways issues amendment slips.

IF you write to tell me of any changes or problems you meet and tell me the paragraph number, I will refund your postage.

IF you send a stamped addressed envelope with a note of what publication(s) you have, I will send you up to date amendment slips. (Enquiries 0121 550 3158.)

John Roberts

Boots & Clothes & Things

These walks are all modest affairs and you do not need to go equipped for mountaineering. If you do not suffer too much the first time and decide to take up walking as a pastime, get one of the many books that offer good advice on boots, clothing and equipment. For beginners, the following note might help with the first couple of walks.

The Midlands gets muddy at times and walking boots are best, but for short walks wellies will do fine if you find them comfortable. Trainers are excellent in dry weather. You do not necessarily need two pairs of socks but a thick woolly padding is a great comfort. The type of footbed used in trainers is helpful. It will usually be sensible to take a hat and waterproof; in winter carry gloves.

Getting There

CARS
We have made sure that there are suitable places for a few cars near starting points, though in some villages these are small. Use a car park if there is one and take great care never to cause obstruction or inconvenience. Never use pub car parks without permission, but this will usually be given on the reasonable condition that you have drink or snack at the end of your walk. It's not a bad idea anyway.

TRAINS & BUSES
Bus and train services are subject to change or cancellation. For each village we note whether there were trains or buses when we went to press and give a phone enquiry number. Good luck with the trains.

General Map

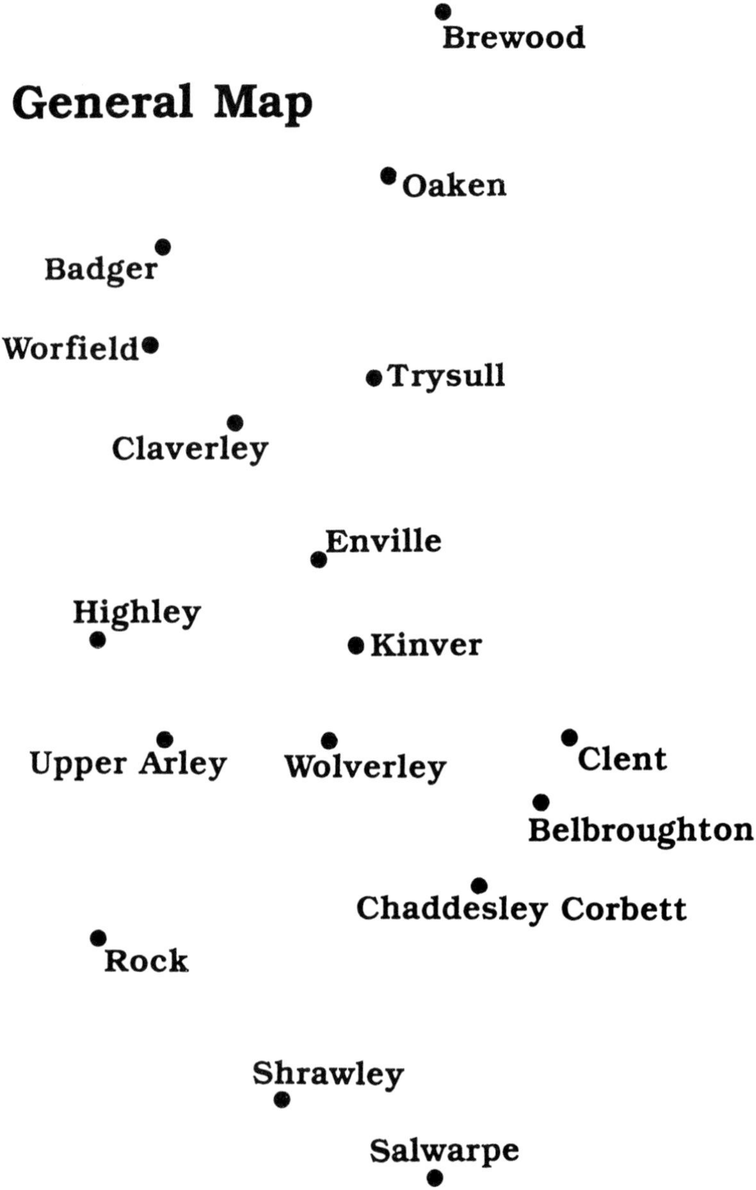

Brewood

Oaken

Badger

Worfield

Trysull

Claverley

Enville

Highley

Kinver

Upper Arley   Wolverley   Clent

Belbroughton

Chaddesley Corbett

Rock

Shrawley

Salwarpe

List of Walks

Working narrowboat at Brewood

Badger

WHERE
About 10.5 miles west of Wolverhampton and just north of the B4176 Dudley - Telford road. Maps: Landranger 138 and 127, Pathfinders 911 SO 69/79 and 890 SJ 60/70. Map reference SO 768997.

TRANSPORT, PARK & START
Buses call; enquiries 01743 253030. There is limited car space by the church and in The Crescent. This is a tiny and beautiful village. If there is any chance you would be a nuisance, ask to use one of the pub car parks and start there. The Stroll and Walk start at the church.

REFRESHMENTS
There is no pub at Badger, but you meet the Red Cow (Free House) at Ackleton on the Stroll or Walk, and on the Walk, the Seven Stars (Pubmaster) at Beckbury.

HOW FAR
Stroll 3.5 miles/5.6 kms, Walk 5 miles/8 kms.

THE VILLAGE
Even the name draws visitors, and no one enticed into this charming, serene village will be disappointed. Tucked away in an unspoilt corner of Shropshire, Badger nestles under steep slopes cloaked in magnificent woodland with the River Worfe curling round it to the west. The village centre is no more than the church, two pools and a clutch of beautiful timbered cottages, red brick and stone houses. One fine example is a thatched house called The Cottage which rests by a pool.

The name derives from *Baegi,* a personal name, and *ofer* a river bank or border. The Manor of Badger once belonged to the Abbey of Wenlock and in the early middle ages the village had a water mill.

St Giles Gothic sandstone church was rebuilt in 1834 and the Norman foundations of the tower are the only remains of the original building. Within the broad nave, the dark oak of the pews sets off the white walls which are bedecked with 19th century monuments and memorials by the sculptors Flaxman, Chantrey and Gibson. The chapel was built in 1886 by the Capel Cure family and contains more monuments. The intricately carved screen separating it from the nave dates from the 15th century. Copies of Titian's "Ecce Homo" and Guido Reni's "Annunciation" are unusual features for any church wall, and were given by the Capel Cure family.

The tranquil pools were once in the gardens of Badger Hall. A seat in the churchyard overlooks one of them; an idyllic spot to do very little. The Hall was a vast mansion remodelled in the early 1780's by James Wyatt, but you are too late because it was demolished in 1952. The ghost of a grey lady is said to have haunted the house, and when they removed it, transferred her presence to the grounds. During later building work an ancient jewellery box containing a ring was discovered, since when the ghost has been at rest.

Badger Dingle which you meet on the Stroll and Walk may be the same as Badgwick Dingle in a novel by P G Wodehouse. He knew the area as a teenager.

THE STROLL
This 3.5 miles is longer than the others but very well worth doing. Near the start you plunge through a gorgeous dingle with old fishponds of the Badger Estate. Look out for the ice house. Later comes the River Worfe, a fine pocket sewage works, a woodland walk, then a track through strange little hills. The dingle paths are steep and can be slippery.

(1) Face church & go L to road junction. Turn L to next junction, then bear R. Pass last house & go 100yds to take falling path L.

(2) Go down to cross dam, then follow rising path to field. Go ahead to phone pole & join fenced path to lane.

(3) Turn R for 450yds to sharp, falling L bend. Enter wide gateway R & cross stile.

(4) Bear R to end of trees & cross stile. Go ahead to bend of river, pass it on your L & cross footbridge. Follow L hedge (via stile & gate L) to corner gate, & cross stile to lane.

(5) Go R over bridge, pass lodge, & go up for 50yds to take gate L.

(6) Follow track 450yds & take gate L into field.

(7) Go ahead parallel with wood R & take gate. Follow green track, circling R to take gate on corner of wood onto woodland track.

(8) Go ahead for 1/4 mile & take gate into field. Follow green track & curve R between hills (past R fork) to T junction of tracks.
STROLL CONTINUES - para (9)

****
FOR WALK - switch to Walk para (1)
****

(9) Go R for 1/4 mile to road. Go R for 1/2 mile to start.

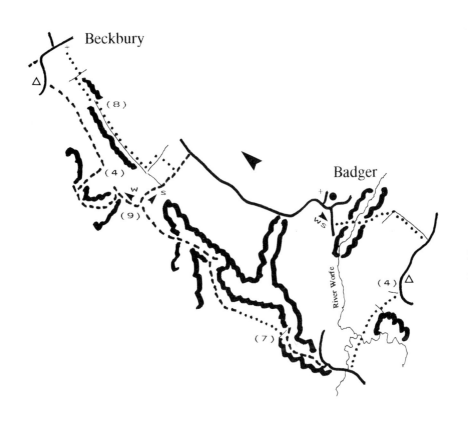

Cottage and pool in Badger

(11)

THE WALK

These 5 sylvan miles follow most of the Stroll and continue through pockets of woodland and pasture to the village of Beckbury. It returns beside more woodland, then across fields which give sweeping views over the Shropshire plain to where the Wrekin and Wenlock Edge rear out of the green patchwork.

(1) Follow Stroll to para (8), THEN -

(2) Turn L then immediately R, & follow track to tip of woodland L. Take gateway into wood & go down. At bottom curve R 100yds to fork. Go R & pass small path L to meet track by post.

(3) Go R & emerge into field. Follow R hedge to its end & continue to tree clump ahead.

(4) Circle L round clump & join an earth track. Follow 1/2 mile to road at Beckbury.

(5) Go R [IF LEAVING Seven Stars go L]   100 yards, & round R bend to church.

(6) Enter churchyard, go behind church & take iron gate to field. Follow R hedge round to R & over crest, then take fence gap into field.

(7) Go L by fence & cross stile. Go R down stone steps to field. Go L by wood 150yds to start of conifers & take track L to field.

(8) Go R by wood for 1/2 mile to field corner. Go L by hedge 150 yards & take gap R. Go ahead & take hedge gap onto track. Go L to lane.

(9) Go R 1/2 mile to start.

Belbroughton

WHERE
On the B4188, just off the A491 four miles south-east of West Hagley. Maps: Landranger 139, Pathfinder 953 SO 87/97. Map reference SO 920770.

TRANSPORT, PARK & START
Buses run; enquiries 01905 763763. Roadside parking in side streets, including Church Road. Both the Stroll and the Walk start at the church lychgate.

REFRESHMENTS
The Talbot (Hanson's), The Old Mill (Free House), and The Queens (Marston's).

HOW FAR
Stroll 1 mile/1.6 kms, Walk 4 miles/6.5 kms.

THE VILLAGE
Belbroughton is a big, attractive village south of the Clent Hills. The satisfying mix of buildings includes 19th century brick and immaculate 17th and 18th century cottages. It is a busy community, with a village hall, a cricket pitch, recreation ground and tennis courts, shops, four pubs and a post office. Bright gardens add a splash of summer colour.

In the 19th century the West Midlands was one of three scythe making areas and Belbroughton was an important centre. Edged steel had been forged here since the 16th century when a mill produced sword blades. The works centred on Belne Brook which flowed through a narrow, easily dammed valley to provide power. Isaac Nash, a local mill owner, bought up more distant scythe mills and created a monopoly.

Belbroughton main works probably housed the first plating forge in 1755 and it worked on until 1967. The brook was already powering five corn mills before the end of the 18th century and also drove the scythe making forges. In the 19th century scythes were exported worldwide. In this century the UK market became the main outlet but it declined after World War II and the trade finished in 1967.

There are survivals. Play spot the grindstone and count the ways that old millstones have been used; in garden walls, as cottage steps and as breakwaters in Belne Brook. An old plating hammer stands on the small village green. It was used in the Nash scythe works until 1968 and moved here in May 1995. The present four pubs may seem ample, but the mill workers once supported eleven.

Holy Trinity church, has 12th century Norman features, notably the doorways and a window on the south side, but is mainly 19th century. An early 17th century pulpit carved with dragons and weird human figures was "improved" in the 18th century, but 20th century renovations restored its original design. The font was taken out when the galleries were installed, but recovered from a village garden in the 1840s. On the chancel arch you can see faint red patches which are traces of underlying paintings. The chancel has one aisle from the 14th century and the other from the 19th.

THE STROLL
A mile around the outskirts of Belbroughton. A narrow path follows the Belne Brook through the village and links with a track to cross fields and pass the cricket pitch.

(1) From lychgate go down Church Road & turn L down Church Hill to High Street. Cross & go L 25yds then take path sharp R, with brook on your R.

(2) Follow it 200yds to drive. Cross stile opposite & follow R fence to cross second stile. Continue through woodland & round R bend to lane.

(3) Go L 200yds & take drive L. Follow till it swings R, then go ahead on track to field. Go L down hedged track to road.

(4) Go L, join pavement & continue 170yds to Queens. Take Church Hill R back to start.

THE WALK

About 4 miles. On fieldpaths from Belbroughton to Drayton Pool you pass an exciting, nautical sewage works, and at paragraph (3), a ruin of the remains of Weybridge Forges. It may have been a gun mill in 1821, but was a plating forge by 1849. Drayton Pool once supplied a mill but is now a tranquil spot fringed with anglers. Tracks take you back to village and give views of the Clent Hills.

(1) Go through lychgate, pass church door & take path by high brick wall to field. Bear L & follow L hedge to take gate ahead (not R). Follow R hedge to cross stile.

(2) Go ahead past works to R bend. Go round plus 10 paces to track junction. Take small PATH opposite into trees a few paces. Fork L & follow wall to cross footbridge R.

(3) Go L by brook & keep same line 1/4 mile (via stiles & fenced path) to cross stile to lane.

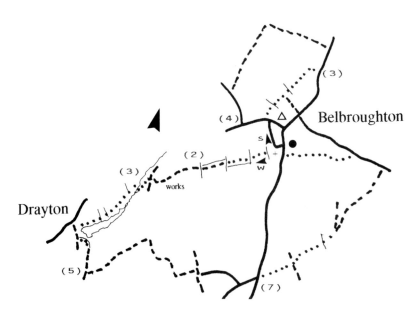

(4) Go sharp L on track to pool's far corner. Turn L into garden & follow its edge past house to gate & track. Go ahead past houses & round R bend to big iron gates R.

(5) Take track L 3/4 mile (via bends) to tarmac lane by farm.

(6) Go ahead, pass farm on your L & walk 300 yds to T junction. Go L 150 yards to T junction at Dordale Road.

(7) Take fenced path opposite 275yds to track. Take small gate opposite & follow R hedge till it bends R. Go ahead past lone tree & take small gate.

(8) Go ahead between banks, pass ruin R & go ahead to take gateway. Follow green track (via gate, when it becomes stone track) to B4188.

(9) Go L 225yds (past Foxglove Cottage R) & take path L. Follow R hedge, pass tennis courts, cross drive & take path back to church

Millstones recyled at Belbroughton

Avenue Bridge over the Shropshire Union Canal near Brewood

(17)

Brewood

WHERE
About 6 miles north of Wolverhampton. Get there from
the A449 or A5. Maps: Landranger 127, Pathfinder
891 SJ 80/90. Map reference SJ 885087.

TRANSPORT, PARK & START
Buses call; enquiries 01785 223344. Free car park off
Stafford Street, which is signed from the centre. The
Stroll and Walk start from the Market Square.

REFRESHMENTS
Lion Hotel (M&B), The Swan (Free House), Bridge Inn
(Burtonwood), plus tea shops.

HOW FAR
Stroll 3 miles/4.8 kms, Walk 6 miles/9.5 kms.

THE VILLAGE
Brewood (locally *"Brood"*) is from the Celtic Bre, meaning
hill, and so means "the wood on the hill". An active Civic
Society produces a leaflet, *Exploring Brewood*, which des-
cribes the history of most of the buildings, and with the
Parish Council they have tried to ensure the village keeps
its character.

Brewood was granted a market in 1221 and developed into
a large community. The Bishop of Lichfield held a group
of manors in the area and built a palace on the east side
of the Market Place. Brewood's importance dwindled in
later centuries, the market ceased in 1621 and the turmoil
of the Industrial Revolution passed it by. Today though,
it is a bustling village with shops, pubs, tea shops, sports,
grounds and hearteningly, schools. The Market Square
has an old pump and a horse trough displaying

flowers. Outside the chemist's shop is a plaque commemorating the birth here of the 19th century engineering contractor Thomas Walker who built the Severn Tunnel. 17th century Brewood Hall was built by Roger Fowke, reputedly on the site of King John's hunting lodge. By far the oddest building is 18th century Speedwell Castle just off the Square. which was funded from the winnings of a bet on the Duke of Bolton's horse, *Speedwell.*

Parts of St. Mary and St. Chad's church date from the 13th century but it was largely rebuilt in the 16th. The massive spire is 168 feet high. The interior is all light and space, and there are four alabaster tombs of the Giffard family of nearby Chillington Hall.

The Shropshire Union Canal runs west of the village and forms part of both the Stroll and the Walk. It was built in the 1830s by Thomas Telford in straight alignments requiring high embankments and deep cuttings.

The Stroll passes the gate of Chillington Hall which is distantly visible. The 18th century mansion is set in glorious parkland which was landscaped by Capability Brown in 1770. Among the ornate park buildings are Gothic and Ionic Temples, an ornamental bridge and dovecote. In 1983 the M54 cut through the south end. Giffard's Cross in the garden of the lodge by the gate commemorates Sir John Giffard's shooting of a panther with a bowshot from the house in 1513. You might not see any because the late specimen was an escaped present.

Belvide Reservoir passed on the Walk was built in 1834 as a feeder for the canal. It is a marvellous birdwatching site with an important winter gull roost which often hosts rarities. It also shelters wildfowl including garganey, teal, shoveler, wigeon, and goosander, as well as migrating waders and terns. In 1977 the West Midlands Bird Club established a reserve, but apart from the track used on the Walk, you need a permit to use other perimeter paths.

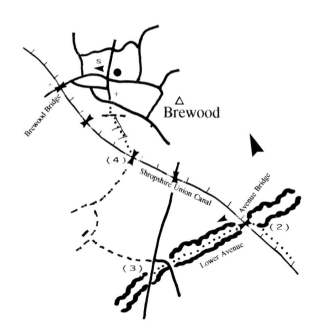

THE STROLL

In 3 varied miles there are fine views of the village, a tree lined canal walk, a woodland avenue and some stony tracks.

(1) Face Lion Hotel & go L 350yds to Bridge Inn. Join canal towpath (DON'T go under bridge) & follow it 1 mile (under 3 bridges), to ballustraded Avenue Bridge.

(2) Go on 50yds & take steps L to avenue. Go L 1/4 mile to lane. Cross & go on to road.

(3) Go R 100yds & take track L. Follow it (via 2 gates) to crossroads of tracks. Go R to T junction, then R to canal.

(4) Cross bridge then stile L & take steps. Cross stile R. Go half L to cross brick bridge, then go ahead via stiles) to track.

(5) Go L 10 paces & take path R to street. Go L, round R bend & back to start.

*Speedwell Castle,
Brewood*

*Cast iron viaduct over
the A5 near Brewood*

THE WALK
About 6 miles on fieldpaths, lanes and tracks, passing the Belvide Reservoir and returning on a superbly beautiful section of the Shropshire Union Canal.

(1) Face Lion Hotel & go L 350yds to Bridge Inn. Cross canal to church & take lane R.

(2) Follow lane (becomes track) 250yds & take gateless track L (Shaftbury Cottage). Follow it past cottage, then continue on wooded green track to its end.

(3) Jink L & join an earth track up to sharp L bend. Go ahead to R of two midfield trees. Turn HALF R to field corner & cross stile.

(4) Go half R to cross stile between bungalow & barns. Go ahead via gate to lane.

(5) Go L 1/2 mile (past Bird Club car park) & take stone track R.

(6) Follow it 250yds (past 2 houses) to its end, & take small gate L.

(7) Go ahead over field & take small gate. Go ahead to cross footbridge, then up L onto pond bank. Follow bank to its corner, then go R by hedge to field corner & take small gate L.

(8) Follow R hedge/fence past wood & via gate to small gate & track.

(9) Go R 1/2 mile to A5.

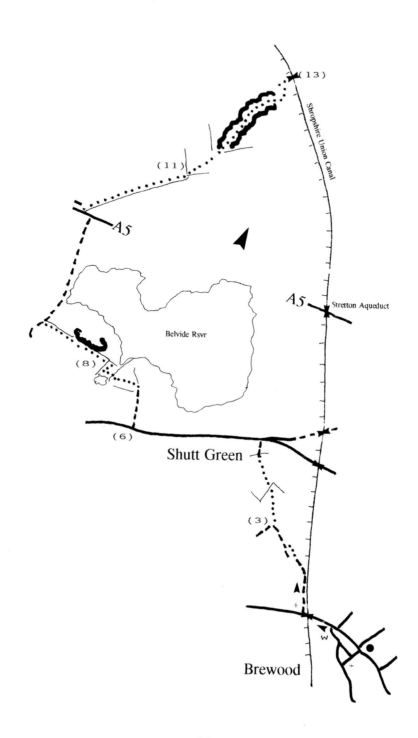

(13)

Shropshire Union Canal

(11)

A5

Belvide Rsvr

A5 Stretton Aqueduct

(8)

(6)

Shutt Green

(3)

Brewood

W

(23)

(10) Go L 30yds, then cross road & take green track opposite. Take small gate & go ahead into farmyard, bearing R to exit by small gate. Follow R hedge (via 2 gates) to gate by track R.

(11) Go half L to projecting hedge corner & take small gate. Follow wooded track 450yds to its end.

(12) Follow L hedge & take small corner gate. Go ahead to concrete track, then L for 100yds to take gate R. Cross canal bridge & turn R to join towpath.

(13) Follow canal for 1 1/4 miles; after aqueduct go under two more bridges to third (No.14, high & white with railings), & just past it take steps L to Bridge Inn. Go R to start.

Font in St Cassian's, Chaddesley Corbett

Chaddesley Corbett

WHERE
Off the A448 midway between Bromsgrove and Kidderminster. Maps: Landranger 139, Pathfinder 953 SO 87/97. Map
reference SJ 893736.

TRANSPORT, PARK & START
Buses pass; enquiries 01905 763763. Roadside parking by
by the church and along the main village street. Both the
Stroll and Walk start from the church.

REFRESHMENTS
The Talbot (Banks's), The Swan (Batham's) and tea shops.

HOW FAR
Stroll 2 miles/3.25 kms, Walk 5 miles/8 kms.

THE VILLAGE
Chaddesley Corbett sits almost on the fringe of the West
Midlands in typical Worcestershire farmland. In 816 AD
the Mercian King Coenwulf granted the land to the Bishop
of Worcester. By 1086, Chaddesley was a prosperous place,
perhaps more important than nearby Kidderminster, with a
similar population of between 300-400. The name Corbett
was added when the Corbett family held the manor from
the end of the 12th century.

In the 14th century the manor passed to the Beauchamps
of Warwick. Part of the estate, including the main street,
was used as part payment to build the Beauchamp chapel
in St. Marys, Warwick. The Corporation of Warwick
was given property in the village at the Reformation.

Chaddesley Corbett has a harmonious mix of buildings,
from Tudor and Georgian to Victorian Gothic. Many of
them have interesting histories which we have no space to

mention, but you can get a booklet from the church which details each one. Although quite beautiful, the village is far from being just a picture postcard, but is live and thriving, with tea shops, pubs, a post office and shops.

St Cassian's is the only church in England with this dedication, after a Roman schoolmaster stabbed to death by his pupils. (No - don't explain, we can guess.) The original church was Saxon and some of the present building is Norman, but significant alterations took place in the 14th century. The font is elaborately decorated with four intertwined dragons, apparently a Saxon design, though carved in 1160.

The tower and spire are the most prominent features of the church, but its glory is the chancel, one of the finest in the county. All three were rebuilt in the 14th century. The stained glass in the east window is nice, standard Victorian stuff, but look at the stonework. Look also at the stone effigy which may be that of Roger Corbett, a Lord of the Manor who died in 1290. This lay first in the north chapel which was built as a manorial chapel in the 13th century by the Corbett family. Also in the chancel is a copy of the Ardebil carpet. The original is held by the Victoria and Albert museum, and was woven in 1512 by a craftsman called Maksaud from the Middle Eastern city of Kashan. Ardebil was a Holy City on the Caspian Sea. The carpet took an incredible 60 years to complete, is 34 feet long, and has over 33 million knots. This copy was woven by a local Kidderminster firm and given to the church by one of the weavers. Elsewhere in the church is a brass to one Thomas Forest who died in 1571, once a keeper of Feckenham forest. Nice one, punster.

Chaddesley Woods is a hilltop remnant of the Royal Forest of Feckenham, which in Norman times reached from Worcester to the Clent Hills, and from the River Severn to Alcester. Designated a National Nature Reserve in 1973, it is an important area of broadleaved woodland interspersed with grassland where traditional management produces flower rich areas. There is a diverse range of wildlife with badgers doing particularly well. Conifers are being felled to allow native trees to regenerate and a nest box scheme encourages woodland birds.

THE STROLL
Around 2 miles of easy walking, with a really thrilling field of rhubarb, an isolated farm, a stream and lots of cow plop.

(1) Put church on your L & go ahead to Swan. Take track opposite 50yds & go L. Follow road to L bend & cross corner stile.

(2) Follow R hedge/fence & cross footbridge. Go ahead on earth track, pass willows on your L & join tarmac path. Follow till it bends, then go ahead to pass power pole with gizmo on your R.

(3) Walk with hedge on your R to edge of orchard, then go R up bank to next field. Go L by hedge to track.

(4) Go R & through farm (via 2 gates), then down track to take first gate L. Continue BESIDE TRACK till it bends R, then head for L pylon. Go down bank & cross footbridge.

(5) Go R (parallel with R hedge) to cross 2 stiles & track. Bear a little L & cross mid-hedge stile. Go ahead (aim just L of steeple) to last low building, & join track.

(6) Go R & follow track round L & R bends to church.

THE WALK

An undulating, sometimes muddy 5 miles through woods, returning across farmland. The woods are particularly splendid in autumn. Take binoculars to spot the birds, and possibly muntjac and fallow deer.

(1) Put church on your L & walk down street to Swan. Take track R, pass end of road L & follow power lines to stile & track.

(2) Go ahead 1/4 mile till track bends sharp L. Go AHEAD with hedge on your L & cross corner stile to field. Go ahead (via stile) & cross stile into woods.

(3) Go ahead to meet track. Go R & climb steeply to T-junction of tracks. Go L, pass track L & go ahead to information board. Cross stile R to field. Go L by wood (via stile) to stile & lane.

(4) Take path opposite & follow wood edge path to cross stile by shed. Go ahead to lane. Turn L 300 yards to bridleway & footpath signs R, & take small gate onto track.

(5) Pass gate L & follow track 1/2 mile (via 2 small gates) to cottage. Take track R 1/4 mile (via gate) to lane

(6) Go R 300 yards (past 2 L turns) to road fork. Go L over stile & bear R to cross corner stile. Go ahead over two stiles & join concrete track. Go ahead (via 2 gates) to its end, & take gateway R.

(7) Bear L to gate on projecting hedge corner, & cross stile. Go L close to fence, then between hedge & trees to cross stile. Follow R hedge to stile, footbridge & track.

(8) Go L 15 paces & turn R to cross plank. Follow fenced path (via 2 stiles) to field. Go ahead to R edge of tree clump & meet track.

(9) Cross & pass R of tree, then follow L hedge/fence (via stiles) to pass pond on your R & cross stile.

(10) Go R on field edge, round L & R corner, plus 100 yards, & cross stile R onto track. Go L to meet outward track.

(11) Go L 1/4 mile (round L & R bends) back to church.

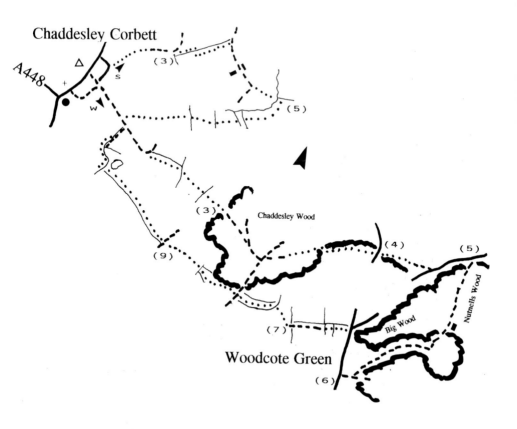

Claverley

WHERE
Some 8 miles south-west of Wolverhampton, best reached
off the A458. Maps: Landranger 138, Pathfinder 911, SO
69/79. Map reference SO 793934.

TRANSPORT, PARK & START
Buses call; enquiries 0121 200 2700. There is limited park-
ing on the main street. Ask permission to use pub car parks.
Start the Stroll and Walk from the church lychgate.

REFRESHMENTS
The Plough (Ansells), The Crown (Banks's), Kings Head
(Free House). On the Walk are the Black Lion (Free House),
Hilton and The Lion o Morfe (Free House) Upper Farmcote.

HOW FAR
Stroll 1.5 miles/2.5 kms, Walk 7.5 miles/12 kms.

THE VILLAGE
Claverley is a picturesque gem set in peaceful and remote
countryside. The name means a clearing where the clover
grows. Flint tools of the Middle Stone Age, 4,000 years
ago, have been found nearby. The village centre, called
the Bull Ring, is a delightful collection of shops, whitewashed cottages and timbered buildings. The 15th century
vicarage is a wonderful timber framed house in remarkable
condition. Next door is the attractive old sandstone school
house; good to see the village still has a primary school.
Claverley can fairly be called a chocolate box village. The
White House in the High Street and its colourful gardens
once featured in Cadbury's advertisements.

All Saints church dates from the 12th century. A massive
wooden door leads into a spacious, bare sandstone interior
which emphasises the vivid colours of the stained glass windows. The church's chief glory are the unique mediaeval

wall paintings in the style of the Bayeux Tapestry which were revealed during restoration in 1902. One on the north arcade may date from 1200 and shows knights in combat representing the Seven Virtues and the Vices. There are still traces of the Last Judgement on the chancel arch.

The church architecture is in several styles including some Norman, the south aisle having been added later. The 14th century chancel has a hammerbeam roof of 1601. The porch, upper windows of the nave and the tower are 15th century perpendicular work. Also in the 15th century, two chapels with two alabaster tombs were built for the Gatacre family, who have been associated with the village for almost a thousand years. There are two notable fonts, one Norman in style and the other early Saxon tub-shaped. On Ascension Day the choir sing from the top of the tower.

In the churchyard is a yew tree with a pitted and gnarled trunk thought to be at least 1,000 years old, which makes it older than the church. The cross by the lychgate dates from 1349 and is a memorial to victims of the Black Death.

Vicarage, Claverley

THE STROLL
A 1.5 mile exploration of some of the narrow tracks which are common in this area. They are usually "white roads", that is, public roads which have not been surfaced. Level and sandy.

(1) Enter churchyard & follow tarmac path round church. Pass seats & join grass path, take small gate & follow hedged path to road.

(2) Cross bearing L & follow hedged path to track. Go L & round L bend to R bend. Go half L across grass to gate & cattle grid. Follow track to lane.

(3) Go R 1/2 mile to meet green track from R, with war memorial ahead.

(4) Take green track R to open field, then go on by hedge to white chalet. Follow new track 400 yards, round R bend by pink house (L) to L bend with red brick house (L).

(5) Cross stile R & head for church, dropping to meet fence. Go R to gate & track.

(6) Go L to next gate & cross stile R. Follow hedged track to road. Cross & follow hedged track into churchyard & back to start.

THE WALK

These 7.5 miles sample the mixed character of landscape to the west of the village. The first half mile seems flat and unpromising, but suddenly there is rolling countryside which you travel on fieldpaths and long, sandy tracks.

(1) Put church & lychgate on your L, then walk down road for 1/4 mile to R bend by Holloway Cottage.

(2) Climb path up bank ahead & follow it to stile & field. Go ahead past R end of sheds to gate, & cross stile to track.

(3) Take track opposite, pass sheds to double gates & cross stile. Go ahead on green track (which jinks R) & follow hedge to field corner. Step into L field, then follow R hedge to double gates & cross stile to lane.

(4) Go R 250 yards to junction & turn L. Go on 1/4 mile to R bend.

(5) Go R 15 paces, then cross stile L. Go ahead, follow L fence round to L, then follow hedge & take small gate. Follow L hedge (which bends L) to gate, & cross stile. Go R & cross 2nd stile to field.

(6) Follow L hedge to field corner & cross stile to an open field.

(7) Go ahead 100 yards to midfield mark post. [IF THERE IS NO POST or marked path, follow L hedge 100 yards to wide gap.] Turn R & head for projecting fence corner & R side of sheds, to cross stile. Go ahead to drive.

(8) Cross to gate opposite, DON'T TAKE IT. Bear L beside fence & follow it to take gate. Follow hedged path to stile & field.

(9) Follow L hedge to cross corner stile, then continue by fence to its end, & cross 2 stiles L. Follow fenced path & cross stile. Go on few paces, cross stile R & go ahead to A454.

(10) Go L 100 yards & take Sandpit Lane L. Follow it 175 yards to double power pole with gizmo, & take lane R.

(11) Pass quarry, then follow track to its end & take kissing gate. Go ahead past midfield lime tree, then bear L to field end gate & cross stile to lane.

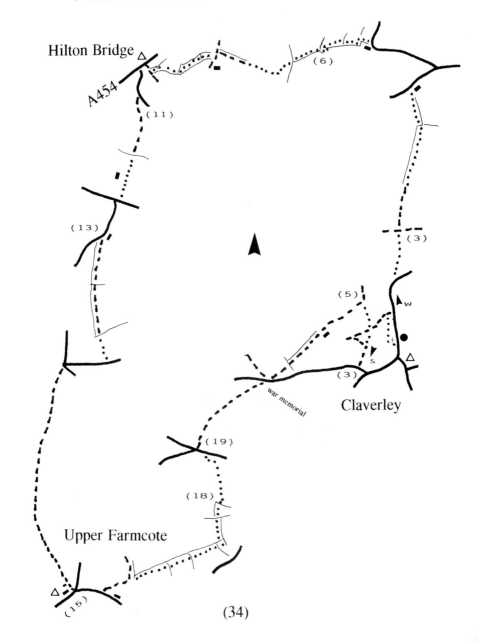

Hilton Bridge

A454

(11)

(6)

(13)

(3)

(5)

W

S

(3)

Claverley

war memorial

(19)

(18)

Upper Farmcote

(15)

(12) Go R 50 yards to T junction. Go L 250 yards & pass 1st farm entrance to 2nd.

(13) Take black steel gate & follow earth track. At end, go on by R hedge & cross corner stile to lane.

(14) Go R 300 yards to junction. Go L & take stone track under power lines. Follow it 1 mile to road junction.

(15) Take lane opposite 200 yards & join track L. Follow it past house to projecting hedge corner.

(16) Go ahead with hedge on your L (crossing an earth track & 2 stiles) to field corner by brick shed, & take gate L.

(17) Go on few paces to hedge corner & turn L (via 2 gates). Pass gateway R, follow R hedge to field corner & take gateway. Bear L to far field corner & cross stile.

(18) Take earth track bearing R for 15 paces, then fork L to far hedge & take double steel gates to road. Go L to road junction & take track R.

(19) Follow it for 1/4 mile to lane & track junction.

(20) Take green track opposite to open field, then go on by hedge to white chalet. Follow new track 400 yards, round R bend by pink house (L) to L bend with red brick house (L).

NEXT - turn to the Stroll para (5)

Clent

WHERE
Start from the south-west tip of Adams Hill which is 2 miles
east of West Hagley on the A491. Get there via Holy Cross.
Maps: Landranger 139, Pathfinders 953 SO 87/97 and 933
SO 86/96. Map reference SO 927799.

TRANSPORT, PARK & START
Buses pass; enquiries 0121 200 2711 or 01905 763763. Car
park near the Hill Tavern at the end of the short road to Adams Hill. Both the Walk and Stroll start from here.

REFRESHMENTS
Hill Tavern (Free House), The Fountain (Hansons) and The
Vine (Free House), The Bell & Cross (Hanson's) and The
Woodman (Ansells). There is a restaurant by the church,
and a burger bar with "amusement" arcade by the car park.

HOW FAR
Stroll 2 miles/3.25 kms, Walk 5 miles/8 kms.

THE VILLAGE
Clent huddles at the foot of the Clent Hills, sliced in two
by the roaring A491, but the oldest part near the church is
tranquil, with a brook bubbling along the main street. Holy
Cross has a newsagent, food shops, a post office and a hair-
dresser. Unusually, the name Clent is the Domesday Book
spelling.

A church has stood here since the 12th century, but the
present St. Leonard's, with its fine tower and huge clock,
was extensively rebuilt in the 15th century and further
restored in the 19th century. The rather gloomy interior
is relieved by the few remaining stained glass windows.
The chancel and sanctuary are higher than the nave and
the 15th century barrel roof is worth a craned neck.

The Clent Hills are mainly owned by the National Trust.
They draw a million visitors a year but few people go far
from the car parks or main paths so there are always peaceful corners. Serious erosion has caused the 270 million year
old coarse sandstone called Clent Breccia to break through
the surface and some areas are fenced off to allow them
to regenerate. On clear days the views from Adams Hill are
about the best in the Midlands. To the north is an impressive
vista over the Black Country, then moving west you see in
turn: The Wrekin, Brown Clee, Titterstone Clee, the Abberley
Hills and the Malverns. To the south and east are Bredon Hill
and Edge Hill in Warwickshire. Sometimes you can see into
Wales as far as the Radnor Forest, Hay Bluff and the Black
Mountains. The Four Stones are not all that prehistoric,
but put up in the 18th century by Lord Lyttleton of Hagley
Hall.

The Arboretum on the south-eastern slopes of Adams Hill is
the only large expanse of tree cover on the hills. Here there
are badgers, foxes and fallow deer, which wander in from
the park at Hagley Hall. The prolific birdlife includes sis-
kins, redpolls, yellowhammers and redstarts.

St. Kenelm's sandstone church has hideously weathered gar-
goyles, a 15th century tower and 16th century porch. Beside
the church is a Holy Well which sprang up where Kenelm,
eight year old Prince of Mercia was chopped into little
bits with an axe. They eventually nicked a hit man called
Askobert who was on a contract from little K's sister. It's
a long story involving a hunt, an old woman, a cow and a
dove, with a walk on part for the Pope. Get the leaflet
from the church, and make sure you pay lots of money.

Walton Hill, at 1035 feet is the second highest in Worcestershire and they say there is no higher ground between
here and the Urals, 3,000 miles east. This less frequented
hilltop is good for birdlife, with ring ouzel, stonechat and
wheatear turning up on migration.

THE STROLL

About 2 miles on the lower slopes of Adam's Hill and through woodland to the summit. Glorious views on a clear day.

(1) From car park, go through vehicle barrier by Hill Tavern & turn R on tarmac path. Follow 300 yds to path R by house. Go L uphill 300yds to draw level with pub below, & cross stile R.

(2) Go ahead & down to foot of slope. LOOK OUT for & take path sharp L, & follow it to stile & track. Go R by fence to junction by steps L.

(3) Take steps & follow path through bushes, wood & wooden barrier onto open hillside. Go ahead & cross a path to main ridge path. Go R to summit of Adam's Hill.

(4) RETURN past first free standing tree clump & path you came on, to clump of Scots pine L. Bear R to pass seat, & when you see Hill Tavern, plunge down to it as you please.

THE WALK

This hilly 5 mile walk includes two steep climbs down green fields, St Kenelm's church and well, two fine ridge walks and a long, sandy track.

(1) From car park, go through vehicle barrier by Hill Tavern onto concrete track. Follow it up to ridge. Go up L to summit. (Just keep on to top, silly.)

(2) Put four stones & trig point on your R & go ahead. Follow ridge path to commemorative stone. Go through barrier & follow R fence down to road.

(38)

(3) Go L 25 paces & cross stile R. Go ahead past markpost & down to field corner to cross stile. Go HALF R to markpost (not one ahead), go R by hedge to markpost, & bear L to cross stile.

(4) Bear a little L from R hedge to midhedge markpost, & keep same line to cross stile. Go ahead into churchyard.

(5) Leave by lychgate & go L to T-junction. Turn R [CARE - walk up verge] to L bend by drive, & cross stile L of gate.

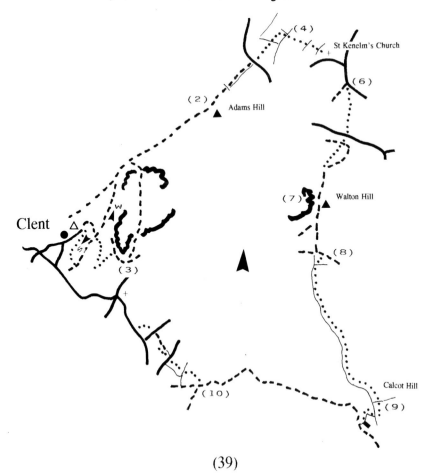

(6) Head up field to just R of power pole & cross stile & road. Take path opposite & climb to track. EITHER go L on easier contour track OR ahead; both ways emerge on shoulder of hill. Go to summit.

(7) Pass trig point & bear L. Head for house, go L & cross drive to take stile.

(8) Bear R to cross corner stile. Follow North Worcs Path along crest of hill (via stiles) for 3/4 mile. When it falls L at stile go ahead 20yds & cross stile R.

(9) Follow L fence round its corner to field corner, & cross stile to track. Go R 3/4 mile to meet track L, & cross stile R.

(10) Go half L to gate & cross stile. Bear a little R to lone pine & power pole without antlers, & cross stile to lane.

(11) Take stile (or gap) opposite, go through gate, follow field edge & cross stile to drive by white gates. Follow it to lane. Take small iron gate opposite & go half L to gate & lane.

(12) Go R 300yds to cross roads. Take Odnall Lane ahead & follow pavement to its end. Cross to opposite pavement, go 400yds & turn R up to car park.

Adam's Hill

(40)

Enville

WHERE
On the A458 5 miles west of Stourbridge. Maps: Landranger
138, Pathfinder 933 SO 88/98. Map reference SO 825868.

TRANSPORT, PARK & START
Buses pass; enquiries 01743 253030. Park by the church,
but leave a lot of money in the wall box inside. The Stroll
and Walk start from the church.

REFRESHMENTS
The Cat (Free House), closed on Sundays.

HOW FAR
Stroll 2.5 miles/4 kms, Walk 5 miles/8 kms.

THE VILLAGE
Enville stands on the Staffordshire border with Shropshire
and is an estate village for Enville Hall. It is split by the
A458, stretching up the hill towards the church and with
newer housing off Blundies Lane. Because of a convenant
in the lease,the Cat Inn is always closed on Sundays. Enville is a thriving community with fund raising activities
which include an annual sponsored ride and walk, garden
parties and local concerts.

The glowing sandstone church of St. Mary the Virgin was
known as St Lawrence in the 16th century. The ornate tower
was altered in 1872 by Sir Gilbert Scott with money supplied
by the Earl of Stamford and Warrington, and is modelled on
the tower of Gloucester cathedral. The tower again needs
repair and this is why we urge you to leave dollops of cash
in the box. The chancel was rebuilt in the 13th century, the
aisles date from the 14th and 15th centuries, the nave and
arcades are much older and typically Norman. Look for
the remains of Saxon stonework, including carved heads

in the north arcade pillars and two figures in the south arcade, which may date from the 7th or 8th century.

Don't miss the gruesome late 15th century misericords in the chancel. Stained glass from the 14th century survives in the east window and the south aisle in the form of heraldic shields of families connected with the village.

Enville Hall is mostly 18th century, and pretty miserable it looks; grey, dull and overbearing. The only redeeming feature is the large stone porch. We would much rather live in the gracious stable block with its jaunty cupola and elegant wind vane. In its heyday, the Hall had formal gardens, a conservatory, pools, a botanical park, summerhouse and Chinese pagoda. The gardens were opened to the public twice weekly in 1853 drawing up to 8,000 visitors a week.

The rolling parkland called The Sheepwalks rises to 675 feet. In the 17th century, the area was known simply as "The Hills". The 7,000 acres were landscaped by William Shenstone, and are a wonderful mix of hills, woodland and pools. Their chief glory is the breathtaking views which stretch from the Malverns to Shropshire and Wales.

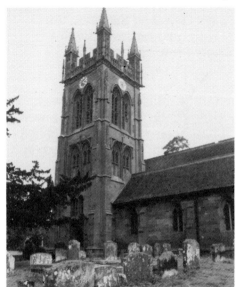

St Lawrence's, Enville

THE STROLL

A low level amble of just under 2.5 miles, with a look at Enville Hall, a woodland track, and fields.

(1) From car park enter churchyard, bear R past yew tree & cross stile. Go half L to midfence gate & cross stile. Go ahead to drive

(2) Go R, pass stable block, enter gateway, & follow fenced drive to pond R. Turn L by fence a few paces & take stile or gate L.

(3) Turn half R to cross midfence stile, then keep same line to field corner & cross stile. Go ahead to lane. Cross & take gap R of gate. Go ahead by L hedge to wall. Go L to its end, then keep ahead to stile & A458.

(4) DON'T CROSS HERE. Go R 150yds (past house R), then cross into track opposite. Follow 1/4 mile to cottage L, plus 75yds, to gate by hedged track L.

(5) Go L on track 1/4 mile (track joins from L), & follow lane up to T junction. Go L 1/2 mile (past lane R) to T junction in village. Go R back to start.

THE WALK

These 5 miles are divided between some remote fields and woodland which are fairly level, and the glorious parkland of Enville Hall and the Sheepwalks.

(1) At church car park, walk away from church to its far corner & join A458. Go ahead until you have CLEAR VIEW of traffic, then cross & continue 300yds, past modern house R to drive.

(2) Turn R into garden, follow L hedge to bottom corner & take small iron gate. Follow green track 400yds into & through wood, to field corner.

(3) Follow R hedge & cross stile to lane. Cross stile opposite, follow L hedge 300 yds to 50yds from wood, then cross twin stiles L.

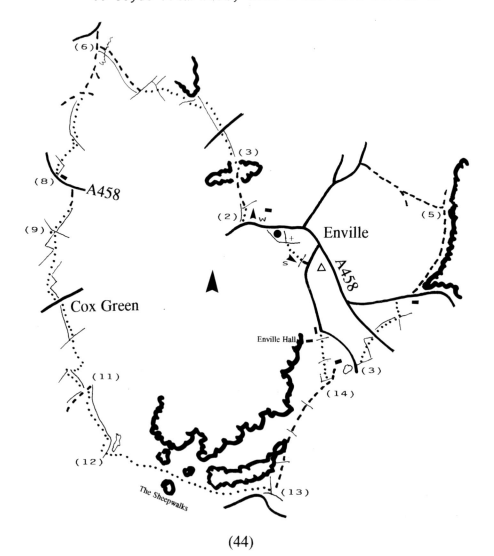

(4) Go half R to gate & cross stile. Cross field diagonally & take corner stile. Bear R & take first of 2 gates.

(5) Go ahead by wood 400yds, (path becomes track & crosses dip) to R bend, then take green track L.

(6) Follow 200yds (past pond) to T junction. Go R through poplar trees to last but one poplar, then take small path L to stile & field.

(7) Go R by R hedge & cross stile. Continue 150yds & cross midhedge stile R. Go L 25yds to big oak. Turn R, cross midfield to power pole & take stile. Cross field diagonally & take corner stile to A458.

(8) CROSS HERE & go L 200yds (past last house L) to enter gap & gateway R. Go ahead with hedge on your L for 300yds thro hedge gap into next field, then cross twin stiles L.

(9) Go half R past 1st projecting hedge corner (R) & 2nd (L) to 3rd (L). Turn L & follow hedge to gate & road.

(10) Take gate opposite, follow R hedge to bottom field corner & take gap. Go ahead midfield & cross stile to thicket. Follow path to field corner. Go L by wood & take corner gap to earth track.

(11) Go L towards gate. DON'T TAKE IT; go R by hedge round field edge to bottom corner. Go R 50 yards & take small path L to cross stile. Go ahead to marker post on edge of field.

*(12) Go ahead to SUMMIT, then keep same line to next summit. **LOOK AHEAD.** Note clump of trees near summit & lone trees to its L. Head just R of lone trees, then past corner of wood L. Keep same line (parallel with wood) down to gate, & cross stile.*

(13) Go half L (parallel with wood), pass midfield tree on your R, & go down to cross stile. Bear L down grass track & take gate. Go on to near farm, & cross stile in fence L.

(14) Go ahead & cross stile. Follow green track & go through covert to cross stile into field. Go ahead to R side of buildings & cross stile to drive.

(15) Go ahead 1/4 mile & pass cottage R, then to end of wooden fence L. Turn L on stone track & cross stile. Go half R to church & cross stile to churchyard.

Highley

WHERE
On the west bank of the River Severn on the B4555 between Bewdley and Bridgnorth. Start from here or from Alveley Country Park on the east bank (SO 751843), which is off the A442 Bridgnorth - Kidderminster road. Maps: Landranger 138, Pathfinder 932 SO 68/78. Map reference SO 742834.

TRANSPORT, PARK & START
Buses visit Highley and Alveley; enquiries 01743 253030. Severn Valley Railway steam trains stop at Highley station; enquiries 01299 401001. From here join the Stroll in para (7) at *. Trains also stop to the north at the new Country Park station, where you can join the Stroll in para (5).

On the WEST BANK park cars and start at the Highley
Mine Park, which is signposted from the village.

On the EAST BANK use the Country Park at Alveley,
signposted from the A442, and start at para (1A).

REFRESHMENTS
Ship Inn (Free House) on both Stroll and Walk by the
river, the Bache Arms (Greenhall) Highley, and the Uni-
corn Inn (Free House) on the Walk at Hampton Loade.

HOW FAR
Stroll 2.3 miles/3.7 kms, Walk 7 miles/11.25 kms. You
can reduce the Walk to 4.5 miles/7.25 miles if you return
by train from Hampton Loade.

THE VILLAGE
Highley sits on a ridge over the glorious landscape of the
Severn Valley, one of the biggest villages in Shropshire
with a population over 3,000. The terraced brick houses
are unmistakably miners' cottages, and the Coop store
with its beehive plaque (1905) and the Working Men's
Club tell the village's social history. So too does the
grim, red brick Methodist Chapel, with its perpendicular style window ready to drop like a portcullis. The
rest of the story can be seen by the river in the remains
of the Alveley and Highley Mines, which are both now
Country Parks.

This area has been quarried for sandstone and mined for
coal since the Middle Ages. Local stone was floated down
the Severn to build Worcester Cathedral. Traces of mineral
railways lie about in the woods round Borle Brook, and at
one time the five pits employed almost 1000 workers. The
last colliery closed in 1969. The buildings are mostly 20th
century, but the area around St. Mary's church could be a
step back in time. The half timbered house by the church
was the vicarage until 1620. St. Mary's was built in 1140;
the oldest building in the village. The chancel walls,

the remains of three windows, a moulded doorway in the south wall and most of the nave are 12th century. Alterations in the 15th century raised the height of the nave roof and added the present tower. More restoration was done in 1880.

The Severn Valley Railway first opened in 1862 and ran 40 miles from Shrewsbury to Hartlebury. It closed in 1963 to passengers but coal traffic continued until 1970. Since then the sixteen miles between Bridgnorth and Kidderminster has become one of the longest, privately owned, restored railways in the UK and it runs throughout the year.

THE STROLL
About 2.3 miles for nature lovers and train buffs on lanes, tracks and fieldpaths. There is a peaceful Severnside path and the country park. Mud warning; in wet weather the farm yard will be a bit deep.

(1) From HIGHLEY MINE car park get onto road & go up to 1st house. Take hedged path R, circling L to B4555. NEXT para (2).

****
(1A) From ALVELEY car park go down to river & cross bridge (directly below old mine buildings). NEXT para (6).
****

(2) Go R 250yds to Library & take Barke Street R. Follow it past last house to electric sub station L, & cross stile.

(3) Go half R to cross midhedge stile (R of power pole) & reach track. Go L round bends & through farmyard (via gates) to stone track.

(4) Go down R to gates, cross stile & continue down to cross railway.

(5) Go ahead to meet path, then turn R 400yds to bridge. DON'T CROSS.

(6) Follow riverside path DOWNSTREAM 1/2 mile, to pass golf course & join tarmac track. Pass cottages to post box by Ship Inn.

(7) Go R up to station, take gate & cross railway. Go L up access track to gate & lane.

(8) Take small gate opposite (Highley Mine) & follow path (bearing L) UP to sandstone cliff. Go R up cutting to path junction by train sign

(9) Go L on grass ride to meet 3 stone paths R. Take any (they meet) & follow looping route past pit wheel to car park.

[IF you started from ALVELEY - NEXT para (1)]

THE WALK

This 7 mile walk is one of the best in the book. Field paths from Highley lead to a wooded brook. Glorious views west to the Clee Hills accompany you over fields to Hampton Loade on the River Severn, before joining the riverside path back.

(1) From HIGHLEY MINE car park get onto road & go up to 1st house. Take hedged path R, circling L to B4555. NEXT para (2).

****

From ALVELEY car park - follow Stroll paras (1A) and 6 to (9), then Walk para (1).
****

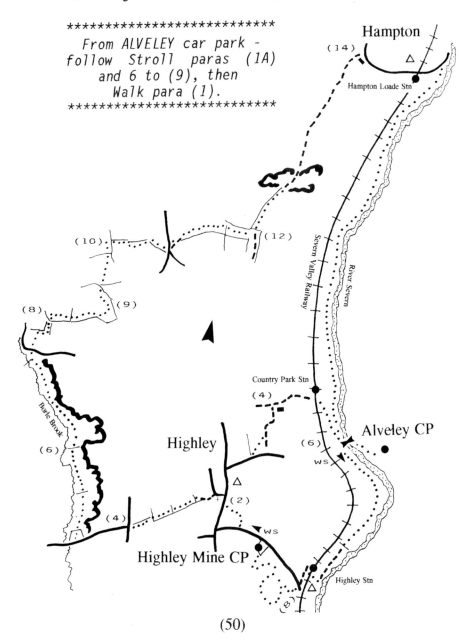

(2) Go R to crossroads, then L to pass church & join gravel track to house, "Springfield".

(3) Fork L & cross corner stile to field. Go ahead by L hedge, & keep this line 1/4 mile (via two stiles) to lane.

(4) Take lane opposite 400yds to near bridge, then cross stile R.

(5) Go ahead & cross corner stile (R of gate). Follow by L hedge & cross 2nd stile. Go ahead through woodland (over fallen fence) 1/4 mile, to meet track from R at double iron gates.

(6) Cross gates & follow edge of wood to take next gate. Follow woodland path to cross stream & take steps. Jink L & follow top of bank, cross wooden bridge, pass paths R, then curve R up to lane.

(7) Take path opposite (via stile & steps) to field. Go ahead to join L hedge, follow it 10 yds to join sunk path, & follow to cross stile

(8) Follow R hedge, cross stile & go ahead through copse to field. Follow R hedge till it bends R, then keep ahead to stile. DON'T CROSS

(9) Go L round field edge to gate & cross stile. Go ahead, bearing R to hedge corner to cross stile by steel gate. Go ahead 50yds & cross stile R.

(10) Go ahead by trees till they end, then bear L to cross stile 10yds L of gate. Go L by hedge to cross stile, then bear R by hedge to gate/stile & road.

(11) Cross, take green track L of Hazelwells Road & take small gate. Follow R hedge (crossing stile & passing stile R) to cross corner stile. Go ahead down narrow field to meet track by power lines.

(12) Go L & take lower gate (Jack Mytton Way). Follow L hedge for two fields & take small gate into wood.

(13) Follow track 1/2 mile through woodland, then between hedges, & through farm to lane.

(14) Go down R 1/2 mile, passing under railway to turning place by river.

(15) Join river bank & follow it downstream 2 miles to bridge.

[IF you started from ALVELEY - Cheerio. IF you started from HIGHLEY MINE, continue with Stroll para (6) to finish.]

Rock houses, Kinver Edge

Kinver

WHERE
WHERE
Off A458, 4 miles west of Stourbridge. Maps: Landranger
138, Pathfinder 933 SO 88/98. Map reference SO 840835.

TRANSPORT, PARK & START
Buses call; enquiries 0121 200 2700. There are several car
parks off the High Street. Both the Stroll and the Walk start
from Ye Olde White Hart Inn.

REFRESHMENTS
In the centre are the George & Dragon (Ansells), The Vine
(Free House), Olde White Hart (Banks), Plough and Harrow
(Batham's), several restaurants and a tea shop.

HOW FAR
Stroll 2 miles/3.25 kms, Walk 6 miles/9.5 kms.

THE VILLAGE
Kinver originally grew up around St Peter's church, high
on a sandstone hill above the flood plain of the River Stour.
The present building is mainly 14th century but the earliest
parts are Norman. Today the village sprawls along its several
roads, but the High Street with its timber framed and brick
buildings provides a focus. The village is hemmed in by the
bulk of Kinver Edge to the south with the River Stour and
the Staffs & Worcs Canal curling round to the east.

Kinver had its industrial revolution between 1820 and 1870.
The river Stour was the source of power and from 1772 the
canal provided transport. During the 19th century there
were five iron mills around the village. Kinver Mill by
the lock was powered by three waterwheels and produced
iron and steel wire. Kinver Light Railway opened in 1901
from Amblecote near Stourbridge; Black Country workers
on days off and Victorian tourists flocked to the area.

Mighty, sandstone Kinver Edge with its caves and hollows and acres of woodland belongs to the National Trust and Hereford and Worcester County Council, who call their bit Kingsford Country Park. From the summit are misty, blue views to the Clent Hills, The Sheepwalks, the Clee Hills, Abberley Hills and Malverns. The ridge is the meeting place of three long distance paths, the Staffordshire Way, Worcestershire Way and North Worcestershire Path.

Cave dwellings carved out of the rosy sandstone at Holy Austin Rock were occupied by hermits in the Middle Ages. During the 1800's, twelve families lived in houses which were later equipped with gas and a piped water supply, and some houses were inhabited until the 1950's. One of the Victorian cottages on top of the outcrop has been restored and is occupied by a warden.

THE STROLL
About level 2 miles beside the river Stour and the Staffordshire & Worcestershire Canal.

> *(1) Face Olde White Hart & go R 500yds (past Police Station) to Mill House. Fork R, pass British Legion & bear R past Community Centre to playing fields.*
>
> *(2) Bear R & follow R hedge. Go ahead 1/2 mile, via gates & fenced paths, to meet track. Go R over vehicle bridge & on 250 yds to canal*
>
> *(3) Go R 1/2 mile, past Hyde Lock & round L bend to Kinver Lock. Leave towpath & follow road R back to start.*

THE WALK

Around 6 miles of exercise, climbing Kinver Edge for an exhilarating ridge walk with superb views, wandering in woodland at Kingsford Country Park, steaming up a rising track and whizzing down a high, green hill to woodland paths on the lower slopes of the Edge. You can also visit the rock houses at Holy Austin Rock.

(1) Face Olde White Hart & go R past library to take Vicarage Drive L. At fork go R to gates, & turn L down fenced path to road.

(2) Go R 200yds to junction by post box. Go L to 30mph sign & turn R up tarmac drive to end.

(3) Take narrow path L of garage & follow it to take gate. Go ahead 50 paces & turn R up steep, sandy path. Follow via wooden steps to grassy shoulder. Go L up to crest.

(4) Go L on ridge path 300yds to where grassy spur veers L. Bear R & follow ridge 1 1/4 miles (passing trig point & meeting of three long distance paths) to fenced reservoir.

(5) Bear L on main path to far corner of reservoir fence. Go R to reservoir gate & turn L 150yds to 5-ways junction. Go R down middle of 3 paths 500yds to wide sandy track.

(6) Go L 500yds to T junction of tracks. Go R to road bend. Go ahead 350yds & take 1st road R to junction by white house.

(7) Go R, then bear L onto track signed Starts Green. Follow 1/2 mile (past 1st & 2nd groups of houses & track R) up to farm entrance.

(8) Take small gate ahead & go ahead to next gate & track. Turn R to cross stile. Head just L of lone tree, cross shoulder of hill & go down to bottom corner fence to cross stile.

(9) Walk by paddock fence 50yds, then turn L & join path to fork. Bear R with (tiny) stream on your R, pass path L to fork, then go R. Cross open area into tunnel of bushes & cross stile. Follow field edge to lane.

(10) Go R 450yds, over cross-roads & up to T-junction. Go L 25 paces & take path R.

(11) Go ahead 400yds; ignore side paths but COUNT 1st & 2nd crosstracks to 3rd. Go L to Y junction of paths, then ahead along foot of Edge. Pass side paths & eventually curve R, to climb stone staircase & steps to crest.

(12) Go ahead to track junction. Take 2nd track from L for 150yds, then take path R to T junction. Go R to next junction by mark post. Go ahead & down. Cross sandy area & bear L to road.

(13) Go R past Meddins Lane plus 100yds & take track R. Pass rock houses & take steep path AHEAD. Curve L via wooden steps & follow path up to grassy shoulder.

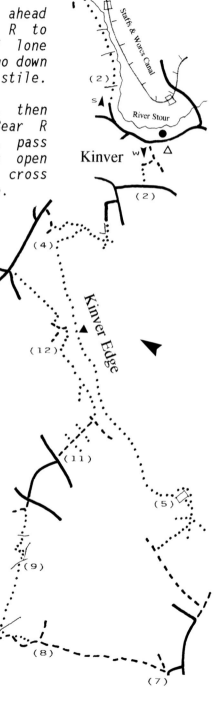

Kinver

(14) Go ahead & down to crossroads of paths. Go L via gate to tarmac drive & follow to road. Go L to junction. Go R 200yds to "Church View" L & take path just beyond. Follow it to track & go R back to High Street.

Oaken

WHERE
About 1 mile west of Codsall, best reached off the A41 midway between Wolverhampton and Albrighton. Turn off at The Foaming Jug pub (see note on parking). Maps: Land ranger 127, Pathfinder 891 SJ 80/90. Map reference SJ 858027.

TRANSPORT, PARK & START
Trains at Codsall station; enquiries 0121 643 2711. From here you can join the Stroll in a few hundred yds, see our map. Buses pass; enquiries 01785 253030.

There is no parking space in the village, use the car park at Oaken Lawn by leaving the A41 at The Foaming Jug. Go 400 yds to the end of the houses and the car park is on the left in the strip of woodland. Both the Stroll and Walk start from the phone box in Oaken but the car park is on the last stage of the Walk. Therefore, if you come by car, start with the Walk para (15), then paras (1) to (14).

REFRESHMENTS
The Foaming Jug (M&B) and The Summerhouse (Banks) on Walk.

HOW FAR
Stroll 1 mile/1.6 km, Walk 5 miles/8km.

THE VILLAGE

Oaken is a quiet, attractive hamlet with flat fields and market gardens to the south and wooded farmland to the west. The Manor of Oaken was given to the Abbey of Croxden by Bertram de Verdun in 1176. They held the land until the dissolution in 1538, then after passing through several owners, the lands came to the Wrottesley family.

In this village of flowery gardens it is a surprise to realise that many of the houses are quite new, but there are older buildings. Codsall and District Civic Society publish a History Trail leaflet which gives the background of most buildings in the village. The Terrace House was built for Henry Wood in the early 19th century. It passed through various hands and is now a nursing home. The Dower House was rebuilt in the early 18th century and became a dower house to the Wrottesley family until sold in the 1950's. Hollybush Cottage, just beyond, was three estate workers' cottages. The Georgian style Manor House, and Oaken Manor opposite are early 19th century.

The Stone Cottage with antlers over the porch is one of the oldest buildings in the village and was once the school. The modern houses in Oaken Lane are on the site of an old smithy and a well. Springfield House on Oaken Drive was probably built around 1850 by William Woodall, an iron and steel merchant, and is now an old people's home. A mill may have existed in Oaken as early as 1230.

The long strip of woods and grassland on the Walk is called Oaken Lawn, and was parkland in the Middle Ages. By the late 17th century it was starting to be developed, with at least six cottages by 1850. Another interesting open area is Kingswood Common by the A41, a family romping place. Both are commons owned by the District Council.

THE STROLL

An easy potter of 1 mile on the outskirts of Oaken passing many of the old buildings.

(1) From phone box, pass terraced house on your L to T junction. Go L 1/2 mile to T junction. [CARE. Use footway till it ends, stay on R to approach bend, then cross.]

(2) Go L round bend for 50yds & take small gate L. Follow fenced path to its end, then take small gate to field.

(3) Go half L (middle path), crossing field diagonally to take stile onto fenced path.

(4) Take small gate opposite, follow R wall/hedge to its corner, then bear L to gate & take small gate to drive.

(5) Go ahead to lane. Go L 300yds (past lane R) to start.

THE WALK

About 5 level and varied miles through wooded farmland on part of the Staffordshire Way, with some parkland and two commons. The going is generally firm.

(1) From phone box, pass terraced house on your L to T junction. Go R 1/4 mile to A41.

(2) Take steps opposite & cross stile to field. Go L by wall & follow field edge round corner, plus 250yds to pass power pole R, plus 100yds, then take gap in L hedge.

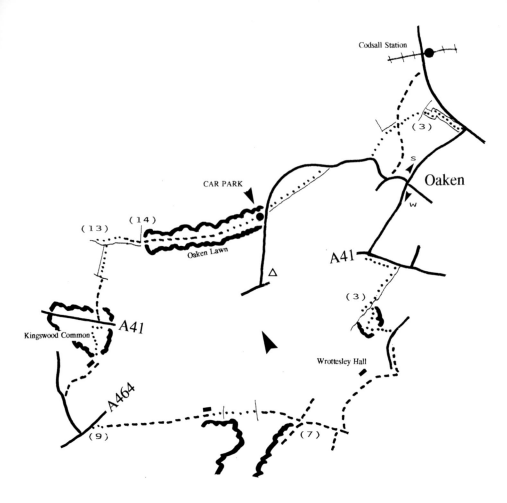

(3) Follow woodland path (over plank) 35 paces, then go R to emerge from trees into nettles. Curve L (past small path R) to join green track.

(4) Follow it (past path right & sign by small gate) to gravel area. Bear L past timber buildings to tarmac drive.

(5) Go R past friendly sign for 150yds, then cross stile L onto track. Go R 1/4 mile to T junction with tarmac drive.

(6) Go R (past drive L) to fork. Go L to end of surfaced drive & take sandy track opposite.

(7) Follow to field corner & take small gate. Go ahead by L fence (past gate L) & take gate. Follow fenced/hedged track to house.

(8) Go ahead on tarmac drive 400yds to T junction by caravans. Take green path ahead (becomes hedged track) to A464.

(9) Go L 100yds to crossroads & take lane R. Go .4 mile to grass triangular & take track R.

(10) Follow track to its end by cottage, then take path ahead to its end at edge of wood. Bear L & find your way to car park by A41.

(11) Face car park entrance, then go R through bushes to open grass area. As soon as you can, bear L & follow paths to A41. Cross & take drive to Park Farm.

(12) Follow past house to stables & cross stile in L corner. Follow L hedge & cross field corner stile onto grass track.

(13) Go R 150yds & take gate to hedged track. Follow it 150yds to join stone track.

(14) Go ahead 1/2 mile;
   - on stone track to cottage,
   - on grass to wood (take L fork),
   - on earth track to car park & picnic site.

(15) Cross stile opposite wood & follow R hedge to stile & lane. Go ahead 1/4 mile (past lane R) to phone box in Oaken village.

Kingswood Common, Oaken Walk

Rock

WHERE
Some 7 miles south-west of Bewdley. get there from the A456
Bewdley - Leominster road. Maps: Landranger 138, Pathfinder
952 SO 67/77. Map reference SO 735713.

TRANSPORT, PARK & START
No buses. There is limited parking on the grass verges oppo-
site the Rock Cross Inn, where the Stroll and the Walk start.
If you patronise the pub, ask for permission to leave the car.
There is some space at the Village Hall at the eastern end
of the village but use common sense if it is in use.

REFRESHMENTS
Rock Cross Inn (Free House) and on the Walk, the Colliers
Arms (Free House).

HOW FAR
Stroll 2.7 miles/4.5 kms, Walk 4.4 miles/7.3kms.

THE VILLAGE
This tiny village sits at 173 metres on a plateau with fine
views over the patchwork countryside between the rivers
Severn and Teme. Its name derives from the Saxon *"Ther
Ak"* (the Oak), and an ancient one stood near the church
until the early 19th century. Older inhabitants still call
the village "The Rock". It seems a healthy place. One
old man who was asked how he had come to live so long
replied that the churchyard was too cold to lie in. Rock
is said to be the coldest village in the county.

The church of Sts Peter and Paul was built around 1170
and is one of the largest Norman churches in Worcestershire. Much of the original work is still in good condition.
Look out for the beautifully carved Norman chancel arch,
the 12th century font and Perpendicular nave arcade. The
corbels have grotesque heads. In 1510 the tower, Lady
Chapel and south aisle were added. Examples of Norman
work can be seen in the marvellous north doorway richly
decorated with masses of zig-zags, faces and crenellations.

In the south chapel is a remarkable altar slab, set incong-
rously on a modern pedestal, which was found beneath the
floor of the nave and may come from the original church.
Most services are now held in the chantry chapel which has
been enclosed and is cheaper and easier to heat. Here is an
engraved slab depicting a priest in mass vestments. This is
unusual because it dates from a time when wearing them
was outlawed by Parliament. Don't miss the stocks and
whipping post near the west end of the church.

To the south are the Abberley Hills, that on the left being
Abberley Hill itself, then Walsgrove and Woodbury Hills
to the right of the clocktower. This amazing object built
in 1884 stands in the grounds of Abberley Hall, which is
is now a private school.

THE STROLL
A 2.7 mile circuit passing the church which gives a taste of
the rolling landscape which the Walk offers. There are fine
views of the Abberley Hills, the famous clock tower and
some ostriches.

*(1) Face Rock Cross Inn, go L 1/2 mile to
church, & opposite tower take path R.*

*(2) Follow it between fences & over two stiles
to field. Go ahead by R fence to its corner,
then keep ahead to bottom of field to cross
midhedge stile.*

*(3) Go L & cross stile into field. Go ahead,
follow L hedge to field corner & cross stile
by gate. Go half L to field corner & take
gate to track by farm.*

*(4) Go R by high fence & follow main track
till it bends R into premises. Go ahead on
green track 300yds to split oak R, & cross
plank & stile L. NEXT - to Walk para (13) at ***

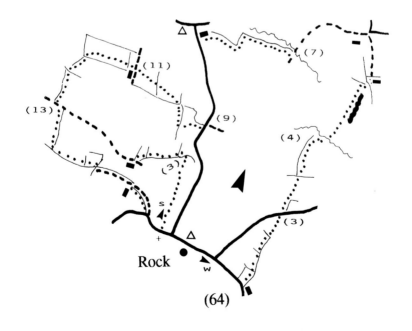

Rock

(64)

THE WALK

A glorious 4.4 miles through a landscape of huge rolling hills and deep, plunging wooded valleys. There are wonderful, sweeping views over half of Worcestershire. In winter it can be muddy.

(1) Face Rock Cross Inn, go R 250yds to just before farm & cross stile L.

(2) Go ahead parallel with R hedge to cross stile. Follow R hedge for two fields & cross stile to open field. Head just L of buildings to gate & lane.

(3) Cross stile opposite, follow R hedge (then barn) to corner, then keep ahead to gates & take stile by R one. Follow L hedge to bottom, pass stile L & bear R to cross footbridge.

(4) Go up to field, then walk R 15 paces along bottom edge. Turn L & go upfield to end of line of trees. Pass them on your R & go on to field corner. WATCH for 2 stiles R, pass 1st & cross 2nd into garden.

(5) Go ahead & take gate onto track. Follow it (becomes lane) 250yds to crossroads.

(6) Go L & down for 1/4 mile to BOTTOM & cross stream. Go on for 30 paces & take small gate R

(7) Go through young trees to field. Go R, follow edge round several bends to corner, & take small gate. Follow track to road.

(8) Go L 1/2 mile to gates of Barratts Court (L) & take gate R.

(9) Follow R hedge to its corner, then bear L to cross midfence stile. Go half R to gate (under tree) & cross stile

(10) Go half L to cross midhedge stile 50yds above field corner. Bear R to R end of steel shed & cross stile to track.

(11) Enter gap opposite by shed corner & take small gate. Go L past sheds to cross midfence stile. Go to far L field corner & cross stile.

(12) Follow R hedge to field corner & cross two stiles. Go L & cross footbridge. Go R by R fence & cross corner stile onto green track.

(13) Go L 50yds to cross plank & stile R. * Follow L hedge to corner & cross stile, then stile L. Follow R hedge to fence corner & cross hurdle/gate. Turn half L & take gate.

(14) Go ahead up stone track, then down past barn. DON'T go ahead, bear R over grass to where fence meets hedge & cross hurdle.

(15) Follow L hedge to corner & cross stile to road. Go L past church to start.

Timber framing at Rock

Salwarpe

WHERE
About 1.5 miles south-west of Droitwich. Get there from
the A38, turning at an eccentric orange coloured pub
called Trotter Hall. Maps: Landranger 150, Pathfinder
973 SO 86/96. Map reference SO 875620.

TRANSPORT, PARK & START
There are no buses. You should be able to park in a few
spaces by the church, except during a service. Both the
Stroll and the Walk start from the church.

REFRESHMENTS
About as close as the buses, on the A38.

HOW FAR
Stroll 2 miles/3.25 kms, Walk 4.5 miles/7.25 kms.

THE VILLAGE
Sleepy Salwarpe is tucked away at the end of a no through
road; a waterside village in the valley of the tiny River
Salwarpe. The substantial village hall and few houses are
scattered along the approach road and around the church.
The meandering river and the partially restored Droitwich
Canal wind through the village way below the level of the
houses. Many of the old buildings have been converted into
new homes, including the barns of Salwarpe Court and Salwarpe House, which was once the Rectory.

St. Michael's church is perched high above both river and
canal. It is mainly 14th century but parts may be Norman.
Inside are 17th century monuments to the Talbots of Salwarpe Court. A magnificent restored Manor House stands
next to the church. This was the birthplace of Richard
Neville, Earl of Warwick (1428-71), often known

as the Kingmaker because of his influence during the Wars of the Roses. The house was later given to Catherine of Aragon. There are yews in the churchyard, but the taller conifers are Western red cedar. They look like cypress but have red bark and an upright leading shoot.

The Droitwich Canal was built by James Brindley in the 1770s to link the Worcester Canal to the River Severn via Droitwich. The River Salwarpe was too shallow and winding to be made navigable, so the new cut was built alongside. It carried mainly salt from Droitwich, but in the 1840's the Birmingham & Gloucester Railway's line took most of the trade, and the canal was abandoned in 1939.

Wildlife is not slow to exploit a disused canal. Reeds, great willowherb, reed mace, white teazel and burdock are among the wildflowers which have colonised the waterway and its margins. Moorhen, coot, little grebe and kingfisher are common, and sedge and reed warblers return in summer to breed among the reedbeds. You may see on the Walk that the canal is being slowly restored.

THE STROLL
An easy 2 miles across pasture and quiet lanes, with a fair sample of the secret and secluded Droitwich Canal.

(1) Face lychgate & go R to War Memorial. Turn R a few paces & cross stile by drive. Follow fenced path & take iron kissing gate to field.

(2) Go ahead, cross stile by house & on, to cross midhedge stile. Go R by hedge to gate & cross stile onto drive.

(3) Go L 50yds to gate & cross stile. Follow R hedge round 1st corner, but as it curves R stay parallel with L fence & go down to cross footbridge.

*(4) Follow L hedge to top field corner & cross
stile L. Cross stile R, then go half L &
cross midhedge stile onto lane.*

*(5) Go R & round L bend to T junction. Go R to
canal & join towpath.*

*(6) Pass cottage & follow canal 3/4 mile. Go
under red brick bridge plus 150yds & take path
L. Go through churchyard to start.*

THE WALK
A pleasant 4.5 miles across mixed farmland in an unspoilt
corner of Worcestershire. You return along the disused canal
towpath with its abundant wildlife.

*(1) Face lychgate, go L 150yds to R bend &
cross stile by gate L. Bear L 30yds to gate &
cross stile L.*

*(2) Get onto towpath. Go R 50yds then turn R
to join path & cross stile L. Follow L fence
via stile to next field corner, & cross stile.*

*(3) Go to far R field corner & cross foot-
bridge. Go ahead, bearing gradually R to far
R field corner. Pass gate R & cross hidden
corner stile. Follow path by L fence to track.*

*(4) Go L 300yds to road. Go L 50yds to gate R,
& cross stile.*

*(5) Go R by hedge till level with projecting
end of midfield hedge. Go L up to its R side.*

**FACE ALONG LINE OF HEDGE, THEN LOOK DOWN R &
COUNT trees in bottom hedge, starting from
small oak at R end.**

Cross field to 7th tree in bottom hedge, &
take hedge gap. Follow L hedge to gap & lane.

(6) Go L to T junction. Turn R 200yds to L
bend & take 2nd gate R. Go down short track &
cross stile L.

(7) Follow R hedge & cross midhedge stile.
Follow R hedge again & cross stile by pond.
Bear R around pond, pass 1st stile R & cross
2nd. Go ahead a few paces, then bear L to
hedge angle & cross hidden stile to lane.

(8) Go R to T junction. Go L 350yds to black
barn R, & take track opposite.

(9) Follow 50yds, then take hedged path L.
Follow down & cross footbridge. Go R by hedge
75yds, then R through gap to next field.

(10) Follow R hedge to field corner & take
small gate. Follow fenced path, cross gated
footbridge, then follow R fence & cross 2nd
bridge R. Follow fenced path to gate & lane.

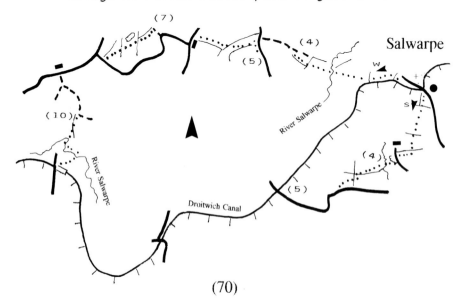

(11) Turn sharp L onto towpath & follow canal 3/4 mile to lane. Go L to junction. Turn R 200yds to steel gateway, & rejoin canal.

(12) Follow 1 1/2 miles to pass under red brick bridge. Go on 150yds then take rising path L & go through churchyard to start.

Shrawley

WHERE
About 3 miles north-west of Ombersley on the B4196. Maps: Landranger 150; Pathfinders 974 SO 86/96 & 973 SO 66/76. Map reference SO 806649.

TRANSPORT, PARK & START
Buses pass; enquiries 01905 763763. Park at the signposted Picnic Site behind the New Inn on the B4196. The Stroll and Walk start from here.

REFRESHMENTS
New Inn (Marston) and Rose & Crown (Marston).

HOW FAR
Stroll 1.5 miles/2.4 kms, Walk 5.5 miles/8.8 kms.

THE VILLAGE
Shrawley is a sprawling, charming village strung out along the road for almost two miles. It has a church, pubs, post office and village hall but dispersed among the houses. Similar settlements are quite common west of the Severn. The nearby villages of Astley, Dunley, Ombersley and Boreley share the same *ley* suffix. This means wooded area, from the vast forest which covered much of Worcestershire into mediaeval times.

Crossing the Dick Brook in Shrawley Wood

St Mary's perches high above the village. No trace remains of the original Saxon church and the existing building is mainly Norman. The nave and chancel were built in the 12th century and the first tower in the 15th century, but it collapsed and was rebuilt in the 17th. In the 15th century, the roof was replaced and a porch built. Inside, wall plaques depict the Ten Commandments and, unusually, all the 18th century box pews have been retained.

The chancel arch leans alarmingly to the south and the walls seem to lean outwards. In 1936 two buttresses were added to the south wall to prevent collapse, but in 1985 the church had to be closed for urgent repairs. Through massive local efforts the money was raised and the church re-opened two years later. In the churchyard are the remains of the 14th century village cross, now surmounted by a sundial.

Shrawley Wood is a mere remnant of the ancient forest. Although fairly common in Worcestershire, very few lime woods survive in Britain and this one is vitally important. Huge, coppiced trunks rise from centuries old stools throughout the wood. An old name for lime wood was whitewood, and coppicing produced huge lengths of grain free white timber. Part of the wood was taken over by the Forestry Commission in 1959 but the rest is in private hands. The Commission's Forest Enterprise arm are bringing back traditional coppicing methods, and in 1992 a management plan was formulated which should secure the wood's survival.

The woodland flora is incredibly rich. In May a massive drift of bluebells covers the forest floor, following the wood anemones in March. The autumn colours are equally spectacular, although a visit at any time of year will reveal something new. The wood is rich in birdlife. Quiet walkers with binoculars may see woodpeckers, jays, treecreepers, nuthatches, most of the tit and finch families and garden and willow warblers. Chiffchaffs call their name from high in the canopy.

The Dick Brook forms the northern edge of the Walk. In the mid 17th century a local man, Andrew Yaranton, used flash gates to enable barges to navigate some 600 yds of the brook to an iron furnace and forge. Both canal and furnace may be the first of their kind in Britain. The plant later became a flint, paper and bobbin mill, and excavations have turned up pottery fragments.

THE STROLL
An easy 1.5 miles which wanders briefly over the fields before diving into Shrawley Wood.

(1) From car park go to lane & turn R. Follow 400yds & curve L through farm to take wooden gate.

(2) Go down by R hedge & cross corner stile. Go L by hedge & cross corner stile. Go ahead via stile to field corner & cross hidden stile.

(3) Follow fenced path to drive & turn L to
B4196. Go R to Rose & Crown, then take track
opposite by phone box.

(4) Follow between buildings to pass black
steel shed. Follow L hedge to gate & cross
stile. Go on to corner of wood & crossroads of
tracks.

****
     For WALK switch to WALK para (1)
****

(5) Go L 400yds (first with open field on your L, then into wood) to crossroads of paths by red banded post.

(6) Go L 1/4 mile (rejoining wood edge) to gates, & take small gate onto drive.

(7) Follow to B4196. Cross & return to start.

THE WALK

A fine 5.5 miles through parkland and glorious Shrawley Wood. You meet a strange sandstone outcrop called Oliver's Mound which is said to have been inhabited by hermits. Their trick was rescuing abandoned babies from the river, caring for them and christening them all with the surname Severn. There is an alder bog and a walk by the river.

(1) Follow STROLL paras (1) - (4)

(2) From crossroads of tracks go R by high fence to gate, & cross stile.

(3) Go half L, bearing away from wood. When you see white house, head to its L & cross stile. Cross wooded area to gate & cross stile. Go ahead parallel with R fence to gate, & cross stile into wood.

(4) Follow track 200yds & cross bridge with cemetery railings, then stile. Go L by wood, cross footbridge & pass pool R. Continue by wood edge, climb to gate & cross stile.

(5) Go ahead to farm, take gate & curve L between buildings to track fork. Go R to gate & cross stile.

(6) Follow track 1/4 mile (via 2 gates) to pass sandstone outcrop on your L.

(7) Curve around it & follow green track between tongues of woodland, curving R between bogs to river bank.

(8) Go L (upstream) 1/2 mile (via gates & stiles) till track ends at gate. Bear L by wood 1/4 mile & cross corner stile.

(9) Go ahead a few paces to 3 way path junction. Take middle path & follow brook 1/4 mile to stepping stones.

(10) Go half L & follow rising path 1/4 mile to T junction of tracks. Go L to track junction by gates, & take small gate to drive.

(11) Follow to B4196 & cross back to start.

Trysull

WHERE
Some 2 miles north-west of Wombourne, get there from the B4176 or the A449. Maps: Landrangers 138 & 9, Pathfinder 912 SO 89/99. Map reference SJ 852943.

TRANSPORT, PARK & START
Buses pass; enquiries 0121 200 2700. Be very careful about parking. There is limited space near the school on School Road. Better; ask one of the pubs for permission to park. The Stroll and the Walk start from the church.

REFRESHMENTS
The Bell (Holden), The Plough (Banks). There is also a tea shop at Wombourne Station on the Walk.

HOW FAR
Stroll 1 mile/1.6 kms, Walk 5 miles/8 kms or 3 miles/5 kms.

THE VILLAGE
Trysull (locally *Treesul)* timbered cottages, impressive brick
houses, an attractive pub and church between trim, colourful
gardens. The handsome iron and brick bridge over the brook
replaced a horse bridge in 1952. A church has stood here
for over a thousand years. Your impression on entering the
present All Saints is of light and air, with two vivid Victorian stained glass windows giving an almost three dimens-
ional picture. The tower arch and blocked north door are
the only Norman features. The aisle was added in the 13th
century and the tower rebuilt in the 15th.

The Staffs & Worcs Canal features in several of these walks.
On this one you pass the three Bratch Locks which drop the
canal 30 feet into the Smestow valley. The little octagonal
building was the toll house, and the keeper's cottage overlooks the top lock. You leave the canal at Awbridge, with
its unusual parapets of nine pillars. This is the only
original bridge on the canal, and thought to be the Engineer, James Brindley's, first bridge on a public road.

Severn Trent pretend that the magic building in shiny, red
brick with four corner turrets and dazzling cabalistic panels
over the windows is a pumping station. They say it was
opened in 1897 to supply Womborne and Bilston and that
the original steam engines have been preserved. But it is
obviously a gingerbread castle with resident witch.

The Kingswinford Railway Walk follows the old Great
Western line between Dudley and Wolverhampton which
closed in 1965. The cuttings and embankments are now a
precious wildlife corridor through a heavily farmed landscape. Sixty species of butterfly have been recorded but
the fields have few. Birds include sparrowhawk, kestrel,
linnet, whitethroat, yellow hammer, three species of
owl, brambling and most finches.

THE STROLL
A 1 mile shuffle along local footpaths and meadows by the Smestow Brook, with some fascinating buildings.

(1) From church go to junction of School Road & turn R, then L down Holloway. Cross Brook & take lane L.

(2) Follow 350yds, pass brick shed R plus 150yds & take small gate L. Go half L to bottom L field corner & cross stile. Go ahead to gate & cross stile onto road.

(3) Turn L 200yds to just past red brick Manor House, & take track R. Follow it to end of brick wall R at field. Go L by hedge to take small gate, then follow fenced path & take another small gate. Follow green track to School Road & turn L to reach church.

THE WALK(S)
This 5 mile stretch has a 3 mile alternative. They are level but fascinating, with a gingerbread castle, the Bratch Locks, the Kingswinford Railway Walk and the Staffs & Worcs Canal. Lanes and brook-side paths lead back to Trysull.

(1) From church, follow School Road 200yds, & just past Croft (R) turn L on hedged path. Follow it & take small gate into field. Cross diagonally past nearest power pole to gate by far hedge. DON'T TAKE IT. Go R by hedge to field corner, & cross stile to drive & lane.

(2) Go L down lane, pass first track R, cross Smestow Brook, rise to second track R & cross stile L.

Toll house at The Bratch

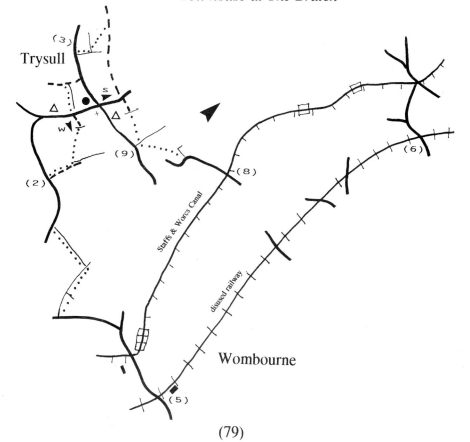

(79)

(3) Follow L hedge to corner & cross stile. Go R by hedge (via stile) to cross stile onto lane. Go L to T junction. Turn R down to canal. NEXT - paragraph (4)

****
SHORT ALTERNATIVE
(4a) Join canal & go UP locks. Follow towpath .8 mile to Awbridge Lock with its nine pillared brick bridge, & join lane. NEXT - paragraph (8)
****

(4) Follow road up & pass under railway bridge. Turn L up drive, then take path L onto track bed.

(5) Go R past station & follow line 2 miles. NOTE bridges; pass Nos 36, 37 & 38 (with road under) to No 39 with road over. Go under plus 50yds, then L up to lane.

(6) Go R 450yds (past lane L) to canal; join towpath on far side.

(7) Follow towpath 1 mile to Awbridge Lock with nine pillared bridge & join lane.

(8) Cross canal bridge to pass houses & go 350 yds to sharp L bend. Take gateway ahead into field. Follow R hedge to its corner, then keep ahead past power pole (not pylon). Head R of white house & cross field corner stile.

(9) Go ahead past shed to gate & cross stile. Follow wooded track to lane. Go L over bridge to church.

Upper Arley

WHERE
By the River Severn 3.5 miles north of Bewdley. Head for
Shatterford on the A442 Kidderminster - Bridgnorth road
and follow the lane 2 miles to the river. Maps: Landranger
138, Pathfinders 952 SO 67/77 and 932 SO 68/78. Map
reference SO 765803.

TRANSPORT, PARK & START
Buses call; enquiries 01905 763763. Severn Valley Railway; enquiries 01299 401001. Large pay car parks by the
river. We offer two Strolls which you can combine to make
a short Walk. Both start on the EAST (church) bank at the
end of the bridge.

REFRESHMENTS
The Harbour Inn (Free House) is on the west (railway) bank,
and you can get snacks at the station. There is a restaurant
and a cafe on the east bank.

HOW FAR
Stroll (1) 2 miles/3.25 kms, Stroll (2) 2 miles/3.25 kms,
Combined Stroll 4.3 miles/7 kms.

THE VILLAGE
Upper Arley is enchanting; a tiny river port by the mighty
Severn. The steep lane from Shatterford gives wide tree-
top views over the valley but offers no clue that a village
is nearby until you reach the river. There is a post office
cum village shop and two tea rooms. Up the hill are a
school and a memorial hall with a busy sports ground.

St Peter's sandstone church overlooks the river. Although
Victorian in appearance from restoration in 1885, parts of
the church are Norman. The nave and tower date from 1135,
other parts from the 14th and 15th centuries. Inside is the

effigy and tomb of a Crusader knight, possibly Sir Walter de Balun who once held lands in Arley. The original coffin lies against the north wall. A Doom painting of a skeleton symbolising the plague was discovered during the 19th century, but has since faded.

The River Severn is Britain's longest river and once carried a huge volume of traffic as far as Welshpool. Today navigation stops just north of Stourport. The charmless tubular footbridge was built in 1971 to replace a ferry which had docked at the slipways on each bank of the river since the 13th century.

Arley Station on the Severn Valley Railway has won awards for Best Kept Station. For details of the line see *Highley*. A famous railway feature nearby is the cast iron Victoria Bridge, which has featured in TV and film productions. When built in 1861 it was the longest cast iron span in the world.

Trimpley Reservoirs were built in the 1960's to supplement Birmingham's Elan Valley water supply. The buildings and noise are intrusive and the reservoirs not too attractive, but the setting is spectacular. The wooded slopes of Eymore and Seckley Woods hang on either side of the winding, silver Severn. The areas of open water are a valuable stopover for migrant birds, particularly gulls, terns and waders which use the Severn as a route into the Midlands.

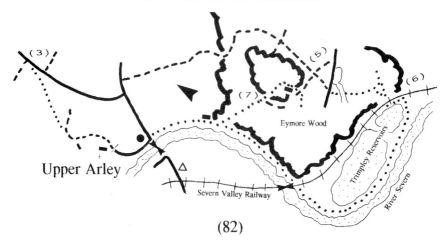

STROLL (1)

Around 2 miles on paths and tracks. You visit the parkland of Arley House and the conifers of Eymoor Wood, returning on part of the Worcestershire Way and a riverside path.

(1) At end of bridge, face river, & go R 200 yds to end of road.

(2) Take small gate ahead & follow tarmac drive (via 2 gates) to fork by millstones. Stay on drive 100 paces till it bends R, then go ahead to pass tree clump on your L. Head for top R field corner, cross stile onto track & join lane.

(3) Go R 1/2 mile to T junction.

(4) Go L 80yds & take gated track R. Follow 1 mile (entering wood, falling to cross bridge, rising over crest & crossing track) to crossroads of tracks by 3 mark posts.

****
TO JOIN Stroll (2)
switch to Stroll (2) para (4a)
****

(5) Turn R & follow track 250yds (past track R, path L & track L) to iron gates.

(6) Cross stile R & follow L hedge to take small gate. Go half L via hedge gap & cross bottom stile into wood.

(7) Go down R, pass track from R & take next steep path R down to cross footbridge.

(8) Go ahead by river to start.

STROLL (2)

A glorious 2 miles which meets the river twice, but also soars up through Eymoor Wood and crosses a wildflower meadow. You circle the Trimpley Reservoirs and are never far from the railway, which carries frequent steam trains.

(1) At end of bridge, face river & go L. Follow concrete path, then riverside path 1/4 mile, to cottage L.

(2) Bear L to cross footbridge & go L. Keep CLIMBING (past falling track L) to R bend, & cross stile L.

(3) Follow green path through hedge gap & take small gate. Follow R hedge & cross stile.

(4) Go L & follow track 250yds to crossroads of tracks by 3 mark posts. Go R to gate & road. NEXT paragraph (5).

****

IF joining from Stroll (1) -
(4a) Go ahead to gate & road.
NEXT - para (5)

****

(5) Cross road & take gate opposite. Follow woodland path across green ride & down (past path L) to fork. Go R to cross railway.

(6) Go L & circle lake to river side, then as you choose, drop down to join riverside path.

(7.) Go upstream 1 1/2 miles back to start.

Wolverley

WHERE
About 3.5 miles north of Kidderminster off the B4189 at its junction with the B4190. Maps: Landranger 138, Pathfinders 933, SO 88/98 and 953 SO 87/97 Map reference SO 829793.

TRANSPORT, PARK & START
Buses pass; enquiries 01905 763763. There are some spaces in the village centre and limited space on the one way street by the church. Both the Stroll and the Walk start from the village centre, by the Queen's Head pub.

REFRESHMENTS
Queens Head (Banks), Live & Let Live (Free House), The Lock, (Banks) and The Anchor (Free House).

HOW FAR
Stroll 2 miles/3 kms, Walk 5 miles/8 kms & 3 miles/5 kms.

THE VILLAGE
Wolverley is a startling village built mostly in 18th or 19th century brick. Many of the houses have decorative barge boards and some have been colour washed in pink, whites and creams. It is wonderfully isolated in a deep, sandstone hollow by the wooded valley where the River Stour runs by the Staffordshire & Worcestershire Canal. Cave cottages were cut into the cliffs in the 19th century to house workers in the iron industry. During the middle ages, a court was held here. The Court House of 1620 is a Jacobean extravaganza, not so much attempted mediaeval Gothic as Hammer Horror. Perched on sandstone cliffs, the dark red, brick church of St John the Baptist (1772) glowers over the village. It was built to an Italianate design, very forward looking, for it resembles a vengeful Victorian gas works. Behind an iron gate at the base of the hill, a path winds up through the rock to the churchyard.

The canal meanders between wooded sandstone banks. It was built by James Brindley in 1722 to link the Trent & Mersey Canal at Great Haywood in Staffordshire to the Severn, 46 miles away at Stourport.

THE STROLL

A happy amble of 2 miles around the edge of Wolverley on a muddy woodland path, the canal and various paths and tracks.

(1) Face Queen's Head & go R 300yds (past traffic lights & pub) to last house R.

(2) Take lane R [Short Yard] 250yds to pass last house R, & take gate.

(3) Turn R, follow R hedge to its corner, then keep ahead down middle of dip into wood. Follow hollow track through it & cross stile.

(4) Follow R fence to cross plank then stile onto track. Follow to white house. Bear R, pass track & gates R, & follow path to canal.

(5) Follow towpath 600yds to Lock pub & B4189. Continue under road plus 400yds & cross steel footbridge R.

(6) Follow R fence to pass cottage R. Take tarmac drive (becomes track) to bend of road.

(7) Go ahead to B4189 (DON'T CROSS), & turn R to roundabout. Go to its R side, cross road & take lane (3 tonnes) back to start

THE WALK(S)

Walks of 5 or 3 miles on fields, pebbly tracks and canal towpath. You pass beetling sandstone cliffs and a canal tunnel, which in its day was the longest in the world.

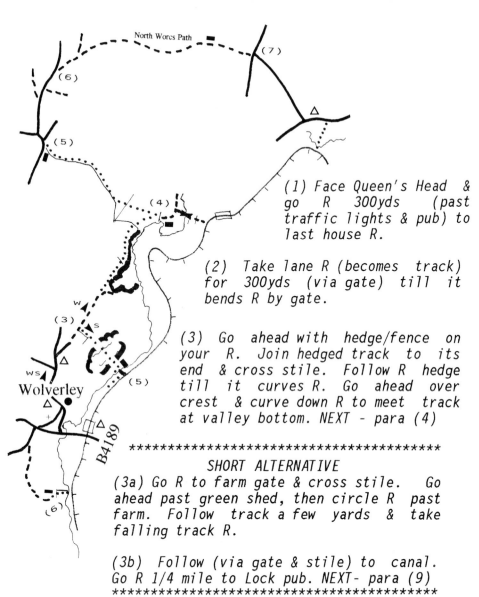

North Worcs Path

(7)

(6)

(5)

(4)

(3)

W

S

WS

Wolverley

(5)

B4189

(6)

(1) Face Queen's Head & go R 300yds (past traffic lights & pub) to last house R.

(2) Take lane R (becomes track) for 300yds (via gate) till it bends R by gate.

(3) Go ahead with hedge/fence on your R. Join hedged track to its end & cross stile. Follow R hedge till it curves R. Go ahead over crest & curve down R to meet track at valley bottom. NEXT - para (4)

****
SHORT ALTERNATIVE
(3a) Go R to farm gate & cross stile. Go ahead past green shed, then circle R past farm. Follow track a few yards & take falling track R.

(3b) Follow (via gate & stile) to canal. Go R 1/4 mile to Lock pub. NEXT- para (9)
****

(4) Go L in valley to far fence corner & cross (?bust) stile. Go ahead up bank to projecting fence corner. Go with fence on your L 1/2 mile to corner gate, & cross stile to road.

(5) Go ahead past lane R, round R bend & continue 400yds (past hedged track R) to sandy entrance R.

(6) Go R past WOODEN gate & follow track 100 yds to fork. Take track R 1 mile to road junction.

(7) Take road opposite 1/2 mile to T junction. Go L to Anchor, plus 100yds, to take small gate R. (Before track.)

(8) Follow path 200yds & cross River Stour to canal towpath. Go R 2 miles to Lock & B4184.

(9) Go R through car park & take lane R. Follow 100yds to cross two bridges, then take small gate L. Go up to church & join lane. Go R to start.

Steel wheel works at Cookley on the Staffs & Worcs Canal

Worfield

Off A454 10 miles west of Wolverhampton and 3.5 miles
north-east of Bridgnorth. Maps: Landranger 138, Pathfinder
911 SO 69/79. Map reference SO 758957.

TRANSPORT, PARK & START
Buses call; enquiries 01743 253030. Park in Village Hall
car park; leave much cash in the church later. The Hall,
where the Stroll and the Walk start, is just off the A454,
well before you reach the village.

REFRESHMENTS
The Wheel (Banks) is on the A454. The one village pub is
both The Davenport Arms and The Dog (Free House).

HOW FAR
Stroll 1.25 miles/2 kms, Walk 5.5 miles/8.8 kms.

THE VILLAGE
This attractive village huddles between the River Worfe
and a steep, sandstone cliff amongst green, wooded hills
with quaint villages and meandering rivers. The main
street is a harmonious mixture of half timbered cottages,
stone and modern brick houses with a pub, stores and
a school.

St Peter's church replaced a Saxon building. The lofty
tower was rebuilt in the 15th century and the spire added
much later. Most of the stained glass is Victorian except
for part of the east window in the south aisle where mainly
14th century glass depicts the Crucifixion. The King to
the right may be Richard II and the Bishop on the right
may be Bishop Scrope of Lichfield. Look at the reredos
behind the high altar, a beautiful sculpture enhanced by

subtle lighting so as to seem translucent. Each June the villagers hold a famous flower festival, and every five years perform a Passion play in the church.

Opposite the church is Jacobean, timber framed Lower Hall, set in a beautiful walled garden. Davenport House was built by Francis Smith of Warwick in 1726. A dovecote stands near the entrance drive to the landscaped park and a ruined tower on a hill looms over the village. The Davenport Estate still owns most of the village.

THE STROLL
An ambly 1.25 miles with a riverside wander and a look at the village.

> *(1) From Village Hall go L 250yds (passing on R, white gate, small black iron gate, then matching double gate) then turn R past black garage.*
>
> *(2) Go ahead & L of brown doored garage to cross stile. Go ahead parallel with river to projecting hedge corner. Go R 20yds to gate & cross stile. Follow green track to junction of tracks.*
>
> *(3) Go L via bends to main street. Go L to T junction by War Memorial. Go L 450yds to start*

THE WALK
This 5.5 miles starts on fieldpaths and quiet lanes; pleasant but level and ordinary. Then the scene changes abruptly to an upland landscape - a delightful shock.

> *(1) From Village Hall, go L 450yds to T junction by War Memorial.*

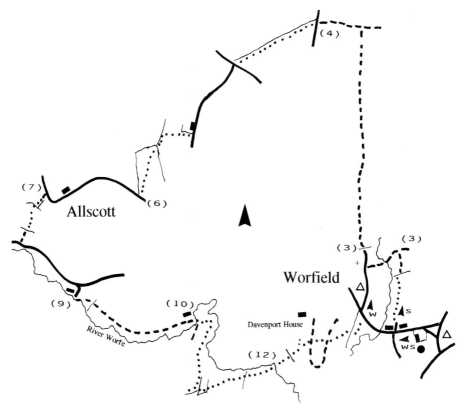

Allscott

Worfield

Davenport House

River Worfe

(2) Go R past school, pub & church. Ignore L turns & follow No Through Road to take steel gates.

(3) Follow green track 3/4 mile to T junction with stony track. Go L to road.

(4) Take L of 2 gates opposite, & follow R hedge to gate & road. Take road opposite 1/4 mile, pass between farm buildings, & just past last house take gateway R.

(5) IF there is clear path bearing L, follow it. IF NOT follow R hedge to its corner, then keep ahead to far fence. Go L 50yds & cross 2 stiles R into field corner. Cross diagonally to gate & lane.

(6) Go R 1/2 mile, pass between houses & round sharp R bend, plus 50yds, to cross stile L by gate.

(7) Follow hedged path to field. Follow L hedge down 80 yds & cross stile L. **LOOK AHEAD** to distant red farm; head across sloping hillside to dip below it & take gate.

(8) Follow wooded track to lane. Go L for 1/4 mile to hamlet. Round sharp R bend & at L bend, bear R into mill gateway.

(9) Curve L onto track & pass cottages to take gate. Follow track 1/2 mile to cross river bridge & pass white cottage. Bear R off drive to gate, & cross stile.

(10) Pass steep track R & follow sandstone cliff 200yds to cross stile into wood. Go ahead 250yds & pass cottage L to power pole. Cross stile L & bear L to take gate.

(11) Follow power lines to field corner & cross stile. Follow river bank 200yds to cross footbridge.

(12) Go ahead under power lines & take gate. Follow track up L to fork. Go R to tarmac drive.

(13) Cross to pass end of fence, then bear slightly L & find easy descent to tarmac drive. Cross stile opposite.

(14) Go half L to field corner & cross stile. Go L to road. Go R 450yds to start.